EL ADEM GAMBUT RESEGH TO   SIDI OMAR   FORT MADALENA
                 CAPUZZO BATTLE CRUSADER OPENS

                                                  HALFAYA   .   /

'C.

  9 DEC.   19-28 NOV. 41

'CE

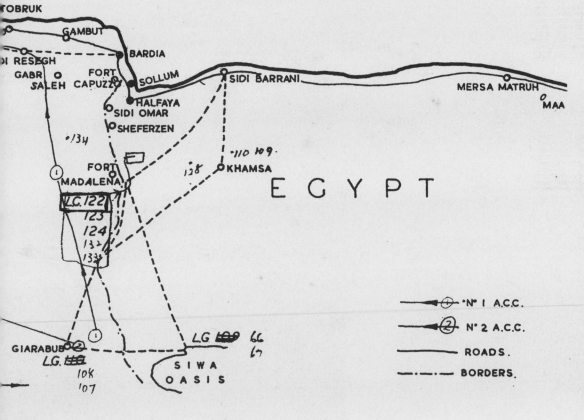

'1 FEB.
VICINITY

LINE STABILISED MID. FEB.
GAZALA TO TENGEDER.

  3 FEB.

  1 FEB.

THROUGH ADVERSITY

The History of
the Royal Air Force Regiment
1942-1992

Her Majesty Queen Elizabeth II
Air Commodore-in-Chief of the Royal Air Force Regiment
(From the original portrait by Huseph Riddle RP and reproduced by kind
permission of the artist)

THROUGH ADVERSITY

The History of
the Royal Air Force Regiment
1942-1992

Kingsley M Oliver

FORCES & CORPORATE PUBLISHING LTD

First published February 1997
by Forces & Corporate Publishing Ltd,
Hamblin House, Hamblin Court, 92-94 High Street,
Rushden, Northamptonshire NN10 0PQ, England.

ISBN 0 9529597 0 4

Typesetting and design by Forces & Corporate Publishing Ltd.
Printed by Impress Printers, Corby, England.

Preface

by

Marshal of the Royal Air Force
Sir Michael Beetham GCB CBE DFC AFC DL FRAeS

The Royal Air Force Regiment was formed for the same basic reason that the Army formed its own Air Corps and the Royal Navy its Royal Marines and Fleet Air Arm. In theory there should have been no need because the major user of the particular element, be it land, sea or air, should be best able to provide the necessary support for the others. However, in practice no one Service has ever had sufficient resources and, human nature being what it is, priority always seems to be given to one's own.

In spite of promises, the Army was unable to give RAF airfields the protection so crucially needed when the threat developed in World War Two and, against stiff opposition in many quarters, the Royal Air Force decided to 'go it alone' and form its own Regiment.

For RAF officers, with their eyes primarily on the flying task, their view of the need for the Regiment probably depended in earlier days on whether their airfield was, or had been, under ground threat. I commanded RAF Khormaksar in the mid 1960s at the height of the terrorist campaign in Aden and my major concern was to prevent the airfield being blown up. Two Regiment Squadrons, one permanently based and one on roulement, were needed. During that time I came to recognise their outstanding professionalism and dedication and I was forever grateful to them.

In an ideal world, every RAF operational station should have its own Regiment Squadron. While this is clearly impractical with resources available and probably not necessary anyway in peacetime, the current cutbacks in regular Regiment manpower give considerable cause for concern. That is why the formation of the Royal Auxiliary Air Force Regiment Squadrons in support of the core of Regular Squadrons has become such a vitally important feature of our Defence posture. When an emergency arises, a rapid source of some reinforcement is available.

In its first 50 years the RAF Regiment has proved its worth in every theatre of operations and firmly established itself as an integral part of the Royal Air Force. It has shown too that it can stand comparison with the best Army Regiments. It is highly appropriate that the Royal Air Force Regiment's distinguished history, born out of adversity, should be recorded in this book.

Acknowledgements

I am indebted to many individuals in various fields for the information and assistance so willingly given in the researching of material for this book. In addition to those whose contributions are acknowledged in the notes to various chapters, I would especially thank:

Air Commodore Tim Thorn and Air Commodore Ian McNeil, successive Commandants-General of the RAF Regiment, who cleared the official channels to enable me to undertake this work.

Group Captain Ian Madelin and Sebastian Cox Esq, successive Heads of the Air Historical Branch in the Ministry of Defence, for allowing me access to the RAF Regiment records there, Group Captain Tony Stephens who gave unsparingly of his time to assist me in my searches in the archives of the AHB and Squadron Leader Peter Singleton whose advice and assistance on the selection of photographs from the AHB library was invaluable.

Huseph Riddle Esq RP, for allowing his portrait of HM The Queen to be used as the frontispiece to this book.

Squadron Leader George Adamson MBE TD AE MA RAuxAF for his scholarly research into the proper translation of the Corps motto from Latin into English – which has been used as the title of this book.

Squadron Leader Nicholas Tucker RAF, for allowing me to draw on his very detailed researches into honours and awards granted to members of the RAF Regiment, and for his practical help in selecting photographs and maps, as well as researching and updating the indexes.

Dr Stephen Hart, for undertaking a comprehensive research programme into the RAF records from 1918 to 1960 at the Public Record Office on behalf of the RAF Regiment Fund.

Dr Michael Dockerill, of the War Studies Department at King's College London, and Patricia Methven of the Liddell Hart Centre for Military Archives.

Squadron Leader MP Casano MC for his recollections of the RAF's armoured car companies before the war and in the campaigns in the Western Desert.

Charles Beddow Esq MBE, for his advice and guidance on RAF Regiment photographic records.

David Parry Esq for his advice and assistance in researching the Imperial War Museum's photographic archives.

Alastair McInnes Esq, Head of Air Defence Sales, British Aerospace Defence Ltd, Stevenage, for material on the development of the Rapier missile system for the RAF Regiment.

Margaret Cronan BSc (Econ) for her skill in indexing the text of this book.

Those serving and retired officers, RAF units and members of the Associations of the RAF Regiment, who contributed so generously towards the 50th Anniversary Fund, one of whose aims was the production of this history.

The many serving and retired RAF and RAF Regiment personnel who have provided me with first-hand material from their own experiences.

The RAF Regiment History Editorial Committee for the guidance and support which they have given so freely, from the inception of this project to its conclusion. My sincere thanks go to the Chairman – Air Vice-Marshal Donald Pocock CBE – and the members – Air Commodore Marcus Witherow, Group Captain Keith Batt MBE, Group Captain Bob Fishwick RAF and Group Captain David Bremner ADC RAF – not forgetting the indefatigable Secretary to the Committee, Squadron Leader Paul Bruning RAF, who, as the Depot Co-ordination Officer, made my visits to the RAF Regiment Museum and Archives so productive and rewarding.

Finally, my wife, Audrey, for tolerating my concentration on research and writing to the exclusion of almost everything else, and for her skilled secretarial support in the preparation and production of my drafts.

Kingsley Oliver
London, October 1996

The
Royal Air Force Regiment

The Royal Air Force Regiment is a Corps established by Royal Warrant of His Late Majesty King George VI on 1st February 1942 as an integral part of the Royal Air Force. Her Majesty Queen Elizabeth II is the Air Commodore-in-Chief of the Corps.

RAF Regiment officers and NCOs are responsible for advising and planning for the defence of RAF airfields and installations against ground and low level air attack by conventional attack, for measures to mitigate the effects of nuclear, chemical and biological weapons, and for training all combatant RAF personnel in these skills. RAF Regiment squadrons are allocated, as available, to RAF airfields and installations to provide defence against ground and short-range air attack so as to maintain their capability to operate effectively in war.

During the Second World War the RAF Regiment served alongside the Royal Air Force in the United Kingdom, the Middle East, North Africa, Sicily, Italy, Greece, the Balkans, India, Burma, Malaya, Indo-China, the East Indies, North-West Europe, West Africa, the Azores, Norway and the Cocos Islands as well as being detached to support operations in various other theatres. Since then, the RAF Regiment has served wherever the Royal Air Force has operated – in the United Kingdom, Germany, Cyprus, Arabia, Singapore, Malaya, Malaysia, Hong Kong, Borneo, Belize, the Caribbean, Northern Ireland, the Falklands and the Gulf.

Contents

Photographs

Maps

(Reproduced courtesy of the RAF Regiment Museum)

1

Straws in the Wind

Air supremacy may in the long run become as important a factor in the defence of the Empire as sea supremacy.

General JC Smuts, 1917

The Royal Air Force

When the Armistice of November 1918 silenced the guns of the "war to end all wars" the Royal Air Force was little more than six months old. The world's first independent air arm had been brought into being on 1st April 1918, following the Cabinet's acceptance of the Smuts Report of 1917,[1] by merging the Army's Royal Flying Corps with the rather smaller Royal Naval Air Service to produce a third Service with a strength of some 400 squadrons and 300,000 personnel. However, the "peace dividend" which followed the end of the war reduced the size of all three Services dramatically – by 1920 the RAF alone had shrunk to a force of merely 25 squadrons with an establishment of 28,000 officers and airmen.

The Struggle to Survive

In order to ensure that the Treasury was able to maintain tight control of naval, military and air force expenditure, the Cabinet endorsed the "Ten-Year Rule" proposed by Lloyd George in 1919. This was that "the British Empire will not be engaged in a great war during the next ten years and no expeditionary force will be required in that period." The annual observance of this policy as an overriding priority ensured that the Treasury was able to keep the defence vote under continual pressure and this in turn made all three Services compete for the limited funding which was made available each year.

This was not an unreasonable political aim as Lloyd George had, as prime minister, brought the British Empire's costliest and bloodiest war to a successful conclusion and he was intent on rebuilding the nation's shattered economy and developing the social policies on his party's agenda. It was also a shrewd alternative to his preferred option – a unified defence ministry controlling a single defence budget for maintaining all three Services – on which he had been defeated. Where the ten-year rule was to fail the country was in its renewal, year after year, without any consideration of the changing international situation and the consequent threats to national security.

While the demarcation between the primary roles of the Navy and the Army was undisputed, the fact that both had controlled their own air arms prior to 1918 made their staffs aware of the spoils – in terms of manpower, equipment and money – which they might claim if the assets of the fledgling Royal Air Force could be dismembered and redistributed to their former owners.

For the Royal Air Force this meant a struggle for survival – and survival would only be assured by proving that air power could discharge some military roles more effectively, and at less cost, than the other Services. As Chief of the Air Staff, Sir Hugh Trenchard's aim in those difficult days was, first and foremost, to develop a sound framework that would generate an adequately trained and equipped air force which would then be capable of producing whatever time might show to be necessary in the future. His foresight was critical in providing the foundations on which the RAF was able to expand from 1935 onwards.

An opportunity of demonstrating Trenchard's philosophy of "doing more with less" fortuitously arose as early as 1919 when the Colonial Office was considering how best to recover a large area of British Somaliland from the control of the so-called "Mad Mullah". Mohammed bin Abdullah Hassan was a religious leader whose campaign against the colonial power had begun more than twenty years earlier. Several military expeditions had been mounted against him from 1900 onwards, but without any great success, and by 1918 his followers controlled half of Somaliland. The War Office's proposal for an expeditionary force consisting of two infantry divisions, and a campaign planned to last at least a year and costing several millions of pounds, was politically unpalatable and the Cabinet sought a more acceptable way of resolving the problem.

The Secretary of State for War & Air at this time was Winston

Churchill and he had no hesitation in recommending the alternative course of action proposed by the Chief of Air Staff to the Cabinet. This was, in essence, that a single squadron of aircraft, supported by the small garrison already in the colony, could drive the Mullah's adherents out of Somaliland within three months. This proposal was infinitely more pleasing than a large-scale military operation – on both political and economic grounds – and to the dismay of the Chief of the Imperial General Staff[2] the Cabinet opted for the use of air power rather than ground forces.

The Somaliland Campaign

Early in January 1920 12 DH9 aircraft drawn from various RAF squadrons in the Middle East, and designated "Z" Unit, were placed under the command of Group Captain Robert Gordon[3] and detached from Egypt to Somaliland. There they joined the resident military forces: the Somaliland Camel Corps, augmented by tribal levies and a battalion of the King's African Rifles.

Air operations began on 23rd January 1920 and the bombing phase was completed a week later, by which time the Mullah's strongholds had been destroyed. The Camel Corps pursued the demoralised rebels, who were harassed by further air attacks, for another two weeks before the Mullah took refuge in Abyssinia, where he died not long afterwards. So ended "the cheapest war in history" which lasted less than a month and cost the British taxpayer a mere £77,000.[4]

The Wider Uses of Air Power in Peacetime

To the Air Ministry, however, this colonial sideshow was of incalculable value in justifying the effective role of air power in disrupting and defeating dissident tribesmen, with the need for only comparatively few lightly-armed troops to re-establish law and order within a dependent territory. In the following year, Winston Churchill – now Secretary of State for the Colonies – convened a conference in Cairo at which arrangements for the administration of the British mandated territories in the Middle East were to be decided.

Mindful of the success of the policy for the pacification of Somaliland, Churchill insisted on taking Trenchard with him in order to support his enthusiasm for the concept of replacing large military garrisons by small numbers of aircraft. In developing this radical solution, Churchill was advised by Colonel TE Lawrence – "Lawrence of Arabia" – who was present at the Conference with an agenda of his own. This was to support the interests of the Arab leaders – including the Emir Feisal – with whom he had fought during the war. Nevertheless, Lawrence's practical experience of the value of aircraft in operations in the desert, allied to Churchill's propensity for unconventional solutions to military problems and Trenchard's unswerving commitment to the doctrine of air power, combined to defeat the strong opposition to such radical ideas from the representatives of the War Office and the Colonial Office who were present at the Conference. In the end, Trenchard's case that a small but flexible force of aircraft would provide better insurance against unrest than large numbers of soldiers – and at a fraction of the cost to the British Treasury – proved an unassailable argument as far as the politicians were concerned, and the generals and the civil servants were forced to concede defeat.

Air Power and Imperial Policing

Thus Churchill had his way and it was agreed that by the end of 1922 the RAF would become responsible for the security of those former Turkish territories in the Middle East which had been passed to Britain to administer under League of Nations mandates. Iraq, Kuwait and Transjordan were to be policed by eight squadrons of aircraft, instead of a large garrison of infantry, artillery and cavalry, together with their supporting services, but – as in Somaliland – it was recognised that some ground forces would be necessary to exploit the advantages of air control.

When the post-war dismemberment of the Ottoman Empire had been proposed by the Treaty of Sevres in 1920, it was intended that the vilayets – or provinces – of Baghdad and Basra should be combined to form the new state of Iraq while the vilayet of Mosul would be added to part of Turkish Anatolia to form a separate Kurdish state. Unfortunately for the subsequent stability of the region, this plan was frustrated by a combination of political and economic demands which prevented the ratification of the treaty. Firstly, Kemal Ataturk – as president of a Turkey which had rapidly regained its military strength – refused to cede any part of his nation's already much reduced territory. Secondly, the expulsion of the Emir Feisal from Syria by the French forced the British government to honour its support for one of its war-time allies by placing him on the newly-created throne of Iraq.

Feisal then insisted on the addition of the mainly Kurdish vilayet of Mosul to his kingdom on the grounds that Iraq would not be economically viable without the revenues from the Mosul oilfields. As a result, the reconstruction of the Middle East from the rubble of the Ottoman Empire was not settled until the Treaty of Lausanne, which replaced the Treaty of Sevres, was signed in 1923. Even this did not unravel the results of the complex pattern of diplomatic and military intervention by the European powers which had been a feature of the struggle to acquire the assets of the Ottoman Empire since the beginning of its political and economic decline in the early years of the 19th century. The result was that the remnants of that once-great empire were to become a carcass over which European and Middle Eastern powers were to squabble – with disastrous results.

Officers and men of the Iraq Levies.

As the result of placing the Hashemite monarchy on the throne of the mandated territory of Iraq (itself an unstable creation) the British government was committed to involving the RAF in a series of air and ground operations against Kurdish rebels on behalf of the Iraqi government; in the long term this political misjudgment was to cause continuing problems to both Britain and Iraq, with consequent instability in the Middle East.

The Royal Air Force in Iraq

On 1st October 1922 Air Vice-Marshal Sir John Salmond[5] became the first Air Officer Commanding in Iraq, in succession to the outgoing Army commander who relinquished responsibility for the area. In addition to river gunboats and an armoured train, the RAF inherited a locally-enlisted force composed of Arabs, Kurds and Assyrians commanded by officers seconded from the British Army. The Iraq Levies of that time consisted of three cavalry regiments, four infantry battalions, two artillery batteries and a machine-gun company, totalling some six thousand men. Under RAF control the size of the force was progressively reduced, to less than a quarter of its original size by 1931, and its structure modernised. Nevertheless, it remained a useful military asset, under the command of the Air Officer Commanding, to support the policy of air control.

During the Second World War the Iraq Levies expanded to a force of 12,000 men in over 80 independent companies, including a parachute-trained unit, and was deployed outside Iraq on security and operational tasks in Middle East Command. As a result, the force was renamed "The Royal Air Force Levies, Iraq" in 1943 in order to clarify its identity and role in the RAF's command structure.

Despite the acquisition of the Iraq Levies as a ready-made military force, there was a need for more mobility and firepower on the ground, which could be deployed rapidly to secure forward airstrips in the desert and protect the aircraft there on the ground. In view of the close relationship between aircraft and ground forces when both were far from base, there were obvious benefits in providing RAF personnel for the ground support element. In terms of mobility, firepower and protection, the best answer to this problem was the RAF-manned armoured car – but this provided the War Office, smarting at the Army's losses and the Air Force's gains in the

Middle East, with the opportunity to resist further expansion of the RAF's role. When, even after lengthy discussions, the Army still refused to transfer any of its armoured cars to the RAF, the Air Ministry took the decision to act independently and build RAF armoured cars on the model of those used by the Royal Navy for land operations in the 1914-18 war.[6]

A batch of Rolls-Royce chassis, with the twin rear wheel modification used for the Admiralty's 1914 pattern vehicles, was purchased and fitted with armoured bodies at the RAF's No 1 Stores Depot. The design was generally similar to the Admiralty's except that the armour plate was thicker and more extensive, which made the RAF's "Rolls-Royce Standard Type A" armoured car different from the Navy's 1914 model and the Army's 1920 and 1924 versions.[7] The RAF version weighed slightly more than four tons unladen and the 7.5 litre Rolls engine, developing 65 bhp, drove only the rear wheels – which was to lead to mobility problems in soft sand conditions. The main armament was a turret-mounted Vickers .303" machine gun, although Lewis guns were usually carried as well for dismounted action by the four-man crew.

In order to provide a comparable degree of mobility for riflemen

HMAC Conqueror (1 Armoured Car Company) at speed in the Iraq desert.

(from the Iraq Levies or the Desert Police – or even co-opted RAF tradesmen) to support the armoured cars, a limited number of Lancia armoured personnel carriers – similar to those used by the Army – were purchased from 1921 onwards. These had a single Lewis gun mounted in the enclosed cab with an open-topped armoured body capable of carrying up to ten men but, with a smaller 5 litre 35 bhp engine driving the rear wheels only, their cross-country mobility was not always as good as the Rolls-Royce armoured cars. Other supporting vehicles used by the armoured car companies at this time included Model T Fords and Rolls-Royce Silver Ghosts with truck-type bodies. Both these types were unarmoured but carried Lewis guns for self-defence. In 1928 the range of support vehicles was extended to include a number of Crossley six-wheelers, built on either the 30/70 or 38/110 chassis.

The Armoured Car Companies

1 Armoured Car Company was formed at Heliopolis in Egypt on 19 December 1921 for service in Iraq, where it was joined in November 1922 by a wing headquarters and four more companies, numbered 3, 4, 5 and 6. 2 Company had been formed at Heliopolis on 7th April 1922 for service in Transjordan and remained at Amman, unaffected by the reorganisations which took place in the Iraq armoured car wing, where the wing headquarters itself was disbanded in November 1924. In the following April 3 Company was disbanded and in April 1927 the remaining companies were disbanded and reorganised as eight sections within an armoured car wing. The wing headquarters and four sections remained at Hinaidi (Baghdad), two were based at Kirkuk and one section each was deployed to Mosul and Basra. Finally, in April 1930 the armoured car strength was reduced to four sections and reformed as 1 Armoured Car Company at Habbaniya.

The RAF armoured cars were manned by personnel drawn from various officer branches (including those from the General Duties Branch who were either over the age of 35 or unfit for flying duties) and aircraftman trades of the Royal Air Force. Most served for a single overseas tour in the Middle East but there were some – mainly officers – who were attracted by the lifestyle of independent operations in the desert and who volunteered to stay for longer periods.

Thus was established the first ground combat element in what was otherwise a Service formed specifically to fight in the air.

The armoured car sections were used extensively in mapping and developing routes across the desert from Damascus and Amman to Baghdad, Basra and Kuwait, escorting road convoys and securing the advanced landing strips used by aircraft engaged in peace-keeping operations among the desert tribes. The most serious tribal disturbances in this period were the incursions, by fundamentalist Saudi Arabian tribesmen known as the Ikhwan, or Brotherhood, which threatened the stability of Transjordan, Iraq, and Kuwait.

In 1924 the Ikhwan invasion of Transjordan was driven back – at Ziza, only 20 miles from Amman – by the aircraft of 14 Squadron and the armoured cars of 2 Armoured Car Company. Sporadic Ikhwan incursions continued until 1930 when they were defeated, and their leaders captured, in the desert near Kuwait. The final battle was won by a mixed force of aircraft, bluejackets and Royal Marines landed from HM ships lying offshore – and the concentration of an imposing force of forty-eight RAF armoured cars from the wing in Iraq.[8] The armoured car companies resumed their roles in Iraq and Transjordan and until the outbreak of war were primarily engaged in internal security tasks – particularly in Palestine from 1935 onwards.

The success of the policy of air control in the Middle East led to its extension to the colony and protectorate of Aden in 1928, replacing the conventional garrison which had been provided there by the Indian Army. A locally-enlisted force, the Yemen Light Infantry, which had been raised during the First World War when the colony was threatened by Turkish forces, had been disbanded in 1925. However, the RAF had no difficulty in recruiting Arab tribesmen into another British-officered infantry unit – the Aden Protectorate Levies, usually abbreviated to APL – in 1928 to provide the ground element for internal security operations carried out by the single squadron of aircraft stationed in Aden.

It was not long before it became clear that air operations in the interior of the Aden Protectorate needed armoured car support as well and this was provided by a detachment from the armoured car wing in Iraq, which became "D" flight of the resident flying squadron in Aden. The war-time commitments of the APL led to its expansion, by 1945, to ten infantry companies, a light anti-aircraft wing and an armoured car section, all still under the control of seconded British Army officers and NCOs.

The Hendon Air Display -July 1929

Following the collapse of Germany and Russia as major military powers, the absence of any potential threat from the European continent had been used to justify maintaining the defence budget at the lowest possible level. This, combined with the political lethargy which derived from an inability to foresee any possibility of changes in the attitudes of other nations, had inhibited the modernisation of all three Services in the post-war period.

As far as the Royal Air Force was concerned, this retarded any realistic progress being made to develop the potential of air power – which had been described in a visionary book[9] published shortly after the war by Trenchard's contemporary, the Italian airman General Giulio Douhet. Equally, there was no indication of any awareness of the vulnerability of aircraft on the ground to attacks by either ground or air forces.

The first RAF open day at Hendon had been held in 1920 and the programme for the tenth Hendon air display in 1929 gave an insight into the training and tactics of that time. Apart from pure flying displays, the set-piece demonstrations included "Army co-operation aircraft swooping down low and collecting messages strung between two up-ended rifles", "artillery observation from the air of guns registering on an unseen target", "the convergent bombing of an encampment" and the "thrilling fights between single-seaters and fast day bombers".[10] It was, in essence, a reflection of the Royal Flying Corps at war in 1914-1918 but extended by the experience of keeping the peace in the post-war empire, albeit expanded by the need to produce a visual spectacle for public consumption.

Back to Basics

The RAF's success in the role of imperial policing in the Middle East undoubtedly gave credibility to the usefulness of the new air arm, but it did not open the door to a wider acceptance of the importance of air power in imperial defence. In India, for example, the Army remained firmly in control of defence policy – particularly on the North-West Frontier where the RAF was relegated to the supporting roles of reconnaissance, ground attack and transport. In the Far East, the Cabinet's rejection of Trenchard's arguments for basing the defence of the Singapore naval base on aircraft and air power undoubtedly contributed to the inability of all three Services to develop a unified strategy for its defence. This dysfunctional approach to war was to lead to disaster and defeat at the hands of the more single-minded Japanese.

Unfortunately, despite the development of aircraft, armour and weapons of all types, and the progressive replacement of horse-drawn transport by motor vehicles, military – and political – thinking remained heavily influenced by the strategy and tactics of the 1914-18 war. In the United Kingdom the Army had the responsibility for both land operations and anti-aircraft defence, which covered – in theory at least – the protection of RAF airfields and installations, but the deployment of aircraft to bases outside the United Kingdom raised the question of providing security for airfields in those theatres. After some deliberation, the Overseas Defence Committee of the Committee of Imperial Defence took what seemed to be the least contentious, and certainly the least expensive, option when it ruled, in 1926, that the Army should have similar responsibilities in overseas theatres to those which it exercised at home.[11]

It was a decision which was acceptable to all three Services (as it made the Army responsible for the defence of ports as well as airfields) because it avoided incurring expenditure in what both the Navy and the RAF viewed as secondary activities, even though it added weight to the Army's case for additional units to fulfil these tasks. As long as the unpleasant realities of a modern war could be ignored, it was a very satisfactory endorsement of the status quo which enabled everyday life to continue without raising disturbing thoughts of what might actually happen in the next major conflict.

The Period in Retrospect

Due to the economic restraints placed on the Services in this period, which effectively precluded the introduction of new operational concepts, there had been little opportunity to study what the future might bring in terms of improved equipment, new weapons and the roles of all three Services in a major war, whether operating singly or jointly. As a result, the ways in which the roles of the RAF extended into the domains of the other two Services were either resented as an intrusion into established practices or dismissed as irrelevant to real war at sea or on land.

This lack of finance and political direction combined to limit strategic thinking: the Admiralty and the War Office concentrated on ways in which the battles of the 1914-18 war might be re-fought more successfully, while the Air Ministry was uncertain of how best to develop new policies in an environment which was overshadowed by uncertainties in the continuing existence of an independent air arm. At the same time the aircraft carrier, the tank and the monoplane fighter were all being resisted as innovations which threatened accepted values and in such a climate it is perhaps understandable how issues such as the security of air bases never saw the light of day in scenarios which remained firmly rooted in the past.

Notes

[1]   "And the day may not be far off when aerial operations with their devastation of enemy lands and destruction of industrial and populous centres on a vast scale may become the principal operations of war, to which the older forms of military and naval operations may become secondary and subordinate".(Extract)

[2]   Field Marshal Sir Henry Wilson Bt GCB DSO, (1864-1922) who had summed up his opinion of the RAF as a force "coming from God knows where, dropping its bombs on God knows what, and going off God knows where" in an address to the Army Staff College at Camberley after the war. (Quoted in *Trenchard* by Andrew Boyle (Collins) 1962 p383

[3]   Later Air Commodore Robert Gordon CB CMG DSO (1882-1954). Retired 1925

[4]   AIR5/428, 846, 1309, 1310-14, 1315, 1422 (PRO)

[5]   Later MRAF Sir John Salmond GCB CMG CVO DSO (1881-1968)

[6]   Andrew Boyle – *Trenchard* (Collins) 1962 pp387-8

[7]   RJ Peters *Armoured Cars of the RAF* (Military Modelling) 1972. Part 3 pp200-201

[8]   EG Godsave *Tales of the Tin Trams* (Unpublished MS) c.1930 (RAF Regiment Museum Archives)

[9]   *The Command of the Air*, published in Italy in 1921

[10] *The Times* 13th July 1929

[11] CID 519 11th September 1926 (PRO)

2

The Lull before the Storm

All the business of war, and indeed all the business of life, is to endeavour to find out what you don't know by what you do.
Arthur Wellesley, Duke of Wellington[1]

The ten-year rule had been successful in containing expenditure on defence but less successful in ensuring that Britain – and the British Empire – would have an adequate military posture in a hostile world. Inevitably, many countries – including Great Britain – had counted on the League of Nations to provide the means for the peaceful settlement of international disputes so as to make major wars avoidable and unlikely. Consequently, among the by-products of these policies was stagnation in British defence capability since little or no additional funding had been made available to enable the armed forces of the Crown to develop, modernise and expand in order to meet the growth of militarism, and the drive for territorial expansion, in countries such as Germany, Italy and Japan.

Planning for War

In March 1932 the Cabinet accepted the increasingly obvious political and military signals from abroad and yielded to demands from the Chiefs of Staff for improvements in the capabilities of all three Services: the ten-year rule was formally declared to be dead and buried. This did not, of course, result in an immediate outpouring of public money; apart from the fact that the Treasury did not relax its normal cautious approach to expenditure of public funds, military plans had to be recast, new equipment evaluated and ordered, personnel recruited and trained, and new installations built – all of which would take time. Nevertheless, by the end of 1932 the Air

Ministry was well advanced in planning aircraft deployments at home and overseas and the problem of defending RAF installations and aircraft on the ground appeared on the Air Staff agenda.

While the 1926 decision of the Committee of Imperial Defence had ruled that the Army would be responsible for the general defence of the land areas in which RAF stations were located, arguments arose over the small print in the agreement. The Army took the traditional view that local ground defence was a unit responsibility – in this case that of the RAF station commander – and that the local Army commander was responsible only for providing reinforcements in the event of superior enemy attack.[2] From the Royal Air Force's viewpoint, such a policy represented too little, too late since personnel on flying stations were fully committed to maintaining air operations and there would be no surplus manpower available to defend airfields until the arrival of Army reinforcements – by which time the damage would have been done. Thus, by setting in peace time goals which were to prove unattainable in the realities of war, were the seeds of disaster sown.

Whatever the Air Staff might have felt about the likelihood of enemy ground forces penetrating the Army's forward defences and attacking RAF airfields behind the front line, the threat of enemy air attack on RAF stations was taken more seriously from November 1933 onwards when it was decided that the Air Force would be responsible for its own anti-aircraft (AA) defence against low flying enemy aircraft. Despite this, the provisioning of suitable weapons was not given much attention, partly because little research and development had been carried out but largely because of an overriding sense of pessimism about any possibility of effectively engaging modern aircraft delivering attacks at low level and high speed.

In the early 1930s the Royal Navy had studied the results of the United States Navy's investigations into the defence of warships against air attack in 1927, and had not found these very encouraging either. The USN's trials had established that the .303" machine gun lacked the necessary range, rate of fire and hitting power and estimated that the concentrated fire of at least four pairs of Lewis guns would be needed to engage each attacking aircraft with even the minimal prospect of deterrence, let alone the possibility of inflicting lethal damage. The American conclusion was that the .50" machine gun was the smallest calibre weapon which could be effective in the anti-aircraft role.

Later trials by the Royal Navy and the British Army confirmed that the .50" machine gun was more effective than .303" weapons – but proved that the 20mm (Oerlikon) and 40mm (Bofors) were better still. Given that none of these weapons were readily available in the United Kingdom, there was consequently more support within the RAF for passive defence measures (camouflage, dispersal, trenches and sandbagged walls) than for anti-aircraft machine guns.[3]

In 1935 the Air Ministry "Committee on the Defence of RAF Stations against Air Attack" held its first meeting, under the chairmanship of Group Captain R H Peck,[4] to examine the existing Air Staff policy that the probable scale of air attack on RAF stations, irrespective of geographical location, did not justify the expenditure which would be incurred in providing AA defences. By the end of that meeting, having considered the results of the Navy's trials with AA machine guns, the committee had decided that the Air Staff should review the need for AA defence of airfields. In addition to tasking staff officers to carry out further research into the progress which the Navy and Army had made in this area and establishing a study into the RAF's operational requirements for AA defence, the committee also concluded that there was a case for providing all RAF stations in England south of the Tees with such defences.[5]

The Low Flying Threat to Airfields

By 1938 the threat of low flying attacks on airfields was such that it was clear that active defence measures against air attack had to be introduced, although these would have to be based on what was available rather than on what was desirable. A further series of studies within the Air Ministry revealed the dilemmas which faced the RAF: there was a reluctance to opt for weapons which would be unfamiliar to Air Force personnel, but even so there were inherent cost and supply problems in adapting aircraft armament for effective ground use – and the limited effectiveness of the .303" calibre machine gun in the ground-to-air role was well known. RAF trials with the naval two-pounder pom-pom had been inconclusive and the .50" (12.7mm) machine gun, in a quadruple mounting, was considered to be more suitable for the RAF requirement for airfield defence than the naval system – whose two-pounder HE shells did not self-destruct before striking the ground – and more effective than the .303" machine gun which was in general use, in several versions, in the RAF.

The Army had, after a series of trials, opted for the 40mm gun which had been developed by the Swedish firm of Bofors, but the cost of re-equipping the Royal Artillery with this weapon was more than double the amount provided for in the Army estimates. The Treasury, economical as ever, was therefore able to exploit these inter-Service differences on the grounds that the limited funding available should be disbursed in accordance with accepted priorities and single-Service principles. Consequently, the RAF had to settle for the simpler option and the cheaper weapon – the machine gun. Unfortunately, the .50" machine gun was not readily available in a suitable ground mounting so the solution had to be found by adapting a weapon which was in plentiful supply, even if it were not the preferred choice, This forced the RAF to accept the .303" Lewis light machine gun, as used both on the ground and in the air during the previous war, as an interim weapon for ground use against low flying aircraft. The Lewis gun was an obsolescent and temperamental weapon which was subject

RAF Ground Gunner manning twin Lewis AA machine guns.

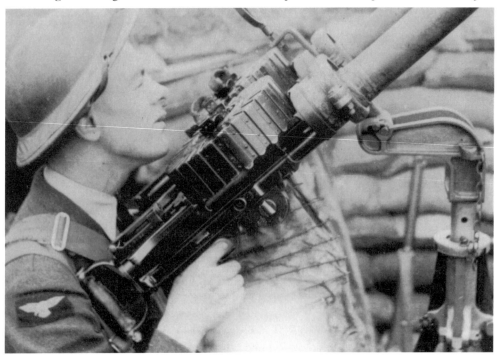

to frequent stoppages, and the expectation was that it would be progressively replaced by the more modern Vickers "K" gun with its higher rate of fire. As the Vickers was being phased out of aircraft use in favour of the Browning machine gun, surplus Vickers guns were expected to become available for ground use.

The difficulties of trying to adapt aircraft weapons to the ground role – for which they had not been designed – were subsequently appreciated by at least some RAF officers. Early in 1938 the Deputy Director of Plans[6] in the Air Ministry challenged the conventional wisdom of relying on limited numbers of .303" machine guns for low level air defence when he wrote to the Deputy Chief of Air Staff: "I don't know what the answer will be in terms of guns or their cost. I think it may be most unpalatable but we have to face the facts and it is my considered opinion that if we can't get the money and men by any other means, then we must be prepared to cut bomber squadrons to find it. It's better to start the war with 800 bombers operating from reasonably secure bases than with 1,000 bombers, of whom perhaps more than half will be unable to operate because their aerodromes have been put out of action. I think we ought to order some Bofors guns for our most exposed aerodromes....and I don't think we should make heavy weather about it being an 'artillery weapon'; I believe we'd soon train our chaps to use it, and we'd do it far cheaper than the Army would, and just as well."[7]

Here were the first stirrings in the Air Staff of an understanding of the threat to aircraft operating from vulnerable airfields in the as yet unproven conditions of modern war. The realisation of the existence of such an Achilles' heel was – after it had been devastatingly proved in the reality of combat – to lead the RAF inexorably to the protection of its own resources on the ground by the formation of the RAF Regiment four years later.

In July 1938 the Air Ministry issued a policy letter[8] setting out the allocation of anti-aircraft machine guns to RAF stations on scales of either four or eight guns, depending on factors of both location and type of station, and making provision for the establishment of aircraftmen to man them. Nevertheless, there were still differing opinions among senior officers about the value of active defence for RAF installations. Apart from those who saw it as an inappropriate and diversionary role for an air force, there were others who regarded the deployment of such defences as an unwelcome advertisement of the existence of a possible target for enemy attack.

Air Vice-Marshal Bradley, the Air Officer Commanding (AOC) Maintenance Command, reacted to advice from the Air Ministry on the deployment of anti-aircraft defences by writing to the Under-Secretary of State to say "the presence of guns might....become an actual source of danger...and draw attention to the unit. Evasive siting and camouflage are the primary aids upon which our depots and units depend for security and the aim is that it should be possible for enemy aircraft to fly close by, or even overhead, without observing them."[9] Predictably, this negative approach to a positive threat did not meet with much success once war broke out.

Joint Service Responsibilities

Hitler's disclosure of the existence of the Luftwaffe in 1935 had concentrated the minds of the General and Air Staffs with the result that Army and RAF commanders were jointly tasked to examine their respective responsibilities for aerodrome defence in the United Kingdom. Neither Service had resources to spare and the conclusions were much as before: the Army remained responsible for area defence and the provision of reinforcements for RAF stations in an emergency, as well as for providing anti-aircraft artillery and searchlights as part of an overall air defence system. Although the Army was, in principle, also committed to providing AA guns to protect RAF airfields sited outside the Army's anti-aircraft defence zones, the slender resources available made it doubtful if it would be possible to honour this commitment adequately in war.

Inter-Service agreement was reached on the understanding that defence against low-level attack for RAF airfields and installations was an RAF responsibility which would be fulfilled by anti-aircraft machine guns manned by aircrafthands trained as ground gunners.[10] At the same time, much greater emphasis was placed on those passive defence measures which had been ordered in the previous year, such as camouflage, dispersal and shelters while new criteria were issued for buildings which were essential for operational purposes and therefore had to be strengthened against the effects of bombing.[11]

The results of these policy decisions were not encouraging either to RAF commanders – who had to divert precious manpower to both ground and low-level air defence tasks when they were also required to operate aircraft at maximum intensity – or to RAF staff officers who had to find the resources to provide anti-aircraft machine guns and the personnel to man them. The intelligence view at the time was that low level air defence would not be necessary at stations in the Middle East but even without that commitment it was estimated that the additional number of airmen to crew AA machine guns on RAF stations would amount to war establishment increases of 3,000 men for such tasks in the UK and the Far East. The planned deployment of AA machine guns in the United Kingdom was based on the assessed threat to airfields, depending on whether they were located in front of, within or behind the main air defence zone. The original concept of quadruple machine gun mountings operated by one man proved to be impossible to resolve in practice and the result was that more numerous single or twin gun mountings had to be used, with a consequent increase in the number of personnel required to man them.

Advance warning of the fragility of the agreed inter-Service responsibilities for the defence of RAF installations had been given during the Arab-Jewish disturbances in Palestine between 1935 and 1938 when the large Army garrison there was frequently unable to provide reinforcements for RAF stations threatened by terrorist attack. Station commanders met this situation by using sections of No 2 Armoured Car Company, as allocated to them by the AOC, which were then supplemented in the ground defence role by armed station personnel withdrawn from their primary duties. The diversion of technical tradesmen from aircraft servicing tasks adversely affected flying operations and when the AOC Palestine and Transjordan, Air Commodore AT Harris,[12] complained about this, and the Army's failure to meet its commitments to the RAF, he received the prescient response from the AOC-in-C Middle East that "if war should come it would be extremely difficult – if not impossible – for the Army to provide adequate defence for RAF establishments."

The Unarmed Service

By 1937 the Air Ministry was under pressure from the War Office to release rifles for Army use. Accordingly, the Air Council ordered the withdrawal of all .303" rifles, other than those required for recruit training, competition shooting and ceremonial purposes.[13] But the intention was not to leave the Air Force completely defenceless and it was reassuringly stated that the withdrawn rifles would be replaced by a "light repeating automatic weapon fired from the shoulder." Unfortunately, no one knew what this weapon might be or when it would be brought into service.[14] In an attempt to bridge the gap it was decided to issue .38" revolvers to ground personnel and to supplement this level of defence by a few Vickers "K" guns "modified for firing from the shoulder." However, the limited supply of Vickers guns was such that few could be spared for ground defence purposes and the problems of adapting those that were available "for firing from the shoulder" proved to be insurmountable and the project was abandoned.

Commanders-in-Chief were not slow to realise the implications of the withdrawal of rifles – without replacement by another type of personal weapon – on the defensive responsibilities with which they had been charged by the Air Ministry. Air Marshal Sir Charles Burnett, AOC Training Command, wrote to the Air Ministry in February 1938 expressing his dismay at the situation – of which the Deputy Chief of Air Staff immediately disclaimed any knowledge.[15] As a result, prompt staff action was initiated by the Air Ministry to scale weapons and manpower for station defence.

This became even more urgent following the crisis in the summer of 1938 when, following the annexation of Czechoslovakia by Hitler, war with Germany appeared imminent. In order to ensure the defence of selected RAF Vulnerable Points (VPs) in the UK, a joint force – of six officers and 331 other ranks provided by the Army and one officer and 332 airmen drawn from Training Command units – was formed to cope with this task. Inevitably, such an ad hoc approach proved to be quite inadequate – in terms of numbers, training, organisation and equipment – to meet the VP defence requirements to the RAF's satisfaction and the situation was re-examined in the hope of developing a better system for the future.

As prime minister, Neville Chamberlain had bought time for Great Britain at Munich and the onset of war was deferred for a further year during which plans were revised and updated while the new fighter aircraft – Hurricanes and Spitfires – were brought into service and more aircrew were trained. Development of the chain of

Radio Direction Finding (RDF) stations, as the early radar units were known, was accelerated and achieved the operational status which enabled the early warning system to operate effectively by the time the Luftwaffe turned its attention to the British Isles after the battle of France. Had war come in 1938, it is more than likely that the result of a Battle of Britain in 1939 would not have been the victory which was so narrowly won in 1940.

The Revision of Arming Policy

In January 1939 the Air Ministry reintroduced the rifle as a personal weapon for airmen serving overseas and established pools of rifles and revolvers on stations at home for issue to airmen when on guard or defence duties. HQ Far East Air Force submitted requirements for rifles for stations in Singapore and Malaya but specified that bayonets were not required as well "despite the dictum that you can do anything with one but sit upon it".

Arrangements were made for Territorial Army detachments to be deployed to RAF stations at home on mobilisation, pending the enlistment and training of "National Defence Companies" which would subsequently take over these tasks from the TA. Even so, the resources available were insufficient to cover all the RAF's requirements and RDF units which were not provided with Army support had to make do with "unclimbable wooden fences", two pistols and two rifles and bayonets apiece.

At this time, 406 RAF stations were scaled for up to 8 machine guns each for defence against low-level attack but only 124 of these were within the Army's anti-aircraft artillery defence zones. The number of RAF installations which could rely on the close protection of Army two- pounder or 3" LAA guns as well was further reduced by the very limited availability of these weapons, which were also required for the defence of the Field Army against air attack.

By July 1939 the Air Ministry was seriously concerned at the inadequacy of measures for the ground and low-level air defence of RAF stations at home and those in France to which the squadrons of the Advanced Air Striking Force would be deployed. The establishment for manning AA machine guns was increased to six aircrafthands per gun at home and overseas and increases were authorised in the numbers of locally-enlisted personnel in Singapore and Malta for defence and security duties. In the Middle East it was considered that adequate defences already existed with the presence of the Iraq and Aden Levies, the Transjordan Frontier Force and the RAF armoured car companies.

The Race against Time

Nevertheless, there were serious shortfalls in the provision of defence weapons of all types and the additional personnel had still to be recruited and trained, let alone deployed to their war stations. The chillingly prophetic words of Air Commodore Douglas Evill,[16] Senior Air Staff Officer at HQ Bomber Command, who wrote in 1937 that "no works or equipment not provided in peace, and no measures of defence and protection not practised in advance, will be found of any effect in the opening stages of an emergency when the need for them will be at its height"[17], were to serve as a constant reminder of the results of the practical problems of preparing for war in an era of financial parsimony when the RAF had to live from hand to mouth and from day to day. By a quirk of fate, Air Vice-Marshal Evill was SASO at HQ British Air Forces France in 1940 and was able to witness the fulfilment of his prophecy at first-hand.

Rearmament in Retrospect

Although the Air Staff had recognised the inadequacy of station defences, and the consequent vulnerability of vital installations and precious aircraft, the flow of orders and counter-orders which characterised the prelude to the outbreak of war in August 1939 was not conducive to the clear thinking and logical planning needed to resolve these problems. Furthermore, the RAF was operating under the serious constraint of not possessing any competent advisers of its own to plan and organise airfield defence, which had to be done on an ad hoc basis by staff officers with neither the necessary training nor experience.

The Army had priority over the RAF for ground defence weapons and equipment and although the Army had accepted responsibility for the protection of RAF installations, the resources for such tasks were to prove inadequate in many cases and non-existent in most others. In any event, Army officers did not necessarily appreciate the modus operandi of the RAF and the need for continuity in air operations, regardless of the threat of enemy attacks on airfields. Indeed, on more than one occasion Army representatives suggested that military forces had the right to direct the evacuation and destruction of RAF airfields and installations to accord with the land battle, in order to prevent them falling into the hands of the enemy, rather than to defend them at all costs to ensure the continuation of air operations.[18]

The result was to be that the RAF entered a war with a major European power without any coherent organisation of its own for the defence of its installations and aircraft on the ground.[19] Even worse, RAF commanders assumed that their assets would be effectively protected by adequate forces of British infantry, armour and anti-aircraft artillery. Subsequent events made it clear that they were wrong and the consequences of this were to prove disastrous for the RAF when it encountered skilled and determined enemies in the opening stages of war in France and the Far East. The rewards of gallantry in the air were to be, all too often, negated by the results of inadequate organisation for defence on the ground.

It is therefore worth remembering the German solution to this problem: at the outbreak of war in 1939 the strength of the Luftwaffe was one and a half million officers and men – of whom two-thirds were in anti-aircraft, airborne and parachute units which – together with the elite Hermann Goering Regiment – were part of the Luftwaffe's order of battle. With these properly trained and equipped troops at their disposal, German Air Force commanders – unlike their British counterparts – had few problems in ensuring the security of their airfields and installations against enemy attack.

Notes

[1]   *The Croker Papers*, vol 3 p276

[2]   AIR5/503(PRO) – memo from S6 to D Org 20 Feb 1935

[3]   AIR9/51(PRO) – memo from D Plans to DCAS 10 May 1932

[4]   Later Air Marshal Sir Richard Peck KCB OBE MA (1893-1952) Assistant Chief of Air Staff (General) 1940-45

[5]   AIR2/2701(PRO) – 14 Jun 35

[6]   Group Captain J C Slessor, later MRAF Sir John Slessor GCB DSO MC (1897-1979) Chief of Air Staff 1950-52

[7]   AIR19/91 – Pt I (PRO)

[8]   S.32948(PRO) – 5 Jul 38

[9]   AIR2/2994 (PRO) – AOC Maintenance Command to US of S (Air) – 25 Mar 39

[10] S.22660/IV – 30 Aug 38/S.46238 – 3 Sep 38/S.35123 – 15 Sep 38/S.46351 – 28 & 30 Sep 38/S.32948/I – 25 Sep 38 (All PRO)

[11] S.38103/S.6(PRO) – 22 Feb 1937

[12] Later Marshal of the Royal Air Force Sir Arthur Harris Bt GCB OBE AFC (1892-1984). AOC-in-C Bomber Command 1942-45

[13] Air Council 75(PRO) – 23 Mar 1937

[14] AIR2/270 (PRO). In June 1936 an Air Ministry committee had considered a range of options for replacing the rifle. These included .303" Lewis guns fitted with Bren magazines, BSA automatic rifles, Austrian Neuhausen 9mm machine pistols, Hungarian Kiralyi rifles and Italian Scotti automatic rifles. The Vickers 12mm automatic gun was also considered as a possible anti-aircraft weapon. No decisions were taken for provisioning any of these weapons for RAF use

[15] AM/S.41239(PRO) – 14 Mar 1938

[16] Later Air Chief Marshal Sir Douglas Evill GBE KCB DSC AFC (1892-1971). VCAS 1943-46

[17] AM/S.35134/1 (PRO) – 12 Oct 1937

[18] AIR2/7266/3 (PRO)

[19] "Moreover, inadequate as were the air forces for the support of the army, the army provision for the support of the air – AA and ground defence of air bases, provision of engineers for airfields, etc – was even more inadequate." Tedder – *Air Power in War* p24

3

Trial and Error

The surest and most effective way of achieving this end is to destroy the enemy air force at its bases. This is the principle which governs the situation: it is easier and more effective to destroy the enemy's aerial power by destroying his nests and eggs on the ground than to hunt his flying birds in the air. And every time we ignore this principle, we commit an error!

General Giulio Douhet[1]

The Move to France

The outbreak of war in August 1939 was followed by the deployment of the British Expeditionary Force (BEF), with its Air Component of twelve RAF squadrons, to France in September and October. The airfields from which these squadrons operated were within the BEF area and the policy for ground and low-level air defence which had been agreed by the War Office and the Air Ministry was followed, as far as it was possible with the resources which were available.

The ten RAF squadrons in the first echelon of the Advanced Air Striking Force (AASF) were not so fortunate: deployed in two-squadron wings on five airfields to the south-east of the BEF area, they were entirely dependent on 75mm guns of the French Army, and French air companies armed with Hotchkiss machine guns, for local defence. It was not long before the French notified the British of their intention to withdraw their troops from the airfields on which the AASF were deployed in order to protect French aircraft elsewhere.

In the rush to provide a measure of defence for the AASF, now deployed on ten airfields, additional Lewis guns were provided and

235 aircrafthands were flown from Bicester to man them. Unfortunately, they had no experience of anti-aircraft machine guns of any type and had to be trained as they arrived in France. The late reintroduction of the rifle as a personal weapon resulted in elementary training courses having to be carried out on operational stations at home and abroad. At that stage it was discovered that all RAF .303" ammunition was supplied in boxes – ready for aircraft use – and without the chargers and bandoliers which were essential for ground defence purposes. As a result airmen armed with rifles had to carry loose rounds in their pockets and load them one by one into their weapons.

Experimental Air Defence Systems

Meanwhile, the Scientific Adviser to the Air Ministry[2] had been investigating other means of augmenting airfield defences against low-level air attack. In September 1939 he reported on trials carried out at the University College of the South-West at Exeter on his behalf.[3] The concept was to use rockets, spaced sixty feet apart in lines across the likely approaches to a vulnerable point, in order to project a barrier of steel cables, each with a breaking strength of one ton, to a height of 400 feet to intercept attacking aircraft. A parachute, three feet in diameter, would open at the top of each cable to delay its descent while another, which was attached to the lower end of the cable, would remain in a sleeve in the ground until an aircraft struck the suspended cable. Then the momentum of the aircraft would pull the cable clear of the ground sleeve and deploy the second parachute. The effect of this would be to retard the aircraft's flight by 400 feet of steel cable, with a parachute at each end, and this was expected to bring the aircraft down.[4]

The rockets were fired, in salvos of 25, by command switches operated by one airman (or one airwoman, as operators later included members of the Women's Auxiliary Air Force) who had to judge the correct moment to fire in order to intercept attacking aircraft. Such was the state of desperation about the adequacy of defence against low-level air attack that the Air Ministry immediately placed an order for 5,000 "Rockets Parachute and Cable" (abbreviated to PAC) at a cost of £25,000. By June 1940 PACs were deployed operationally at eleven airfields and nine factories. This was increased to a total of 59

PAC defended airfields in the UK, as well as several in the Middle East, by the end of 1941.

This PAC system was in fact the first phase of an ambitious scheme, the second of which was to add larger rockets and longer cables so as to increase the effective height of the barrier to 2,000 feet. In this phase, the parachute at the bottom of the cable was to be replaced by a high-explosive charge which would be drawn towards the aircraft by the parachute on the upper end and act as an aerial mine to destroy the target. In the third phase the intention was to replace the rockets and cables with 250lb high-explosive bombs, placed on angled ramps facing outwards and upwards around airfields. Each bomb would be detonated automatically by a photo-electric cell as attacking aircraft flew over them and it was hoped that this would produce sufficient blast and splinters to destroy or disable low-flying aircraft. Neither the effectiveness of such a system, nor its implications for the safety of friendly aircraft, appear to have been tested in practice.

Once deployed, the operational limitations of the PAC concept became obvious by the inflexibility of the defence – and its poor rate of success in destroying enemy aircraft – which led to its withdrawal by the autumn of 1942, before phases two or three could be introduced. Thereafter attention returned to more conventional means of defeating, or mitigating the effects of, air attacks on RAF installations.

Problems at Unit Level

The ad hoc provision of manpower for the defence of the AASF airfields in France inevitably resulted in problems of efficiency as well as difficulties in command and control. It was not until April 1940 that junior NCOs had been established to supervise the ground gunners deployed on airfields but even at that late stage no provision was made for armourers to maintain the air defence machine guns. Establishing new posts was one thing – manning them another – and it took time for them to be filled, whether by NCOs or aircraftmen, with suitably trained personnel.

Inevitably, the age and serviceability of the variety of machine guns allotted to airfield defence caused problems at unit level: 70% of these were the Lewis Mk VII guns which had been fitted in aircraft in World War I and which were already obsolescent. The only common feature of the wide variety of mountings and sights provided was that none had been designed originally for ground use against aircraft flying at low level and high speeds.

In April 1940, in an attempt to improve the situation, the Air Ministry approved the temporary release of 500 surplus 20mm Hispano aircraft cannon to supplement the existing aircraft .303" machine guns issued for the air defence of stations. Training for the personnel to man them was arranged at a ground defence gunnery school at RAF North Coates but before the 100 Hispanos and the gunners earmarked for France were ready for deployment, the German offensive had begun. On the day on which the German attack was launched, the RAF's airfields in France were defended by only 433 .303" machine guns manned by 835 ground gunners, in addition to 72 assorted anti-aircraft artillery weapons provided by the Army.

Blitzkrieg – and the Battle of France
At first light on 10th May 1940 the Luftwaffe launched attacks on French Air Force installations and the RAF airfields of the AASF. At 0545 the Blenheims of 114 Squadron were still on the ground at Conde Vraux when the airfield was attacked by a squadron of twelve Dornier 17 light bombers. In the space of ten minutes six of the aircraft were destroyed and the remainder damaged. The attack also set the aviation fuel dumps ablaze and damaged the buildings on the airfield. Surprisingly, the sixteen Lewis guns defending Conde Vraux airfield claimed to have destroyed ten of the attacking "Heinkels", but there is no confirmation of this and the claim is annotated "all most unlikely!" in the records of the AASF.

This was the Royal Air Force's first experience of effective counter-air operations and it provided a salutary example of the effectiveness of co-ordinated air attacks on airfields and their installations. The vulnerability of aircraft on the ground, and unprotected support facilities, had been graphically demonstrated to RAF commanders at all levels – fortunately in time for some remedial action to be taken in the United Kingdom before the Battle of Britain began.

To make matters worse, as the RAF withdrew from its French airfields and columns of its vehicles retreated towards the Channel coast, it was discovered that the RAF convoys were particularly vulnerable to air attack as machine guns could not be mounted in an AA role on their vehicles. Conversely, the pilots of RAF aircraft soon discovered that the advancing German columns had well- organised light anti-aircraft defence weapons which could be brought into action while on the move. The last elements of the RAF were withdrawn from France in June 1940 and preparations to resist German attack on the United Kingdom were accelerated.

Unfortunately, there are no records of individual actions by ground gunners in the confusion of what came to be known as the Battle of France, although the reasons for the losses suffered as the result of inadequate ground and low-level air defence were included in a comprehensive despatch by the AOC-in-C British Air Forces France,[5] who summarised the lessons which had been learned in the disastrous campaign. Among these were: insufficient anti-aircraft weapons for airfield defence, a lack of personal weapons resulting in inadequate defence against ground attack, unawareness of the importance of camouflage and dispersal, the need for mobile reserves – including armoured vehicles – to reinforce ground defences and the shortfall in Army units assigned to defend RAF airfields. Among his recommendations was the provision of specially trained and equipped airfield defence battalions to prevent a repetition elsewhere of the disasters experienced by the Royal Air Force in France.(6)

The full implications of his report were, inevitably, overtaken by other events but in the wider context of conducting air operations against a formidable enemy it seems probable that those who had not experienced the situation at first-hand could not grasp the extent of the threat. Nevertheless, the Air Staff was quick to appreciate the significance of the Luftwaffe's tactics and a Ground Defence branch was hastily formed within the Air Ministry, even before the last British aircraft had left France for home.

By this stage of the war it was clear to the RAF that it could no longer rely upon the Army for the close defence of RAF installations; indeed it was only in circumstances far removed from the reality of a major war that politicians and senior officers of both Services had been able to shelter behind the illusion that the British Army would have sufficient resources to do everything from fighting the land battle to defending the bases on which the Royal Air Force depended for air operations. The unhappy position in which the RAF found itself in 1940 can be traced to two main causes: an unquestioning reliance upon an unproven policy for the provision of those defence measures which were of primary importance for the exercise of air power, and the lack of expertise within the Air Ministry and RAF Commands to enable ground defence measures to be planned and executed in conjunction with the needs of air operations.

New Policies for Airfield Defence

In January 1940 the War Office had appointed Colonel WE Davies to be the Inspector of RAF Vulnerable Points, with the aim of rationalising (from an Army viewpoint) the RAF's requests for military support. At the same time, the Air Ministry established a number of flight lieutenant posts, to be filled by officers of the Administrative Branch, for station defence duties on selected RAF stations. However, prompted by the unexpected German success in destroying RAF airfields in the battle of France, the Air Ministry lost no time in taking action to create a branch of the Air Staff to deal with the planning and organisation of defence measures within the RAF as a whole.

On 27th May 1940 the Directorate of Ground Defence, with Air Commodore APM Sanders[7] as its first Director, was formed in the Air Ministry. Its task was to co-ordinate arrangements and issue instructions for the ground defence of all RAF stations in the United Kingdom, liaise with the other Services and Ministries on such matters, and deal with questions relating to passive defence measures against air attack for the country as a whole.[8] The Treasury grudgingly gave approval for the establishment of the Directorate on a temporary basis for three months only, on the understanding that its work would be completed within that period of time.

One of the first tasks of the new Directorate was to obtain approval for the establishment of 100 airmen per flying station for defence duties and by the end of the year 29,000 men, wearing the new Ground Gunner armbadge, were employed in this role as Aircrafthands/General Duties/Ground Gunner (ACH/GD/GG). An initial evaluation of the station defence task indicated that 100,000 men (half the strength of the pre-war Regular Army) would be required to provide adequate defence for every RAF station in the

United Kingdom[9] and Commands were soon competing with each other for these resources. Even Maintenance Command reversed its pre-war view about the undesirability of siting anti-aircraft weapons near its units and appealed for such defence for its aircraft storage and equipment depots.

The next problem was to find officers with the appropriate training or experience to take charge of station defence planning and exercise command over the airmen who were now being posted to form RAF defence units. The most obvious source was the pool of Army Emergency Reserve (AER) officers who were too old for service in the field Army and by September 1940 some 800 such ex-officers, mainly over 53 years old, had been recruited. But more were still needed and the Army agreed to provide a further 125 serving majors and lieutenant-colonels as local defence advisers for RAF and RN airfields. In many cases, however, the elderly AER officers were not suited to their unfamiliar roles (one station commander reported that his defence officer had refused to climb the ladder to the defence observation post on a water tower because he was afraid of heights) and the RAF began recruiting younger men who could be trained and commissioned in the Administrative (Special Duties) branch for employment as station defence officers.

The Taylor Report

A joint study by Major-General GBO Taylor (Director of Fortifications) (Army)[10] and Air Commodore APM Sanders (Director of Ground Defence) (RAF) was issued on 31st July 1940 as the Taylor Report.[11] While this recommended a series of improvements in defence measures on RAF stations, it neither addressed nor resolved the fundamental problems which resulted from the divided responsibilities between Army and RAF commanders: once again, the critical factor in the equation was avoided as being too contentious to resolve.

On 2nd September 1940 the Director of Ground Defence attempted to clarify the RAF's position by proposing to VCAS that the RAF should form its own ground defence corps on the lines of the Royal Marines.[12] But the War Office remained resolutely opposed to any diminution of its responsibilities for overall ground defence of the home base and had no difficulty in finding allies in the Air

Ministry who considered that this proposal would be a dangerous diversion of RAF resources. United in maintaining the status quo on the basis of principle and precedent, neither the Air Staff nor the General Staff could – or would – suggest any means of improving the patently unsatisfactory situation which faced hard-pressed RAF commanders on the ground.

Preparation and Improvisation

By the end of June 1940 the enemy were in possession of the continental coastline facing England from Land's End to the Shetlands. The deployment of the Luftwaffe to its newly-gained forward airfields posed a threat to almost every RAF installation in the United Kingdom. At the same time, the likelihood of invasion meant that vulnerable points between the Bristol Channel and the Humber became potential targets for airborne attack as a prelude to large-scale landings, both by air and sea.

This situation was radically different from the one which had existed when the Allied armies and air forces were deployed in France and all three Services had to adjust rapidly to the possibility of fighting the next battle on English soil as well as in the surrounding airspace and coastal waters. Frantic efforts were made to increase the number of anti-aircraft machine guns for airfield defence and by September 1940 it had been possible to augment the dwindling stocks of .303" Lewis, Vickers and Browning guns available for this role by .300" Lewis and Vickers guns obtained from the USA. Despite the supply problems caused by different ammunition requirements, these additional weapons were gratefully received.

Improvisation remained the order of the day for both the anti-aircraft and ground defence of RAF stations. Anti-aircraft machine guns – mainly Lewis guns, with some Vickers "K" and Browning guns – were deployed on a variety of twin mountings. A quadruple Lewis gun mounting was devised but it was too cumbersome and slow to traverse for engaging fast, low-flying aircraft. Adaptation of whatever MT chassis could be spared from other tasks produced a remarkable range of vehicles intended to provide mobile firepower for station defence forces. It was perhaps fortunate that these improvised weapon carriers were never tested in combat against well trained and well equipped Luftwaffe parachute forces.

Experimental quadruple Lewis AA machine gun mounting.

The first such vehicle was the Armadillo – built at the London, Midland & Scottish Railway's workshops at Wolverton, mainly on the 30 cwt Bedford chassis. The Mark I had an armoured cab and mounted a single Lewis gun in an open-topped wooden box superstructure in which protection was provided by filling the 6" space between the inner and outer boxes with shingle. The Mark II had an armoured radiator and fuel tank as well and mounted twin Lewis guns in the box body. The Mark III was built on the Bedford 3 ton chassis and was fitted with a $1^1/2$ pounder COW (Coventry Ordnance Works) gun. 312 of the Mark I were delivered and these were followed by 295 Mark IIs with 53 of the more powerful Mark III version completing the order.

Other vehicles which were modified with some form of protection and used for airfield defence at this critical time included the Morris Type E armoured car – of which about two thousand two hundred were manufactured – in Mark I and Mark II form, and Bisons – produced by Concrete Ltd and named after the firm's bison trademark – which carried a concrete pillbox on flatbed 4x2 trucks. The "tender, armoured, Leyland, type C" – also known as the Beaver-

Armadillo with AA and ground to ground weapons.

Eel – was an open-topped steel body on a Leyland Retriever chassis, carrying either a 20mm cannon or a $1^1/_2$ pounder COW gun. There was also the Cockatrice flame-thrower, mounted on an AEC 6x6 chassis and – presumably as a last resort – Triumph motorcycles fitted with armour plate on one side only and mounting a Bren light machine gun.

Perhaps the most successful of these improvised station defence vehicles was the Beaverette light armoured car designed and built by the Standard Motor Company on their ordinary motor car chassis. The first Beaverette Mk I was designed and built in 24 hours, although it took ten days to produce the Mk III version, (which became known as the Beaverbug) and both types continued in use throughout the war. Some 2,800 of these vehicles were eventually produced and those in RAF service were fitted with either an LMG (the Mk I) and used as reconnaissance vehicles or with twin Vickers "K" guns (the Mk.III) for use as mobile anti-aircraft posts.[13]

Another improvisation upon which the Air Ministry pinned high

Beaverette Mk I armoured car.

The Disappearing Pillbox

Now you see it…

…now you don't!

hopes for its contribution to airfield defence was the disappearing pillbox. This was described in a memorandum to ACAS(G) on 26th July 1940 as being "rather like two cocoa tins, one inside the other, sunk vertically into the ground, the bottom half being larger than the top. The construction is of concrete drain pipes, which have withstood the test of rifle fire. Inside is a hydraulic jack attached to the roof which raises the upper portion approximately thirty inches above ground level. Loopholes are cut in the portion raised above the ground, from which machine guns can be operated." It was estimated that three or four would be required for each airfield in the "invasion area" – a total of 350 pillboxes at a cost of £200 each.

The Battle of Britain

The Luftwaffe began a three-phase attack in July 1940 with the aim of gaining air superiority over southern England before the end of August so as to enable the invasion to be launched from the Channel ports. Of the 900 raids mounted by the Luftwaffe in this period, some 300 were directed against RAF airfields and installations. As the station defences were not autonomous, there are no separate records of anti-aircraft actions as a whole but from the operational reports of those stations which were attacked, some of the results can be extracted. Overall, PAC defences destroyed one aircraft and damaged another, while ground fire from .303" machine guns and 20mm cannon claimed 15 aircraft destroyed and six damaged. A number of station personnel – including ground gunners – received gallantry awards during these actions. Among the latter were Corporal BSC Jackman who fought his twin Lewis guns at RAF Detling until severely wounded and AC2 DG Roberts[14] who, as a PAC operator, achieved the first success with this system at RAF Kenley. Both were awarded the Military Medal.

As three Dornier bombers approached the northern edge of the airfield at Kenley on 18th of August 1940, AC2 Roberts pressed his firing button and a salvo of nine PAC rockets soared upwards, each with 600 feet of steel cable snaking behind them. Whatever the kill probability of the PAC system might have been, the German pilots found the sight unnerving "suddenly red-glowing balls rose up from the ground in front of me. Each one trailed a line of smoke about one metre thick behind it, with intervals of 10 to 15 metres between each.

I had experienced machine-gun and flak fire often enough, but this was something entirely new."[15] Of the three enemy aircraft, one eluded the cables completely, a second was struck on the wing, but managed to slip the cable, while the third – with one engine already ablaze – was dragged down as the cable and parachutes grasped it firmly.

This first live firing of PAC rockets had an unforeseen result in that the descending parachutes were mistaken for a German airborne attack and a widespread – but unnecessary – ground defence alert was generated.

Meanwhile, at RAF Hornchurch, AC Lightbody was manning a 20mm Hispano gun when an aircraft appeared over the airfield. Recognising it as a Dornier, he fired a burst of nine rounds before it disappeared into low cloud – and was promptly accused by an irate station defence officer of opening fire, not only without orders but also on a friendly aircraft, which the officer claimed to have been a Blenheim. While that dispute was raging between officer and airman, the Dornier reappeared out of the clouds – this time with the black crosses clearly visible on its wings and fuselage.

Hastily revising his earlier opinion, the officer urged the gunner to engage the enemy aircraft. Realising that he had only 36 rounds left in the Hispano magazine, Lightbody waited until the aircraft was over the WAAF block – and therefore well within range – before opening fire and he had the satisfaction of seeing his tracer curve into the target. Unfortunately, the Hispanos had been issued only with ball, and not high explosive, ammunition so the Dornier was able to stagger away towards Grays, where it was intercepted by a pair of patrolling Spitfires and shot down.

In this period the threat of invasion created turbulence and uncertainty and while the RAF's successes against the Luftwaffe created a wider understanding of the importance of well-defended airfields, the forces available for defence tasks were constantly changing as the Army's deployments varied in accordance with changes in the tactical plans of the GOC Home Forces. The only constant factor was the RAF's own defence force, which was integrated into the structure of operational stations in an attempt to meet the Air Ministry directive that RAF stations should become "local fortresses" within Army areas of responsibility.

The fall-out from the Taylor report at this critical period was that both the Army and the RAF took steps to augment their respective forces for the defence of RAF stations. The War Office, anxious to demonstrate its responsibility for ground defence, proposed to discharge this by deploying "Young Soldier" battalions to replace the Field Army units allocated to existing RAF stations. Furthermore, as new RAF stations opened the Army undertook to assume responsibility for their defence.

At the Chiefs of Staff meeting of 27th August 1940, the Commander-in-Chief Home Forces made it clear that while the Army would proceed on the basis of joint responsibility for airfield defence for the time being, its long-term aim was to become completely responsible for this task. Pressure continued to be exerted on the RAF to accept greater Army control of station defence and on 17th November 1940 the Air Ministry agreed that all local defence advisers at RAF stations would be drawn from the Army to the extent that RAF officers already in those posts would be transferred to the Army – in their equivalent ranks. This uncompromising attitude was underlined in a memorandum dated 20th December 1940 when HQ Home Forces advised all Army Commands that although the RAF's defence organisation would remain for the time being, the defence of all airfields would ultimately become the prerogative of the Army.

The Air Ministry endeavoured to justify its acceptance of the failed inter-Service policy in a letter to RAF Commands in the UK which stated: "The Air Council has given careful consideration to the proposal that a RAF Ground Defence Corps should be created to undertake the whole of this commitment, but has decided that, whereas such a solution would undoubtedly possess certain advantages, it would be inconsistent with the principle of single responsibility for a single form of defence activity which has always been the basis of Air Ministry policy." It went on to make the point that it would be uneconomical for the RAF to duplicate facilities which the Army already had and that as the Army had undertaken to defend airfields, there would be no increase in the existing levels of defence already provided by the RAF.[16] It was a convenient form of window dressing by both parties which did not address the fact that new problems usually require new solutions. However, it would not be long before the Germans again demonstrated this fact to the British.

The frustration felt by RAF commanders-in-chief and group

commanders, who were not included in the chain of command for the defence of their stations, was evident in an exchange of correspondence between Air Vice-Marshal Sir Richard Peirse, SASO at HQ Bomber Command and Air Chief Marshal Sir Wilfred Freeman, VCAS, in December 1940. Peirse made it clear that defence measures at stations were an integral part of the operational capability of those stations – but it was the one area in which station commanders were subject to direction by the local Army commander and not by their respective AOCs at RAF group and command headquarters.

Despite this, commands and groups were subjected to seemingly endless instructions from the Air Ministry on defence matters, regardless of the fact that it was powerless to exercise operational control over station defence. Even so, RAF headquarters were required to produce voluminous reports on various aspects of station defence for the Air Ministry. The result was that HQ Bomber Command was "much overburdened by a superfluity of paperwork…which detracts from our ability to get on with the war." Peirse stressed the high standards of ground defence training and preparedness which had been achieved on Bomber Command stations and echoed the annoyance of station commanders when key defence personnel were arbitrarily posted on instructions from Air Ministry without reference to their superior headquarters. Freeman sent a reassuringly anodyne reply – and the situation continued without any perceptible change.

The Inspector of Aerodrome Defence
In January 1941 the War Office appointed Major-General CF Liardet[17] to be Inspector of Aerodrome Defence and in the same month the Army became responsible for the ground defence of.204 airfields, leaving 246 to the RAF's ground defence forces – which continued to provide anti-aircraft machine gun crews, PAC detachments and Armadillos across the whole spectrum of RAF stations and installations. The amorphous defence units were given a clearer identity by being formed into organised squadrons and were later in the year, in accordance with established RAF organisation policy, numbered from 701 to 850. In January 1941 DGD complained to the Director of Personnel that the RAF was still short of 352 station defence officers and he accused the Air Ministry of not giving the

problem the attention it deserved at a time when the threat to airfields was greater than ever.

However, by April the Army was also admitting to manpower problems, which resulted in reductions to the defence forces which it had promised to provide. Despite this, and the fact that the "Young Soldier" battalions allocated to airfields often consisted of recruits who had never fired a rifle, and were therefore not allowed to carry live ammunition when on guard duties, the Air Ministry began to solve some of its own manpower shortages by transferring ground gunners to other trades.

Improvised armoured vehicle for RAF station defence.

The Assault on Crete

This atmosphere of unreality was soon dispelled by another German initiative. Some 25,000 British, Australian and New Zealand troops had been evacuated from Greece to Crete after failing to halt the German advance from the Balkans. Most of their heavy equipment had been lost and they landed in Crete with only their personal weapons and joined the small British garrison of less than 5,000 men at Suda Bay. The German attack on Crete began, by air and from the sea, on 20th May 1941 and after failing in the initial assaults on the airfields at Heraklion and Retimo, the enemy succeeded in capturing the fighter airfield at Maleme – now without any British aircraft – by the use of parachute and glider-borne troops. German reinforcements were then flown in to the captured airfield by transport aircraft and the rapid build-up which followed enabled the German forces to overcome the allied defences which were under continuous air attack from German aircraft operating from Greek airfields.

The battle of Crete was over by the end of May, despite stubborn resistance by the British, Australian, New Zealand and Greek troops and by the heroic efforts of the Royal Navy to control the surrounding seas. What had been demonstrated to the world was that an airborne army could – with overwhelming air support – overcome an opposing army, and navy, which had no effective air cover.

The British view of the importance of airfield defence had, for the past twenty-one months, been overshadowed by more strident voices seeking priorities for other interests but in a brief campaign lasting only ten days, Crete had projected the case for airfield defence into the category of first essentials.[18] In the debate in the House of Commons which followed the loss of Crete, Colonel RJR Macnamara, MP for Chelmsford, attracted considerable support when he called for the formation of a specialised airfield defence force to prevent the repetition of such disasters.

The Findlater Stewart Committee

In the aftermath of the loss of Crete, the Chief of Air Staff[19] concluded an Air Staff paper on the defence of aerodromes with the words "the use of airborne troops to attack and destroy aerodromes far beyond the land battle is a new development of war, and demands new methods of defence."

The Air Ministry's immediate reaction was to call for a specialised corps of aerodrome defence troops, provided, trained, organised and administered by the Army – but distinct from field Army units so that it would not be diverted to other military tasks. The Chiefs of Staff appointed Sir Findlater Stewart[20] to chair a committee[21] which was to report on improved methods of defence for airfields. The Committee held its first meeting on 31st May 1941 and submitted interim reports in June on matters which were considered extremely urgent before its final report was placed before the Defence Committee (Operations) on 7th July 1941. The subject was given some impetus at the highest levels by the Prime Minister, who issued a typically Churchillian minute to the Secretary of State for Air and the Chief of Air Staff on 29th June 1941.[22]

As an immediate result of the committee's interim recommendations, the Air Ministry accepted the requirement to arm all RAF personnel, regardless of trade, and undertook to submit proposals to the Committee for the introduction of an airfield defence corps provided by a single Service. The Committee reported again on 21st November, recommending that a Royal Air Force Aerodrome Defence Corps should be formed under the executive control of the Air Ministry. The new corps would become responsible for the defence of 590 airfields with 79,000 airmen, thus releasing 92,800 soldiers for Army tasks. By the time that the Defence Committee (Operations) considered the report on 24th December 1941 the War Office had decided to support the proposal as the easiest solution to a difficult problem and offered to assist the Air Ministry in organising and training the new corps.

Cabinet approval was given the following day and the decision to form the RAF Regiment was announced on 8th January 1942 by the Secretary of State for Air who told the House of Commons "probably few honourable members realise how far we have travelled from the extraordinary, and even alarming, low standard of aerodrome defence which existed in this country after the battle of France." He went on to explain some of the difficulties which the RAF had encountered in sharing defence tasks with the Army such as the varying requirements of successive military commanders, the withdrawal of military units to meet Army tactical redeployments, the lack of contact between RAF and Army commanders, the difficulties which Army commanders had in gaining RAF acceptance for their plans and the fact that RAF group commanders had no say in the defence of stations in their groups. He assured the House that these, and many other, problems would be resolved by the formation of the RAF Regiment[23].

The Way Ahead

The die was thus cast for the RAF to form its own specialised ground combat units, trained and equipped for the task and – most importantly – under RAF command and control. But it would be unrealistic to believe that the Secretary of State for Air (or, indeed, anyone else) could transform a pumpkin and a few white mice into a glass coach and a team of plumed horses by the single wave of a magic wand – even in the House of Commons. There were enormous problems of logistics, recruitment and training to be overcome before RAF Regiment squadrons could begin to pay operational dividends; in addition they had to achieve acceptability within the RAF establishment and create confidence in their professional ability to carry out the great variety of tasks which they were expected to fulfil.

Above all, the pool of British manpower and material was finite and there were to be continuing disputes as to how this might be shared out – particularly as the Army, the Royal Marines and the RAF Regiment were competing for the same resources. Coming into existence thirty months after the outbreak of hostilities, the Regiment's achievements in the succeeding forty-two months of a world war reflect great credit on a corps which was constantly under threat from friend and foe alike.

Notes

[1] General Giulio Douhet (1869-1930) published *Il dominio dell'aria* ("The Command of the Air") in 1921 and it was soon widely translated into other European languages. The quotation is from pages 53/54 of the translation by Dino Ferrari, published by the Office of Air Force History, Washington DC, in 1983

[2] Professor Tizard, Chairman of the Aeronautical Research Committee 1933-43. Later Sir Henry Tizard GCB AFC FRS

[3] AIR2/3203 (PRO) – opened 16/09/38

[4] GR Hill *The Protection of an Aerodrome against Low-flying Attack*, University College of the South-West, for ACAS 15/10/39

[5] Later Air Chief Marshal Sir Arthur Barratt KCB CMG MC (1891-1966). Inspector-General of the RAF 1945-47

[6] II H2/414 (PRO) – *Summary of Campaign Lessons*

[7] Later Air Chief Marshal Sir Arthur Sanders GCB KBE (1898-1974). Vice Chief of Air Staff 1948-50

[8] S.61785 (PRO) M1 25/05/405

[9] S.46598/II(PRO) 15/08/40

[10] Later Major-General Sir Brian Taylor KBE CB (1887-1973). As a Royal Engineer officer he had been Chief Engineer to the RAF in Iraq 1929-31

[11] AIR2/7315 (PRO) – the *Taylor Report*

[12] AIR2/7315 (PRO) – *Proposed RAF Ground Defence Corps* 05/08/40

[13] RJ Peters *Armoured Cars of The RAF* (Military Modelling) 1972 Part 6 pp16-17

[14] Later Group Captain DG Roberts MBE MM, Commandant RAF Regiment Depot 1966-68

[15] Price – *The Hardest Day* p72

[16] AIR2/7315 (PRO). DGD had presided over an examination of the problem by a broad-based committee which included the Director of Manning (Air Cdre J W Cordingley – later AVM Sir John Cordingley KCB KCVO CBE) and the Director of Organisation (Air Cdre LN Hollinghurst – later Air Chief Marshal Sir Leslie Hollinghurst GBE KCB DFC). It is clear that DGD's arguments were not supported, at that time, by either D of M or D of O

[17] Later Major-General Sir Claude Liardet KBE CB DSO DL (1881-1966). A Territorial Army artillery officer before World War I, during which he served on the Western Front where he was mentioned in despatches five times and awarded the DSO. He returned to the TA after the war when he resumed his career as a Lloyd's insurance broker. GOC London Division (TA) in 1938. Director-General of Ground Defence and Commandant RAF Regiment, 1942-45

[18] "The ground defence of airfields....called for special measures: special equipment

and armament and special training of the troops." (Buckley – *Crete*, HMSO 1977, p301)

[19] Air Chief Marshal Sir Charles Portal (1893-1971) Chief of Air Staff 1940-45. Later MRAF The Lord Portal of Hungerford KG GCB OM DSO MC

[20] Sir Findlater Stewart GCB GCIE CSI (1879-1960) A member of the Indian Civil Service 1903-30. Permanent Under-Secretary of State for India 1930-42

[21] The secretary to the committee was Squadron Leader DA Boyle, later Marshal of the RAF Sir Dermot Boyle GCB KCVO KBE AFC. (1904-1993) Chief of Air Staff 1956-59

[22] "Further to my minute of June 20 about the responsibility of the Air Force for the local and static defence of aerodromes. Every man in Air Force uniform ought to be armed with something – a rifle, a tommy-gun, a pistol, a pike or a mace; and every one, without exception, should do at least one hour's drill and practice every day. Every airman should have his place in the defence scheme. At least once a week an alarm should be given as an exercise (stated clearly beforehand in the signal that it is an exercise) and every man should be at his post. 90 per cent should be at their fighting stations in five minutes at the most. It must be understood by all ranks that they are expected to fight and die in defence of their airfields. Every building which fits in with the scheme of defence should be prepared, so that each has to be conquered one by one by the enemy's parachute or glider troops. Each of these posts should have its leader appointed. In two to three hours the troops will arrive; meanwhile every post should resist and must be maintained – be it only a cottage or a mess – so that the enemy has to master each one. This is a slow and expensive process for him.

2 The enormous mass of non-combatant personnel who look after the very few heroic pilots, who alone in ordinary circumstances do all the fighting, is an inherent difficulty in the organisation of the Air Force. Here is the chance for this great mass to add a fighting quality to the necessary services they perform. Every airfield should be a stronghold of fighting air-groundmen, and not the abode of uniformed civilians in the prime of life protected by detachments of soldiers.

3 In order that I may study this matter in detail, let me have the exact field state of Northolt Aerodrome, showing every class of airman, the work he does, the weapons he has and his part in the scheme of defence. We simply cannot afford to have the best part of half a million uniformed men, with all the prestige of the Royal Air Force attaching to them, who have not got a definite fighting value quite apart from the indispensable services they perform for the pilots." (Churchill – *The Second World War*, Cassell, 1950, Volume III, pp 692-693)

[23] *Hansard* Vols 361, 362, 372, 373, 376, 377 columns 93-100, 464 & 465

4

Events in the United Kingdom

"That Your Majesty may be graciously pleased to approve the formation of an aerodrome defence corps to be styled "The Royal Air Force Regiment" and to be subject to the executive and administrative control of the Air Council in accordance with the principles set out in the attached memorandum."

This was the preface to the Memorandum[1] submitted to King George VI on 5th January 1942 and the basis of the Royal Warrant establishing the RAF Regiment, which the King signed on the following day. In this document the Royal Air Force Regiment was defined as a Corps in its own right, albeit an integral part of the Royal Air Force. At the College of Arms, Chester Herald – in his capacity as Inspector of RAF Badges – devised a distinctive badge for the new Corps: crossed No.4 rifles, encircled by an astral crown, within the standard frame used for all RAF unit badges. The motto was "Per Ardua", which can be translated as "Through Adversity" – and which has proved to be appropriate for a Corps which has often been required to make bricks with an inadequate amount of straw.

The approval for the formation of the RAF Regiment, which had been given by the Cabinet on Christmas Day 1941, was followed by a flurry of staff action in January 1942 when the decision was publicly announced in the House of Commons after the Royal Warrant had been signed. Major-General Liardet, who had been the Army's Inspector of Aerodrome Defence since January 1941, was seconded to the RAF to become both the Commandant of the new Corps and Director-General of Ground Defence for the RAF as a whole, with DGD – now Air Commodore AP Ledger[2] – as his immediate subordinate in the Air Ministry.[3]

Despite the failings of the policy of divided responsibility which had been demonstrated repeatedly since May 1940, the Air Ministry's memorandum stressed that the Army retained its responsibility for overall ground defence and that the new corps would be under the operational control of the Army's C-in-C Home Forces acting directly through RAF station commanders. This policy continued to contravene the Royal Air Force's chain of command by excluding RAF Commanders-in-Chief of major commands and Air Officers Commanding groups from operational responsibility for the ground and LAA defence of their stations.

Furthermore, the content of the memorandum addressed only the defence of RAF stations in the United Kingdom and conveniently ignored the problems of RAF stations and installations in overseas theatres. Fortunately, these anomalies were to be resolved in the combat zones by a combination of inadequate Army resources and unilateral decisions made by those RAF commanders who were directly involved in operations against the enemy.

In 1941 an attempt had been made to impose some structural organisation on the station defence squadrons and AA flights which had developed in the United Kingdom from the varying responses to the threats – whether real or imaginary – posed by the enemy from the outbreak of war. The defence squadrons had been given numbers from 701 to 850, but this policy had not extended to the AA flights which were left without numerical identities.

With the impending formation of the RAF Regiment, instructions were issued that all RAF defence personnel were to be absorbed into the RAF Regiment.[4] Existing defence squadrons and flights would be reorganised, expanded, re-equipped and form the basis of the new Corps with effect from 1st February 1942.[5] The RAF defence squadrons thus became part of the Regiment's order of battle, being re-numbered 2701-2850, while the three hundred AA flights were given new RAF Regiment numbers in the block 4001 to 4336. The detailed organisation and composition of the RAF Regiment, which followed RAF precedent in terms of rank structure, unit organisation and administrative procedures, was set out in an Air Ministry Order, which also specified the standards of efficiency to be attained by AC2 Gunners Class V for reclassification to AC1 and LAC.[6]

This recognition of the precept that the Regiment was to be an integral part of the RAF ensured that, by utilising the RAF infrastructure for all their support requirements, RAF Regiment units had a very high "teeth-to-tail" ratio and were thus much more cost-effective than their Army counterparts.

Apart from training and equipment, one of the major problems which confronted the new force was that of the physical fitness of its personnel for active operations. No such requirement had existed for station defence personnel and the medical review of airmen in the new Regiment squadrons revealed that a substantial number did not meet the higher standards of individual fitness which were now required. As an interim measure, temporary medical categories were introduced to enable the best use to be made of the manpower available: those fit for full mobile duties (Regiment squadrons) were classified "X" while those fit only for sedentary station duties (eg station AA flights) were placed in category "Y".

A step towards creating a demonstrably separate identity for the new Corps was taken in August 1942 when all ranks of the RAF Regiment were authorised to wear khaki battledress, although with

RAF Regiment trainees – Guards instructors in the background.

blue rank insignia and, of course, the RAF Regiment shoulder titles. In the following year, the Air Force blue beret was introduced to replace the RAF forage cap which had proved unsuitable for combat duties. While eminently more suitable for field operations, the fact that Regiment personnel wore khaki when the remainder of the same Service wore blue undoubtedly served to accentuate the differences – which many were not slow to emphasise – between Regiment officers and airmen and those of the other branches and trades in the Royal Air Force. The absence of such visual differentiation in those overseas theatres where khaki or jungle green were worn by all members of the RAF undoubtedly helped towards achieving a more cohesive attitude in operational situations.

By September 1942 149 squadrons and 62 independent flights of the RAF Regiment were in being and 102 squadrons had been deployed to defend 65 RAF stations. Recruiting, specifically for the RAF Regiment, had begun in order to produce a further 5,000 gunners to replace those who were medically unfit for full RAF Regiment duties.

RAF Regiment training schools were established in various locations in the UK, most being formed on existing RAF stations.[7] The major exception to this was the RAF Regiment Depot, which moved from Filey to Lord Brownlow's seat – Belton Park near Grantham – where it remained until after the war. In order to obtain the number of NCO instructors necessary to inculcate and raise skill levels into the flow of trainees, the Brigade of Guards and the Royal Marines were approached for assistance. Both responded generously and the firm foundation on which the RAF Regiment was established in its formative years owes much to the dedication of the Guards instructors who gave the training machine its elan and professionalism and to the Royal Marines who trained the warrant officers and senior NCOs who were to form the backbone of the new Regiment squadrons.

AC2 Leech, who began his basic training as an RAF Regiment Gunner at RAF Locking in November 1942 described his shock at discovering that the NCO instructors there were drawn from the Brigade of Guards. Having survived the arduous training course, he found that the sense of achievement in reaching the high standards demanded produced a memorable esprit de corps among the trainees.

So much so that when he was medically downgraded and remustered to another RAF trade, he could barely contain his dismay at being forced to leave the Regiment when his comrades were being drafted to the squadrons preparing for the forthcoming invasion of North Africa.[8]

When No.6 Recruit Training Wing moved from Melksham to Butlin's Holiday Camp at Filey, where it became No.1 RAF Regiment School in 1942, it was joined by the RAF Drill School from Padgate, under the command of the legendary Squadron Leader Farey – who was not renowned for his popularity among the airmen who passed through his hands. A mix of Army and RAF Regiment NCO instructors formed the staff of No.1 School and as former Ground Gunners were retrained and promoted, they gradually replaced the Army NCOs who were returned to their units. No.1 RAF Regiment School rapidly established a reputation for inculcating discipline into its trainees – so much so that in late 1942 a draft of airmen from the Royal Canadian Air Force was sent to Filey to improve their standards of drill and discipline.[9]

The initial establishment tables for RAF Regiment squadrons and flights were complex in the extreme, possibly because of the need to cater for a variety of tasks with limited resources in terms of weapons and vehicles. The "standard" field squadron had five flights: one anti-aircraft, one rifle, one mobile rifle, one support weapons and one armoured car flight. The "lower" squadron, with only three flights, was without support weapons and armoured car flights, whereas the "higher" squadron had an additional rifle flight to bring it up to a strength of six flights. The independent flights were of two types: the "special" flight consisting of half a rifle flight and two anti-aircraft half-flights, and the "composite" flight of three half-flights: rifle, anti-aircraft and armoured.

In October 1942 these cumbersome unit structures were replaced by two establishments based purely on the respective requirements of ground and anti-aircraft defence. The field squadron of seven officers and 178 airmen, was organised in three rifle flights, one armoured car flight and a support weapons flight. The independent AA flight of one officer and 60 airmen was equipped with 12 20mm Hispano cannon.

The operational requirement in the United Kingdom was for

147 airfields to be defended by RAF Regiment field squadrons and for a total of 329 stations to have AA defences provided by independent AA flights. The reality was that the Regiment faced a considerable manpower shortage in that of its current strength, some 53,000 officers and men were absorbed by the field squadrons at home and overseas, by personnel in staff appointments, instructional posts and training schools and by non-effectives undergoing training or awaiting remustering or discharge.

This left 22,000 for AA defence tasks – but 16,000 of these were already deployed on stations, manning twin .303" Brownings and waiting for these to be replaced by 20mm Hispanos. In order to achieve operational effectiveness among the field squadrons, a programme of withdrawing squadrons for reconstitution with fully fit personnel and retraining them as formed units began. These squadrons were then deployed to release others to undergo the same cycle of reorganisation and training, with the aim of bringing all squadrons up to the required standards of fitness and efficiency in the shortest period of time and with the minimum disruption to operational tasks.

The other major problem facing the Corps was that of officer manning. The RAF had previously obtained the services of over-age Army Emergency Reserve officers as station defence officers and it was necessary to find more suitable officers for Regiment units. Age limits of 48 for squadron leaders and 45 for flight lieutenants were introduced and an OCTU established to train candidates for RAF Regiment commissions. The immediate shortfall of officers from RAF sources was made up by the transfer of 389 officer volunteers from the Army.

As the threat of invasion declined, Army garrisons on airfields in the South-East of England were being withdrawn from mid-1942 onwards and were being utilised to strengthen the Army in the UK and provide reinforcements for the Army in the Middle East and India. Even at its planned strength of 75,000, the RAF Regiment would have found it difficult to meet the additional commitments imposed on it by the Army's redeployments. The Findlater Stewart Committee had recommended an establishment of 93,000 officers and men for the new RAF Regiment, of whom 79,000 would be in the United Kingdom and 14,000 in overseas theatres; but this figure was never reached and was shortly afterwards amended to a maximum of 85,000 – 75,000 in the UK and 10,000 overseas.

Then the long drawn-out struggle for manpower between the Army and the RAF began with the first reduction of 10,000 men – to a global ceiling of 75,000 – which was imposed on the RAF Regiment in October 1942. It was not long before the War Office, scenting blood, was back again with a demand for more and in December 1942 the second reduction of 17,900 – to 42,100 in the UK and 15,000 overseas – was ordered. The third reduction came in July 1943 when the Regiment lost another 7,100 men, bringing its establishment down to 39,000 in the UK and to 11,000 overseas – a total force level of 50,000 officers and airmen with which to meet the global commitments of three major theatres, and numerous minor ones, all of which were to become more demanding as the war progressed.

The Personnel Staff action taken to implement these reductions revealed that the policy of remustering medically unfit gunners to other trades had not been implemented by the RAF Record Office and that there were over 4,000 medically unfit men still in the Regiment trade group. This added to the problem facing the staff of DGGD but by the beginning of 1943 some 10,000 gunners had been

RAF Regiment 75mm field gun detachment.

remustered to other trades and almost 4,000 others were earmarked for transfer overseas: for the landings in North Africa[10] and the reinforcement of Regiment units to be used in the invasions of Sicily and Italy.

In March 1943 a decision was taken to reduce the number of field squadrons and to form Light Anti-Aircraft (LAA) squadrons from the existing AA flights which were armed with 20mm Hispano guns. The new LAA squadrons were to be re-equipped with 40mm Bofors guns and some would be made available as replacements for the Royal Artillery LAA batteries which were to be transferred from Anti-Aircraft Command to the Field Army. In this way, 115 LAA squadrons were formed but equipment shortages precluded the uniform re-equipment of complete squadrons with 40mm guns. Instead, 70 became composite LAA squadrons with one 40mm Bofors flight and two 20mm flights each while 45 AA squadrons remained equipped with three flights of 20mm Hispano guns each.

In addition, a mobile force of 40 squadrons (21 field and 19 LAA) was formed and held in readiness for deployment with the 2nd Tactical Air Force which would accompany the Army back into Europe. This was later adjusted to 25 LAA squadrons and 12 field squadrons. This reorganisation of the Regiment's resources from a defensive to an offensive posture led to changes in station defence organisation to compensate for the withdrawal of Regiment units. This resulted in RAF Regiment officer and NCO instructors being allocated to RAF units to train station personnel to form their own defence flights and to operate AA machine guns.[11]

The 25th anniversary of the formation of the Royal Air Force was marked by the RAF Regiment mounting guard at Buckingham Palace and St James's Palace from the 1st to the 4th of April 1943. A hand-picked body of officers and airmen had been trained for the task at the Guards Depot and carried out their duties – in No.1 RAF Dress with steel helmets – in exemplary fashion and earning praise for their turnout and drill from the succession of senior RAF officers who gathered in the forecourt of Buckingham Palace each day to witness the guard changing ceremonies. Among the spectators was MRAF Lord Trenchard, who may have been pleased to see how his original concept of ground forces as an integral part of the RAF had developed under the pressures of war.

The effect of the force level reduction imposed on the RAF Regiment in July 1943 meant that its strength would be limited to 39,000 in the UK, 8,500 in the Middle East and 2,500 in India. The cumulative effect of the series of these savage reductions in strength inevitably cast doubt on the ability of the Regiment to defend many of the RAF stations in the UK. The Chiefs of Staff Committee therefore decided that the Army now had sufficient manpower to resume its role of providing forces to defend RAF stations in Great Britain and Northern Ireland against ground attack, leaving the anti-aircraft defence of RAF stations in the hands of station personnel

The RAF Regiment takes over the guard at Buckingham Palace on 1st April 1943 – the 25th anniversary of the Royal Air Force.

and such RAF Regiment units as were available. Accordingly, greater attention was devoted to ground defence training and stations were once more ordered to form their own defence forces. Eight twin Browning .303" guns were scaled for AA defence on each station and sufficient rifles and support weapons were provided for the defence flights and – in some cases – Beaverette or Morris armoured cars were provided as well to enable the defenders to have some mobile firepower in the defence of their stations.

In addition, some of the newly-formed Regiment AA squadrons were deployed to South Coast towns to provide a measure of defence for the civilian population against the "tip and run" raids which were becoming more frequent. In May 1943 LAC Dean – a former ground gunner who had previously manned Lewis guns and later twin Brownings – was a member of a 20mm Hispano gun detachment on the cliff top road above Bournemouth when a group of FW 190s appeared over the sea, flying fast and low – too low for the gun to be depressed for an engagement. The aircraft disappeared inland, reappearing several minutes later over Bournemouth – where they dropped their bombs, killing and injuring a large number of civilians – before heading out to sea on their way home. At that point they were high enough for the various AA weapons to open fire in the brief moments during which the German aircraft were within range – but without obtaining any hits.[12]

Greater success was achieved in the same month by 2892 Squadron at Torquay when the twin Vickers "K" guns mounted on the Beaverettes of the armoured car flight shot down six enemy aircraft in a single daylight raid. The impact made by this achievement led to the formation of a further four specialised AA squadrons[13] equipped with soft-skinned vehicles on which multiple Browning AA machine guns were mounted.

The Situation at the End of 1943

The formation of the RAF Regiment early in 1942 had introduced a sense of order into the improvised defence organisation which had developed within the RAF by reacting to circumstances as they arose without any clear policy guidelines.

The Directorate of Ground Defence, whose staff had been toiling at their tasks since the middle of 1940, had received greater status and recognition and Cinderella – if not universally recognised as a princess – was at least accepted as a member of society instead of a domestic drudge. Suddenly, everyone was trying to organise Regiment units to meet every possible threat but this enthusiasm inevitably foundered on the unyielding principles which govern the allocation of scarce resources. While establishments depended on finance, and were negotiable with the staff branches concerned, the allocation of manpower and equipment depended on the hard facts of availability and priorities. Thus, despite the operational requirement for a specific number of well-equipped RAF Regiment units to serve the Royal Air Force's needs, manpower was to be systematically diverted from the RAF Regiment to meet the Army's apparently insatiable claims for more and more men.

The RAF Regiment squadrons were at the end of the supply line for military stores and this usually meant waiting until the Army's needs had been satisfied before more modern weapons and equipment were delivered. However, with preparations for the invasion of Europe under way, the RAF Regiment staffs concentrated on improving the quality of the smaller number of units which remained to them in

MRAF Lord Trenchard inspecting RAF Regiment gunners at the RAF Regiment Depot, Belton Park.

order to produce the field and LAA squadrons which would be assigned to the groups of the Second Tactical Air Force for operations in North-West Europe. At the same time, it would become necessary to maintain a flow of reinforcements to the RAF Regiment squadrons engaged in operations in the various overseas theatres in which the Royal Air Force operated.

Notes

[1]   "The present methods for the defence of aerodromes whereby the Army and the RAF share responsibility both for the provision of personnel and for the organisation of local defence measures have been found to be in some respects unsatisfactory.

"The Government, after full consideration, have reached the conclusion that, while the responsibility for land defence, including the defence of aerodromes, must remain with the Army, the local garrison defence of individual aerodromes could be achieved more efficiently and with greater economy of effort if it were undertaken by the Royal Air Force on behalf, and under the direction, of the Army authorities. It is accordingly proposed that the Air Ministry (with advice and assistance from the War Office) should raise, organise and train and aerodrome defence corps, and the units of this corps should be allotted to individual aerodromes in accordance with a plan formulated under the guidance of the Commander-in-Chief, Home Forces.

"The operational responsibility for the defence of aerodromes, as of other vital objectives, will remain with the Commander-in-Chief, Home Forces. During land operations, the garrison on an aerodrome, including units of the aerodrome defence corps, would be under his control, and his subordinate Commanders would exercise this control directly through Royal Air Force Station commanders. The Commander-in-Chief, Home Forces, will be entitled to satisfy himself that the training and general disposition of the aerodrome defence corps are in accordance with his policy.

"The title of "The Royal Air Force Regiment" is suggested for the corps. While the strategic function of the corps is inherently defensive, it is essential that it should be trained to act tactically on the offensive, and that its title should be one which should foster a fighting spirit and high morale and not lay emphasis on the defensive role."

[2] Later Air Vice-Marshal AP Ledger CB CBE (1897-1970) AOA HQ Flying Training Command 1950-52

[3] CS 12390(PRO) E.19A – 6 Jan 42

[4] CS 12390(PRO) E.53A – 24 Jan 42

[5] Air Ministry Order N.221/1942

[6] Air Ministry Order A.368/42

[7] RAF Regiment Depot Grantham

No.1 School Filey

No.2 School Whitley Bay

No.3 School Douglas

RAF Artillery School Eastchurch

RAF Regt OCTU Sidmouth

RAF Regt Wing Locking

[8] Mr CG Leech – letter 25 Oct 95

[9] Mr CG Richardson – letter 13 Dec 95

[10] Including 1,500 for RAF units in Operation Torch (Invasion of North Africa) as well as the officers and airmen in the field squadrons and independent AA flights allocated to that operation. This was the first occasion on which RAF Regiment personnel had been sent abroad in formed, combat-ready units

[11] Air Ministry Order A.718/1942

[12] Mr DE Dean – letter 25 Mar 96

[13] 2871, 2872, 2873 & 2874 Squadrons were formed at Belton Park and their vehicles became known as the Regiment's "flak-wagons"

5

The War in the Middle East

*Our first object must be to gain a decisive military success in the
Western Desert and to destroy the enemy armed forces in a battle
fought with our whole available strength.*

Winston Churchill, 18 May 1941

The Emergence of the Threat

British forces in the Middle East, India and the Far East were, in
effect, on the fringes of the war from August 1939 until the
German offensive, which began in Europe in May 1940, gave warning
of the widening of the conflict. Although the situation in the Far East
grew more tense, the uneasy peace there continued while the war
spread to the Middle East when Italy became Germany's ally in June
1940. The presence of large Italian forces in Libya – less than 400
miles from the Suez Canal – and on the borders of the Sudan and
Kenya in Abyssinia required the rapid reinforcement of the British
presence by troops and aircraft from India, Australia, New Zealand
and South Africa. However, with the Iraq Levies and the Aden
Protectorate Levies under RAF command, as well as the RAF
armoured car companies in Iraq and Transjordan, the Royal Air Force
in the Middle East had some organised defence units of its own in
being when war began.

Armoured Cars in the Western Desert

Two sections, each of six armoured cars, were detached from 2
Armoured Car Company at Amman and arrived in Egypt in September
1940 under the command of Flight Lieutenant MP Casano. Attached
to an Army armoured car regiment – the 11th Hussars, with whom
they had operated in Palestine before the war – as "D" Squadron,
they immediately began to participate in reconnaissance and fighting

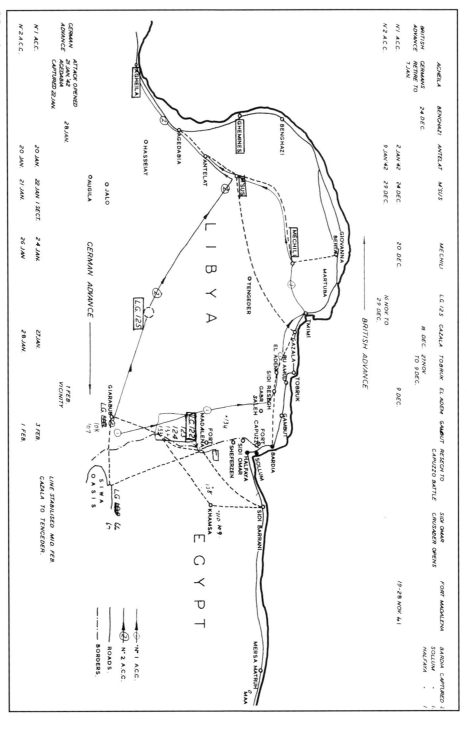

Western Desert 1941-42

Map 1.

patrols by Army units in the Western Desert. When the British offensive opened in December 1940, the RAF armoured cars were used to provide flank protection for the assault on Bardia. From then onwards they formed part of the forward screen for the advancing British force and in January the RAF armoured cars were at Bir Hacheim to secure a forward landing ground from which an RAAF fighter squadron operated. These sustained operations in the forward area resulted in high levels of unserviceability among the RAF armoured cars and a number were lost by enemy action – at this stage, mainly to land mines.

In February the remaining vehicles rejoined the 11th Hussars as part of a composite force of infantry, artillery and armour tasked with cutting the escape route of the retreating Italian army by blocking the coast road at Beda Fomm. The vanguard of the British force reached the coast forty minutes before the head of the Italian column appeared from the east and a fierce gun battle began – and ended in the destruction of 51 enemy tanks and the capture of 8,000 prisoners. From there "D" Squadron continued westward and a patrol commanded by Flying Officer Spearing reached Ghemines to find it still occupied by the enemy. A brisk attack followed and 500 prisoners were taken and handed over to the Rifle Brigade. By 8th February 1941 "D" Squadron was at Agheila, over 100 miles west of Benghazi. By this time the British force had not only overstretched its lines of communication but had also been weakened by the withdrawal of many of its formations to Greece in the vain attempt to halt the German advance through the Balkans.

In this parlous situation the deployment of the German Afrika Korps and the Luftwaffe in North Africa changed the course of the battle dramatically. On 14th February 1941 16 Me.110 aircraft signalled the arrival of the Germans by attacking the airfield at Agheila. One of the RAF armoured cars was hit, and Flight Lieutenant Alan Douglas[1] wounded, but Flight Sergeant Lewis redressed the balance by shooting one aircraft down from another armoured car. Later the same day, the Germans demonstrated their resolve by delivering another attack on the airfield, this time by 20 Ju.87 Stuka dive-bombers.

Faced with this new, more determined and much more powerful enemy, the British began their long retreat back to Egypt.

At the end of February 2 Armoured Car Company was ordered to return to Amman for refitting – which was hardly surprising in view of the age and condition of their vehicles. Rolls Royce had ceased production of Silver Ghosts in 1925 and although the Air Ministry began considering a replacement vehicle for the armoured car companies in 1935 no decision had been reached by the time war broke out. So the best that could be done for their ageing Rolls-Royces was to remove the armoured bodies and turrets and remount them on Fordson truck chassis, which gave them a new lease of life, despite a move downmarket in terms of brand names. During the five month period of intensive mobile operations the detachment had shot down several enemy aircraft, engaged superior enemy forces on the ground and taken several hundred prisoners. In the course of these operations, eight armoured cars were damaged by enemy action and five crew members had been wounded or injured.

In April the whole of the Company, now under command of Squadron Leader Casano, who had been awarded the MC for gallantry in the earlier campaign, was back in the Western Desert. This time the armoured cars were engaged in providing reconnaissance screens, protecting forward airfields and escorting RAF resupply convoys. This pattern of operations was, however, soon overshadowed by the results of a coup d'etat in Baghdad when the pro-Axis party of Rashid Ali overthrew the pro-British Regent and seized power in Iraq in April 1941.

Revolt in Iraq

The British mandate over Iraq had ended in 1932 but the British government was anxious to maintain its privileges in the newly-independent state of Iraq because of the importance of the air routes to India and the Far East. Accordingly the Anglo-Iraqi Treaty which followed the mandate took account of the policy of air control which had been in force since 1922. Under the terms of the treaty, the RAF was allowed to maintain two major air bases in the country: one at Shaibah, south of Basra on the Persian Gulf, and the other at Habbaniya, inland and west of Baghdad. In return, the British government accepted the Iraqi condition that no British troops, other than RAF personnel and locally-raised levies, would be stationed on Iraqi territory. These two RAF stations played a vital role in

RAF armoured car crew in the Western Desert. maintaining British communications by air with India, as well as providing the RAF with bases for the exercise of air power in the Middle East. In accordance with the terms of the treaty, 1 Armoured Car Company and two battalions of the RAF Levies were the only ground forces in Iraq in April 1941 when the balance of power in Baghdad tilted towards the Germans and Italians.

Following the coup in Baghdad, the new leaders of the Iraqi government fomented anti-British feeling and strengthened their links with the representatives of the Axis powers. By the end of April the British government decided that this unfriendly action had breached the terms of the Anglo-Iraqi Treaty and ordered three Indian Army brigades to deploy to Basra to safeguard British interests.

On 30th April 1941, units of the Iraqi army, totalling some eight thousand men with artillery and armour, surrounded the base at Habbaniya and cut its communications – other than by air – with the outside world. The Habbaniya garrison, which included 1 Armoured Car Company, less one section detached to Shaibah, and six companies (four Assyrian and two Arab) of the Iraq Levies, had by then already been strengthened by a battalion of the King's Own Royal Regiment, flown in from Shaibah after landing at Basra ahead of the three Indian brigades.

Having occupied the plateau which overlooked the RAF base, the road from Transjordan to Baghdad and the adjacent town of Fallujah, the Iraqi forces positioned detachments on the road to Baghdad and at Ramadi on the road to Transjordan. They then demanded a complete cessation of military activity at the RAF base – which was immediately rejected by the AOC Iraq, Air Vice-Marshal HG Smart. Deciding that, in this particular situation, attack would be the best form of defence, the training aircraft of No.4 FTS at Habbaniya began to deliver bomb and machine-gun attacks on the Iraqi positions at dawn on 2nd May. Blenheims, Wellingtons and Tomahawks from operational squadrons elsewhere in the theatre reinforced Habbaniya, attacking Iraqi forces on the ground and establishing air superiority over the Iraqi air force and those elements of the German and Italian air forces which had been deployed to Aleppo and Mosul to assist the Iraqis. The favourable air situation thus achieved, and the intensity of the air attacks on the Iraqi positions, demoralised the besiegers as well as inflicting heavy casualties on enemy troops, guns and vehicles.

Under the direction of Colonel Roberts, who had been flown in to take command of ground operations, the garrison forces of RAF armoured cars, Levies and British infantry carried out aggressive patrolling and drove the Iraqis back in critical areas. Even the ornamental 4.5" howitzers, which had stood outside the station headquarters building as souvenirs of the 1914-18 war, were refurbished and brought into action against the enemy. On 6th May 1941 the Iraqi positions on the high ground overlooking Habbaniya were captured and continuing pressure by the much smaller British force – albeit with air support – steadily pushed the Iraqis back. Communications between the Iraqi-held town of Fallujah and Baghdad were cut by the simple expedient of using an Audax aircraft to fly through the telephone wires at several points. On 11th May 1941, 3 Section of 1 Armoured Car Company was escorting an Army convoy to Mujarra where the armoured car crews salvaged an RAF aircraft – which was then flown back to Habbaniya by the 1 Armoured Car Company Commander.

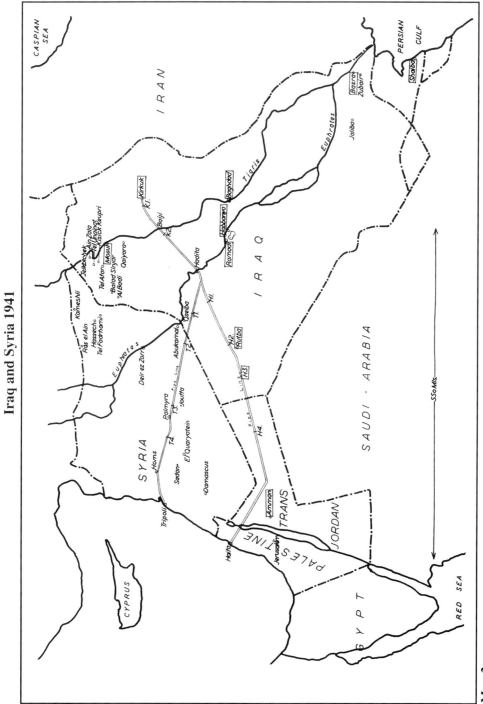

Iraq and Syria 1941

Map 2.

In Transjordan, 300 miles to the west, the commander 4th Cavalry Brigade was assembling a relief column from whatever units could be made available. The brigade intelligence officer described the scene: "We were a motley crowd. His Majesty's Life Guards and the Royal Horse Guards jostled along in their army trucks beside the bedouin of the Arab Legion – Glubb's Desert Patrol, swathed in garish robes, who raced about in trucks armed with Lewis guns. We even embraced eight Royal Air Force armoured cars. Tough stuff, these boys. They had left Sidi Barrani in the Western Desert on Thursday and were reported in action at Rutbah on Saturday, a thousand miles away. They were all rogues, God bless them, for whom the war had come as an eleventh hour reprieve. They were the sort of men to whom legend clung like the cloak of Mephistopheles."[2]

Kingcol (so named after its commander, Brigadier Kingstone) reached Habbaniya on 17th May 1941 and after regrouping moved forward to dislodge Iraqi forces from Fallujah and open the road to Baghdad. Following some brisk fighting on the approaches to Baghdad, an armistice was agreed on 31st May 1941 and the pro-Axis elements in the Iraqi regime were replaced by those more sympathetic to the British. The section of armoured cars at Shaibah had not been inactive either; after routine patrolling and actions against small groups of Iraqi army and police, they participated in the British advance to Basra, after which the armoured car section drove to Habbaniya to rejoin 1 Company.

The total Iraq Levy casualties in these operations were nine killed and 31 wounded while 1 Armoured Car Company had two officers and eight airmen wounded. In his report on the campaign the AOC Iraq, Air Vice-Marshal JH D'Albiac – who had succeeded AVM Smart when he became a casualty during the siege – wrote "Finally, my report would indeed be incomplete if I failed to record the outstanding services rendered by the Iraq Levies and the RAF officers and airmen of No.1 Armoured Car Company. It was on these units that the close defence of Habbaniya Cantonment depended and right well did they carry out their task. Their steadiness under fire, their dash, and complete disregard for danger in attack provided a valuable complement to the action of their comrades in the air and helped materially towards the demoralising of a vastly superior enemy force."[3]

The Campaign in Syria and Northern Iraq

Apart from the need to defend Allied forces in the Levant, the security of oil supplies to the Mediterranean ports required that all Axis influence in Syria and Iran should be eliminated without delay. 1 Armoured Car Company operated with the Army forces which reoccupied Kirkuk and Mosul and patrolled to the northern borders with Iran. The vital oilfields were once more in British hands, and were to remain so for the rest of the war.

The force which had relieved Habbaniya and secured the surrender of the rebellious Iraqi regime in Baghdad was now tasked to join the drive from Palestine into Syria. As a French mandated territory, Syria was garrisoned by some 37,000 French troops, most of whom were supporters of the Vichy regime – which was to bring them into conflict with the Free French forces from Palestine – as well as with British troops. The Syrian campaign opened in June and ended with an armistice on 12th July 1941.

2 Armoured Car Company remained heavily involved in this campaign, still as part of Kingcol, and took part in the operations against the determined resistance of French forces – including the Foreign Legion. Kingcol's intelligence officer wrote "Casano's face was thin and sallow…with a thin pointed nose, arched black eyebrows and mocking dark eyes. I can see him now, when we were back at H.3 after sharing every variety of adventure, preparing for another campaign and leaning forward in the lamplight, as if he were the devil himself, and saying in a long drawn out whisper, "Go-the-whole-hog."[4]

The Second Western Desert Campaign

This period was marked by the reorganisation of RAF fighter squadrons in the Western Desert into three parties – Advanced, Base and Rear – for each squadron in order to ensure that flying squadrons could redeploy rapidly to keep up with the advancing ground forces. The Advanced and Rear parties consisted of about 80 men each, with another 150 in the Base party. The thirty-six Ground Gunners established for each squadron were divided among these groups as required. However, without their own officers and NCOs to provide a command and control structure, let alone discipline and training, and without even any transport of their own, it is remarkable that

2 Armoured Car Company in the Western Desert.

these leaderless little bands of heroes managed to achieve anything at all.

Squadron Leader Casano brought 2 Armoured Car Company back to the Western Desert in October 1941, following a two month refit at Amman after completing their part in the Syrian campaign. In November, 1 Armoured Car Company, under Squadron Leader WO Jones, arrived to join them and by the time that the British offensive began on 18th November 1941, both companies were deployed in support of RAF fighter squadrons operating from forward landing grounds. In the confused situation which developed during the tank battles which followed, aircraft were often flown to the rear area at night, returning in the morning to the landing grounds which had been left to the armoured cars and ground gunners to hold during the hours of darkness. There were some close calls – a German armoured column passed within a few miles of LG 122 where 175 aircraft were on the ground, and at LG 125 2 Company's defensive screen was heavily attacked and nine of their vehicles destroyed or damaged, but the landing ground remained secure.

In January 1942 the pendulum swung again and the German counter-attack drove the British forces back towards Egypt and the two armoured car companies were occupied in providing rearguards for the ground parties of the fighter squadrons as they withdrew eastwards. The 1941/42 campaign saw the armoured car companies used as an integral part of the Desert Air Force's forward fighter operations – in contrast to the 1940/41 campaign when, the RAF having no use for them, they were detached to the Army, which welcomed this addition to its limited reconnaissance capability. It is to the everlasting credit of the officers and airmen of the two RAF armoured car companies that, despite their outdated and unsuitable vehicles, they carried out an invaluable role in protecting RAF resources at a time when the Army was fully committed to a fluid land battle and was unable to divert any elements to the defence of the RAF's forward installations.

The turret-mounted Vickers guns proved to be of little use against aircraft and the armoured car companies relied increasingly on the twin Browning machine guns mounted on top of the turrets to counter enemy air attacks.[5] The RAF report for the period November 1941 to April 1942 states "the fine work of the two RAF Armoured Car Companies in defence of our forward landing grounds when our fighter force moved from Msus to Mechili deserves special mention. No.1 Company engaged a number of enemy AFVs in the area while No.2 maintained patrols well into enemy territory and reported the movements of advanced hostile elements. During the retreat from Msus, No.2 Company was informed by a Tank Corps officer that some tanks had been left behind and could not be brought away because of a lack of drivers. The company commander (Squadron Leader MP Casano MC) returned down the track and he and five of his crews collected the tanks and, although none of them had previously driven a tank, delivered them safely to a tank unit some sixty miles away."[6]

The Takoradi Air Route

With the entry of Italy into the war in June 1940, another way had to be found to ferry aircraft from the UK to the Middle East. In the autumn of 1940, an air route via Takoradi in the Gold Coast (now Ghana) had been established and the Army undertook the protection of the 13 stations and staging posts on this vital link. Following the German invasion of France, and the establishment of a puppet French regime at Vichy, the air route became vulnerable to attack by Vichy-directed forces in the French West African territories. In November 1941 it was decided to deploy AA defences to these airfields and in August 1943 the nine defence officers and 500 Ground Gunners already in West Africa were formed into RAF Regiment AA flights, which subsequently became the foundation of the RAF Regiment squadrons in Gambia, Sierra Leone and the Gold Coast. As the threat diminished with the success of the North African campaign, the Regiment squadrons were withdrawn in January 1943, although Regiment instructors remained to train station personnel in ground defence skills.

The Reorganisation of Ground Defence Measures

In September 1941 the staff structure of HQ Middle East had been revised to include a Ground Defence branch of three officers headed by a wing commander. A training school was established at Helwan, where the emphasis was on passive defence (chemical defence, camouflage, aircraft dispersal, slit trenches and general protective measures) rather than on the organisation and provision of combatant units for the active defence of the Royal Air Force's assets in the Command.

The arrival of RAF Regiment officers in March 1942 signalled the beginning of a period of reorganisation and restructuring of the improvised arrangements for ground defence which had developed during the desert campaigns. The changeover began by making the existing defence officers (of the Administrative & Special Duties Branch) responsible for passive defence tasks while the Regiment officers took over active defence duties. Flying Officers IOB Carlson and RH Blake[7] were the first RAF Regiment officers to be posted to HQ Western Desert as Defence officers at Advanced and Rear Air Headquarters respectively. In order to standardise – and improve –

the training of Ground Gunners throughout the Middle East, additional training schools were established at Maaten Bagush in Egypt and Amman in Transjordan for this purpose.

The "Rocket, Parachute And Cable" (PAC) system, originally developed for the defence of Vulnerable Points in the UK, was deployed to the Middle East by April 1941 when five VPs in the Canal Zone were protected by this means. HQ Middle East was sufficiently impressed by this to order that a further forty-four stations (including forward landing grounds in the desert) were to be equipped with PAC defences. Unfortunately – or possibly fortunately – the Admiralty had been given priority in the allocation of PAC systems and only 11 of the required 44 were available for the Middle East. Mindful of the need for mobility, a trials unit was established at Sidi Barrani in July 1941 to evolve methods of fitting PACs to motor vehicles from which they could be fired. There is no record of how far such trials had progressed before the Air Ministry decided to cease the use of PAC systems in December 1941. Nevertheless, four of the PAC systems in the theatre were deployed to reinforce the air defences of El Adem, south of Tobruk, in March 1942. However, in view of the low morale of the operators and the lack of success of PAC defences against enemy aircraft, the equipment was finally withdrawn in May 1942. The net result of this was that the Air Ministry increased the establishment of machine guns for anti-aircraft defence, and accelerated their delivery to units, to compensate for the loss of PAC defences.

At the beginning of 1942 the Army and RAF staffs began to examine the division of responsibility between the two Services for the ground and low-level air defence of RAF units. As in the United Kingdom, it proved to be an exercise in semantics which was not particularly rewarding for those who actually had to deal with the problem on the ground.

However, in April 1942 defence officer posts were established at group headquarters, on operational squadrons and at permanent stations and maintenance units. When the Command Defence Officer post was upgraded from wing commander to group captain, the inflationary process extended down the line and flight lieutenants became squadron leaders while flying officers became flight lieutenants.

Malta GC

Malta had, of course, been subjected to Axis air attacks from the time that Italy entered the war and the RAF stations were dependent upon the Army for anti-aircraft defence. In June 1942 an attempt was made to reinforce Malta by sending convoys simultaneously from Gibraltar and Egypt. Embarked in the ships which sailed from Alexandria was a makeshift RAF Regiment unit – "Clara Squadron" – which had been formed from the pool of unallocated Regiment personnel in the Middle East with the aim of establishing a coherent AA defence force for the RAF in Malta. Under constant air and surface attack, which caused heavy losses, the survivors of the eastern convoy were forced to return to Alexandria before reaching Malta.

Pilot Officer Lewis was in command of the RAF Regiment personnel on board the SS Potara which was turned back to Egypt but by August 1942 he had reached Malta to become the station defence officer at RAF Ta'Kali where the anti-aircraft defences had consisted of airmen firing rifles from slit trenches at attacking aircraft. Lewis adapted a range of guns from crashed aircraft – 20mm Hispanos, .303" Brownings and even an Italian 20mm Breda – as AA weapons on improvised mountings and trained station personnel and locally-enlisted Maltese to use them. By the time he left for the UK seven months later he had been promoted to flight lieutenant rank and was in charge of the station police and firefighting sections in addition to his duties as station defence officer.

Anti-Aircraft Reorganisation in the Middle East

At this point in time, the Air Ministry issued standard establishment scales for RAF Regiment AA flights, each of which was to be armed with 36 anti-aircraft machine guns. The Air Ministry scales for the Middle East were 4,200 men with the 3,800 guns available distributed among 118 flights – an average of only 32 guns per flight. HQ Middle East considered this to be insufficient and insisted that 6,900 men with 5,800 guns in 193 flights (30 guns per flight) was the minimum to meet the task, for which there were only 2,900 machine guns in the Command at that time.

But this was only part of the problem facing the RAF in the desert: the decline in the operational capability of the armoured car companies – depleted by unserviceability and losses in action – left the defence of the forward landing grounds in the desert largely in the hands of the Army by March 1942. The Gambut group of airfields, exposed on the Army's open flank to the south-east of Tobruk, was defended by a single company of infantry – at a time when the many squadrons of invaluable aircraft were vulnerable to attack by German units such as the Burckhardt Group which had been formed for long-range penetration and sabotage tasks. In fairness to the Eighth Army, the importance of air support to the land battle was by now clearly understood and positive efforts were made to deploy infantry and artillery – including light anti-aircraft guns – to forward airfields. However, given the limited resources which the Army commanders had at the time, it was inevitable that, as soon as a major crisis developed, these troops were drawn into the land battle as the only reserves available to reinforce Army units against attacks by superior enemy forces.

In April 1942 the commander of 12th Anti-Aircraft Brigade issued "Notes on Landing Ground Defence" which was based on experience gained by one of his LAA regiments in the differing conditions of advance and retreat which had occurred in the "Crusader" campaign of 1941/42. The document is a model of clarity and in analysing the deficiencies and mistakes which were made in the past, sets out the fundamental principles for success in the future.

It concludes that "nothing short of a permanent force will meet the requirement" and the final paragraph reads: "Our aim must be to ensure that the Fighter Force is never left unprotected and is free to move at short notice as the situation develops, and to operate with safety from those landing grounds best suited to its task. A properly constituted defence force which could guarantee the local security of the landing grounds from the moment they are occupied would achieve this aim; so long as we rely upon the present haphazard arrangements for the protection of such valuable and vulnerable targets, not only will our action in the air be hampered but we shall continue to run the risk of losing aircraft on the ground on a scale which is alarming to think of. We must have security on the ground if we are to operate efficiently in the air."[8]

The German Drive for Cairo – May 1942

The reopening of Rommel's offensive in May 1942 drew the Army into a series of large-scale armoured battles and – once again – the protection of forward landing grounds was left almost entirely to 2 Armoured Car Company. At one stage the RAF armoured cars were in direct contact with advancing columns of German panzers, against which they directed a series of successful air strikes. The continual pressure on landing ground personnel to maintain aircraft and defend their airstrips in the fluid conditions of mobile warfare brought them close to exhaustion and it was decided to abandon anti-aircraft defence. As the Lewis guns were found to be ineffectual in that role, the Ground Gunners and their machine guns were used to augment the ground defences of the forward airstrips and so relieve the maintenance personnel of routine guard duties. Unfortunately, the Ground Gunners were not trained, equipped or organised for infantry tasks and, when taken from their AA mountings, their Lewis guns were not found to be particularly effective in the ground role either.

Fortuitously, the Director of Ground Defence (RAF) was visiting the Middle East at this time and so was able to see the situation at first-hand and discuss the problems of airfield defence with senior Army and RAF officers. The outcome of these discussions was much as before: the Army was to remain responsible for providing 4,500 troops for the defence of airfields in the forward area – subject to the usual caveat that they would only be withdrawn by mutual agreement between the Army and RAF commanders.[9]

As had been proved on every previous occasion, this undertaking lasted only until a major battle developed, when the Army units were drawn into it, regardless of the consent or otherwise of the RAF commander. The single new feature was the acceptance of DGD's proposal that the policy should be revised once operational RAF Regiment units had been deployed in the theatre. Both the Army and the RAF now recognised that it was increasingly difficult to provide adequate defence for forward fighter wings in the desert without the establishment of a self-contained, permanent defence force with ground and AA defence units allotted as required to protect areas or groups of landing grounds.[10]

As junior RAF Regiment officers arrived in the Middle East to take command of anti-aircraft flights they were posted to mobile units which already had detachments of Ground Gunners. In many cases these were under strength and the airmen displayed low morale and poor gunnery skills as a result of their misemployment for other tasks at the expense of continuation training in their primary role. Thus the Regiment officers had to carry out the whole spectrum of defence duties as well as reorganising and training the men under their command – "a task which many of them are doing very well." In spite of these efforts, there was to be a lengthy transitional phase in which "the whole situation is similar to that which existed in England in the summer of 1940, although rather worse in many ways. The lessons of Greece, Maleme and Malaya seem to have had much more effect at home than out here, certainly as far as the Army is concerned."[11]

RAF Regiment Reorganisation

Preliminary instructions for the formation of RAF Regiment AA flights were issued on 19th June 1942, but these immediately generated disagreement and counter-proposals from commanders and staff officers who were reluctant to change the existing organisation for one which was unknown and unproven. The view expressed in some quarters of the Middle East Command was "we've never had the RAF Regiment, we never asked for it, and we don't want it."

Wiser counsels prevailed and the Desert Air Force (DAF), having evaluated the likely threats, considered that – on balance – ground defence was more important than AA defence. The decision was that RAF Regiment squadrons and flights, controlled by DAF headquarters, should be deployed when and where necessary to meet the ground threat – but with a retained AA capability as well. Conversely, Air Headquarters Egypt wished to retain the status quo of Ground Gunners as individuals on unit establishments and was not anxious to see them reorganised into RAF Regiment flights – as this would mean the loss of a useful pool of manpower, capable of carrying out a variety of tasks – few of which were connected with ground defence.

The dispute was resolved on 14th September 1942 when HQ Middle East Administrative Instruction No.362 authorised the incorporation of all Ground Gunners into the RAF Regiment and issued the establishment scales of personnel and equipment (including MT) for these units. The Command and group HQs stated their requirements to be a total of 231 flights (29 above the latest Air Ministry scale for the Middle East) for which there were 115 officers and 7,700 airmen available in the theatre.

When the final offensive in the Western Desert opened with the second battle of Alamein on 23rd October 1942, RAF Regiment AA flights were still in the process of reorganisation and training and were still part of flying squadron or station establishments. Nevertheless, these flights – some of which were re-equipped with surplus Hispano 20mm guns for improved ground and AA defence – made an important contribution in sustaining the viability of air operations from forward landing grounds as the 8th Army rolled steadily westwards towards the Tunisian frontier. Some 57 RAF Regiment flights accompanied the aircraft of the Desert Air Force in the advance, but their activities were not reported separately and are therefore generally undocumented.[12]

The first landing grounds captured in the advance from Alamein were at Daba and Fuka which were still held by the enemy when the RAF Regiment units arrived. They seized the airstrips, captured some three hundred prisoners, and cleared the area ready for the arrival of the flying squadrons, which were able to begin operations without delay. However, the confusing conditions of mobile warfare in the open spaces of the desert were such that operations did not always proceed in accordance with expectations. As an example, the Regiment flights attached to a Spitfire wing moved forward to secure the next landing ground for their wing and – despite resistance to their passage through the units of 51 (Highland) Division on its main axis of advance – reached the area of the designated landing ground at dusk and deployed under cover of darkness.

As dawn approached, the rumble of diesel engines caused some alarm among the defenders who prepared – without much confidence – to engage the German tanks which they expected to see advancing on their positions. In the clear light of day they saw, instead, the heavy earthmoving equipment of a South African airfield construction unit at work clearing a new runway on the landing ground. The South African engineers cheerfully informed the RAF Regiment commander that they had already spent two days on site without any interference from the enemy, who were busy withdrawing to new defensive positions further west.[13]

The Armoured Car Companies

The noticeable improvement in operational effectiveness which resulted from a proper command and staff structure for RAF Regiment units led to comparisons with the armoured car companies, which were not directed or supported in the same way by a single branch of the air staff at headquarters. As a result, their operational capability was eroded by a lack of training and equipment as well as by shortages of personnel and vehicles. In September 1942 the AOC-in-C Middle East Air Force[14] proposed that Nos.1 and 2 Armoured Car Companies should be incorporated into the RAF Regiment, not only to remedy these deficiencies but also to enable more armoured car companies to be formed.[15] The Air Ministry rejected the proposal out of hand and the unsatisfactory situation continued, to the detriment of an improved operational capability for 1 and 2 Armoured Car Companies in the desert.[16]

The Armoured Car Companies began their advance with the squadrons of 211 Group on 5 November 1942 and – although 1 Company was at half strength due to shortages of men and vehicles – both units moved rapidly forward on separate axes until they met again at Castel Benito in January 1943. Continuing the advance, they met strong German resistance in Tunisia and among the casualties suffered by 2 Company was Squadron Leader Casano, whose wounds prevented him from leading his armoured cars into Tunis.

When the campaign in North Africa ended in May 1943, both Companies were withdrawn to their home bases. They took with them captured German armoured cars, as well as the British and South African vehicles they had acquired, and returned by road to the Canal Zone, from where they continued their respective journies to Transjordan and Iraq.

In addition to carrying out the multiplicity of roles in which they had become practised in three years of desert warfare, the armoured car companies developed techniques of indicating targets and directing fighter and fighter-bomber strikes against enemy positions by radio from the South African Marmon-Herrington armoured cars[17] which they used as forward air control vehicles. This was at a time when, according to the operations record book of 1 Company, "the Army authorities were not sure that forward contact with aircraft was a vital necessity".

The Formation of RAF Regiment Squadrons

The reorganised RAF Regiment AA flights proved their worth in the final desert campaign – which also revealed the weaknesses in the command and control arrangements for these units. When flying squadrons controlled by one group headquarters shared airfields with squadrons from another group, the lack of co-ordination between the AA defences inevitably led to either over or under provision of scarce resources. Towards the end of the campaign the Command Defence Officer proposed that such problems of administration and operational control could be resolved by removing the AA flights from flying squadrons and forming them into RAF Regiment squadrons "at a cost of some 38 clerks and a number of squadron leaders".

While this suggestion was being considered, a decision was taken in December 1942 that the global strength of the RAF Regiment should not exceed 55,000 men. This was 30,000 less than the original planning figure and, as 10,000 posts had already been saved, a further reduction of 20,000 all ranks was required. In response to the Air Ministry's demand for a return of RAF Regiment strength in the Middle East, the information provided in January 1943 showed that 8,100 men, organised into 225 AA flights, were deployed in Libya, Egypt, Aden, Cyprus, East Africa, the Levant, Malta and the Sudan. Defence for 54 new airfields in the Mediterranean theatre would require the withdrawal of AA flights from Iraq, East Africa, Aden and the Levant with the consequent reallocation of local defence and security tasks from the Regiment to the RAF Levies and other locally-raised forces.

It was obvious that the forthcoming reductions in Regiment manpower would require a more flexible organisation which could deal with contingencies on a priority basis, instead of static deployments spread evenly over all RAF installations regardless of the level of threat. Accordingly, the AOC-in-C accepted his Command Defence Officer's recommendations and in February 1943 24 AA flights were withdrawn to Castel Benito to be formed into four RAF

Regiment squadrons,[18] each with an establishment of eight officers and 219 airmen, in three rifle flights and three 20mm Hispano AA flights. Groups of personnel from the disbanded AA flights assembled at Castel Benito airfield over the next few weeks: "some came with transport, some didn't; some brought their tents, some didn't; most, however, brought with them an amazing number of pets of every description." The Operations Record Book of the RAF Regiment at Castel Benito records that on 1st May 1943 all brothels in Tripolitania had been placed out of bounds, and adds the comment "This news left the RAF Regiment in the Western Desert unmoved."

The reorganisation of the remainder of the RAF Regiment in the Middle East followed shortly afterwards with the aim of producing 38 squadrons comprising 304 officers and 8,626 airmen. Apart from the fact that Air Ministry approval for this reorganisation had not been received, there was a manning shortage of 216 officers (including 15 vacant staff posts) and 500 airmen. The shortage of officers for the new squadrons was a critical factor and Air Ministry was asked to give authority for the commissioning of suitable personnel on completion of the five-week course at the RAF Regiment OCTU at Amman.

In the event, authority was received from London for the reorganisation, but with a manpower ceiling of 8,000 all ranks, and the number block of 2900 to 2940 was allocated for the new Middle East squadrons. A training depot was established at Shallufa in Egypt and as squadrons were formed and trained they were deployed to await the next phase of the Mediterranean campaign – the invasion of Sicily and Italy. A further reorganisation took place at this time – the separation of the AA and the field roles and the consequent formation of distinct LAA squadrons and Field squadrons – the latter with a flight of armoured cars (Humbers and later GMC Otters) for reconnaissance and mobile fire support. This made the RAF Regiment unique in combining infantry and armour capabilities within the equivalent of an Army company.

Not surprisingly, in this pause between the conclusion of one campaign and the beginning of another, HQ Middle East ordered the withdrawal of all Army personnel from static guard duties at RAF installations in Egypt. In September 1943 some 3,000 RAF Regiment gunners had to be deployed to replace soldiers on these tasks, to the detriment of their collective and individual training. Apart from degrading the operational efficiency of the units involved, the inability to withdraw personnel for specialist training on new weapons and in new roles also delayed the introduction of the 40mm L60 Bofors gun as the main armament of RAF Regiment LAA squadrons.

The many problems which faced RAF Regiment units in the Middle East at this time were compounded by factors of geography. Headquarters Middle East was a large organisation, situated in Egypt and – as the front line moved westwards – increasingly distant from the combat zone. Thus RAF Regiment staff officers, having no operational control over Regiment units, became remote from operational matters and became more involved in pursuing matters of policy with the Air Ministry and the other branches of the staff in the headquarters.

The most senior Regiment officers in the forward areas were usually of squadron leader rank – and they were fully occupied in commanding their units. The result was that the standards of training and operational efficiency depended on the leadership and ability of squadron leaders, unsupervised and unco-ordinated by more senior Regiment officers, and therefore varied considerably from unit to unit. This was not the case in the Army, where the necessary standards of command and supervision were achieved by the rank structure at battalion and brigade levels. Unfortunately, such formations were non-existent in the order of battle of the RAF Regiment in the Western Desert, and the squadrons suffered until such time as the pressing need for the establishment of wing headquarters was accepted at the Air Ministry.

Operation Torch

The military rationale for the invasion of North Africa was as a pincer movement to crush the Axis forces which were retreating from Alamein between the Eighth Army from the east and the First Army from the west. The political motives were less obvious, but undoubtedly more significant: they were to draw American forces into combat alongside the British and Free French and to put pressure on the Vichy regime in France, whose writ still ran in Algeria and Tunisia.

The RAF Regiment element of the invasion force consisted of

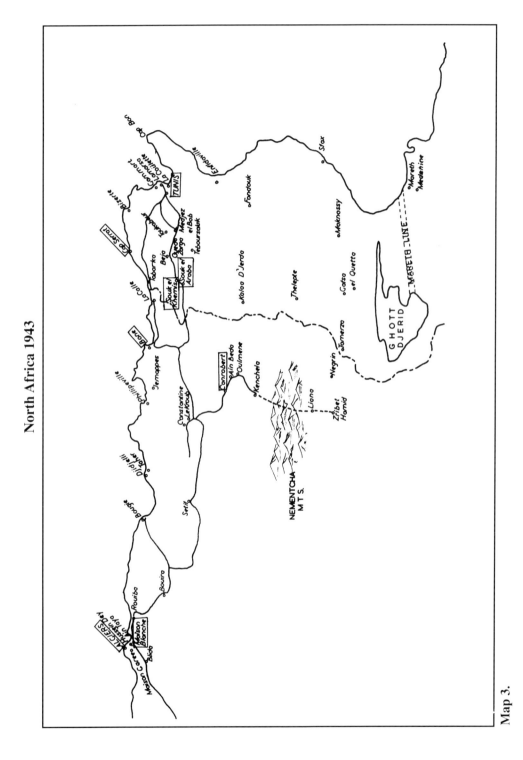

North Africa 1943

Map 3.

five field squadrons and five independent AA flights[19] and additional Regiment personnel were included in flying squadron establishments for local defence duties. The independent AA flights were equipped with the new twin Browning AAMGs, on which they had been trained at the RAF Regiment Gunnery School on the Isle of Man. The senior RAF Regiment officer in the invasion force was Lieutenant-Colonel (later Colonel) H Morrey Salmon, MC[20] an emergency reserve officer of the Welch Regiment who had been attached to the RAF as a station and command defence officer since early in 1941.

The landings in Algiers Bay on 8th November 1942 were unopposed on land but were subjected to German and Italian air and submarine attack. This added to the general chaos engendered by the poor logistic planning, which ensured that what equipment was not sunk was landed in quite the wrong order – at least as far as the Regiment units were concerned. When the SS Strathallan was hit

RAF Regiment landing at Maison Blanche (Algiers).

amidships by a torpedo, some of those on board were premature in jumping over the side, as the Strathallan remained afloat, and one of the RAF Regiment officers on board – Flying Officer FR Dodd of 2788 Squadron – was subsequently awarded the MBE for his work in rescuing men from the dark and oil-filled waters of Algiers Bay.

The RAF Regiment squadrons and flights joined their respective flying wings[21] rather later than intended, due to delays in landing vehicles and equipment, and the Army had to provide ground and AA defence for the airfields until the RAF Regiment units arrived. Colonel Salmon, although technically only the RAF Regiment staff officer in HQ Eastern Air Command, adopted the title of "Commander RAF Regiment" in Algeria and Tunisia and went out into the field to improve the efficiency of his units and ensure that they were used to the maximum effect.

His forthright manner and determined approach were directly responsible for the change in policy which released Regiment squadrons and flights from static duties and enabled them to be deployed as formed units. They were thus available in the forward areas, on a flexible basis, to support RAF operations as they developed in conditions of mobile warfare.

Colonel Salmon's energy and ability raised the standards of training and organisation throughout his squadrons and flights and he did not hesitate to improve their combat efficiency by unorthodox means – including the acquisition of 25 pounder field guns from the Army to improve the firepower of the support flights of his field squadrons. When, after losing a number of field guns to the Germans, the Army sought to reclaim its artillery from the Regiment, Colonel Salmon refused the offer of 40mm Bofors guns in exchange, but accepted six-pounder anti-tank guns instead – which the field squadrons were to find increasingly useful as the war progressed.

During this relatively short and sharp campaign, important lessons were learned for the future. The first was that for an amphibious operation, RAF Regiment units and their equipment had to be loaded together in the same ships, in the order in which they were to land for the assault phase. Although this was not implemented in time for the invasion of Sicily, the lessons were to prove invaluable in the preparations for the invasion of Europe. The second lesson was that RAF Regiment units should not be permanently linked to a flying wing or station; in Algeria the aircraft wings to which the Regiment squadrons and flights were allocated remained at their initial locations in Algeria and as the Army advanced into Tunisia, reinforcement aircraft flew in to forward airfields for which there was no RAF Regiment defence – and the Army had to find resources for this task – to the detriment of the land battle.

The case for changing the inflexible organisation which had suited the particular conditions in the Western Desert was soon accepted by RAF commanders and on 1st January 1943 the RAF Regiment units were ordered to leave their static airfields and deploy to forward areas under the control of the Air Commander. To meet the requirement for increased AA defence, 24 additional AA flights were formed in the theatre on 20th February 1943.[22]

It was not long before the Regiment's forward deployment brought its units into contact with the enemy, as evidenced by award of the MC to Flight Lieutenant AC Langham and the MM to Corporal J Boyd, both of 4337 AA Flight, as the result of fighting patrol actions

RAF Regiment 20mm Hispano detachment – North Africa.

against the enemy ground forces. The MC was also awarded to Flying Officer T Dun of 2788 Squadron and the MM to AC1 R Quigley of 2744 Squadron for separate engagements in which the armoured cars of their respective squadrons were operating ahead of the Army in order to seize airfields in the areas of Cape Bon and Medjez el Bab.

The forward radar units used in tactical air operations were, for security reasons, referred to as "Air Ministry Experimental Stations", abbreviated to AMES. The German forces in Tunisia were putting up a fierce resistance to attacks from both flanks and this was being prolonged by resupply flights to them from airfields in Italy and Sicily. The commander of No.325 Wing – Group Captain David Atcherley[23] – decided that an AMES sited on the coast at Cap Serrat would enable his fighter aircraft, based at Maison Blanche, to intercept German and Italian transport aircraft and so reduce the flow of essential supplies on which the enemy depended. The only problem was that the approaches to Cap Serrat, which was some fifty miles west of

Three-ton truck fitted with Browning twin AA machine guns.

Bizerta, consisted of about one hundred and fifty square miles of scrub-covered, mountainous country with few roads. That apart, the area was still occupied by the enemy who had a network of outposts, connected by patrols operating between them. However, Group Captain Atcherley did not intend to allow such minor problems to interfere with his concept of operations and he assembled a task force to carry out his plan.

At short notice, and without adequate time for preparation or reconnaissance, 2721 Squadron and 4092 AA Flight were ordered to escort 8000 AMES through this unpromising terrain to Cap Serrat where the Regiment units were to defend the radar site against air and ground attack. The column was attacked by FW 190s as it moved through Tunisia during the day, but the AA flight kept the enemy aircraft at bay. In conditions of pitch darkness and rain on the night of 31st January 1943, the advance guard of 2721 Squadron found Group Captain Atcherley, draped in a white blanket to make himself more visible, at the vital crossroads on the muddy track to ensure that the column took the correct route to its destination. Although the AMES was in position on 1st February 1943, further rain soon made the rough tracks impassable to vehicles and the Regiment commander had to organise resupply columns using mules, camels and donkeys. The AMES carried out its task of reporting enemy air movements and, alerted by this, the Germans assembled an armoured column to destroy it.

2788 Squadron was sent to reinforce the Regiment defenders and fierce fighting took place on the approaches to Cap Serrat from 26th to 28th February 1943. By this time, the AMES had fulfilled its role and orders were given for it to withdraw on 2nd March 1943. Although 2721 Squadron lost all its armoured cars and 4092 Flight most of its guns, with 2788 Squadron acting as the rearguard, the force reached the safety of Bone airfield on 7th March 1943. Nevertheless, the Cap Serrat operation had only narrowly escaped becoming a disaster and the units which were involved took the lessons to heart – which stood them in good stead for subsequent operations.

The campaign entered its final phase in mid-April 1943 when 2744 and 2721 Squadrons, with 4091 and 4092 AA Flights, were tasked to support the Army and placed under command of 24th Guards

88   THROUGH ADVERSITY

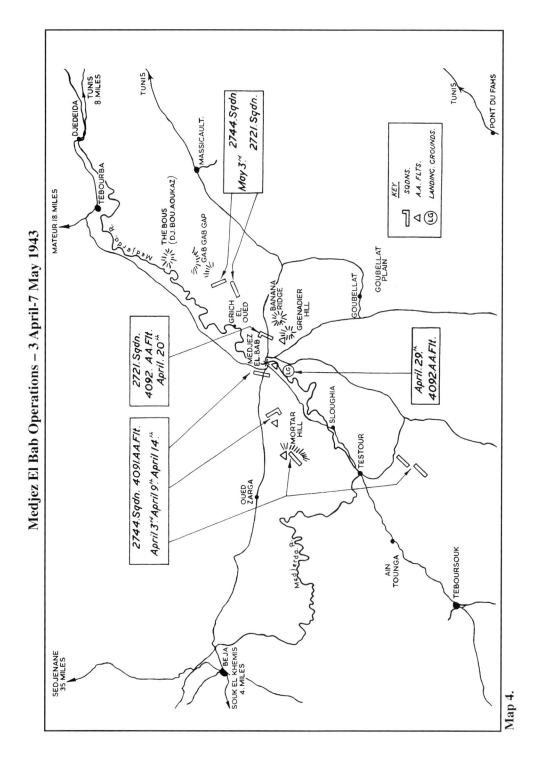

Map 4.

Brigade in the Medjez el Bab sector of the front line. In May 1943, following the Axis surrender in North Africa, "S" Force was assembled with the task of advancing with, or ahead of, the forward army units to seize documents and equipment of value to Allied intelligence before they could be destroyed. The escort force for the motley collection of specialists from all three Services was provided by three RAF Regiment squadrons and three AA flights.[24] "S" Force was disbanded on 11th May, having completed its tasks, but it set the pattern for the future employment of Regiment units to clear the way for intelligence and disarmament teams in the closing stages of the campaigns in Italy and North-west Europe.

The success of this campaign, for the first units of the RAF Regiment to be committed to battle since its formation, was marred by a tragic incident in North Africa in May 1943.

Flight Lieutenant AG Onley, commanding 4347 AA Flight, was preparing to hear a charge of dereliction of duty against one his men when the airman concerned loaded his Sten gun and fired a burst of 9mm rounds into the Orderly Room tent. Onley died of his wounds shortly afterwards and the airman was subsequently found guilty of murder by a court-martial.

As Commander RAF Regiment in North Africa, Colonel Salmon convened a conference of all his RAF Regiment unit commanders on 26th May 1943. For many of them, it was the first occasion on which they had met one another and one result of the pooling of experiences gained in the campaign was the decision to combine the 29 AA flights in Tunisia into 11 AA squadrons in preparation for the forthcoming Mediterranean campaign. A staunch advocate of proper organisation with a sound command and control structure, Colonel Salmon formed the first RAF Regiment wing headquarters in June 1943, without waiting for approval from higher authority. It was not long before the value of such a formation in controlling two or more Regiment squadrons was recognised, and others were established during the campaign in Italy and later in the UK in preparation for the invasion of Europe.

The Dodecanese Adventure

Once the Axis forces had been expelled from North Africa, Middle East Command's interests were in supporting the Central

Mediterranean Command and in controlling the eastern Mediterranean and the land, sea and air routes to India and beyond. Accordingly, the Aegean lay in the Middle East's area of responsibility and it was to the Commanders-in-Chief in Cairo to whom the Prime Minister turned with his strategic plan to bring the Balkans within the British post-war sphere of influence. He saw the Dodecanese islands as the key to the Aegean and, quoting several quite irrelevant 18th century British victories, urged General "Jumbo" Wilson to "dare and improvise" by seizing Rhodes in order to exploit the Italian collapse. Churchill's political aims were, once again, at variance with military realities and his hopes of consolidating post-war British influence in the eastern Mediterranean by launching flanking operations against a determined and competent enemy operating on interior lines, were doomed to failure – as they had been at Gallipoli almost 30 years earlier.

A plan to seize Rhodes and Scarpanto with a large military force, with considerable naval and air support, was already in existence.[25] Despite the fact that the only land, sea and air forces available in the eastern Mediterranean in August 1943 were far less than those originally considered necessary for success, it was decided to implement the plan on the assumption that the Italian garrisons on the Dodecanese islands would rise up against any German forces and support British landings. It was this optimistic premise which was used to justify the employment of totally inadequate forces for an operation of such magnitude.

The first step was to occupy the small Greek island of Castelrosso, some eighty miles south-east of Rhodes, and this was carried out by a detachment from the Special Boat Squadron commanded by Major the Lord Jellicoe[26] – whom the Regiment was to meet again in the Adriatic and in Greece – and two flights drawn from 2907 and 2924 Squadrons. The Italian garrison offered no resistance, but hopes that the 30,000 Italians on Rhodes would do likewise were frustrated by the prompt action of the 8,000 German troops there who seized the key points and disarmed their former allies. Rhodes was not therefore going to welcome the British with open arms, and HQ Middle East would have to look elsewhere for a suitable mounting base.

The islands of Cos, Leros and Samos lay off the Turkish coast to the north-west of Rhodes, and had the advantage of being garrisoned solely by Italian forces. Cos was only 60 miles from German-held Rhodes – but 400 miles from the nearest RAF airfield in Cyprus – and it had an airfield of sorts and some potential airstrips, which made it more suitable for a main base than Leros nor Samos.

It was accordingly decided to establish the main base on Cos and place garrisons on the other two islands in order to establish a British presence in the Aegean. However, the routes to these islands were controlled either from German-occupied Greece and the Cyclades to the west or by the chain of German bases from Crete through Scarpanto to Rhodes from the south. Thus German aircraft, warships and troops formed a noose around Cos, which they could tighten at will to interdict and destroy the much smaller British land and air forces which would be dependent upon support from beyond the German-held perimeter. This impetuous British plan depended for its success on a complete absence of any reaction from the German commander in the Aegean; instead, the British incursion into what was very much a German area of influence provoked an almost immediate counter-attack by the energetic and ruthless German commander in Crete – Major-General Friedrich Mueller[27] – with the more powerful forces at his disposal.

The SBS detachment landed on Cos on 14th September 1943 and received the surrender of the 3,600 Italians on the island. British Army units landed on Leros and Samos, again without any opposition, and Spitfires and Dakotas flew into Antimachia airfield on Cos to establish an airhead. The vanguard of the RAF Regiment deployment to Cos was to be 2909 LAA Squadron – which had only received its first six 20mm Hispano guns in August. The remainder were issued to the squadron at Hadera in September and with barely sufficient time to be trained in the use of these weapons – and without even the opportunity to carry out any practice firing with them – the squadron emplaned for Cos on 15th September, still studying the Hispano training manuals. This was the first recorded occasion on which a Regiment unit had been operationally deployed by air.

By 20th September 1943 the British force on Cos consisted of two officers and 71 airmen of 2909 Squadron RAF Regiment with 16 20mm Hispano guns, 363 officers and men of the 1st Battalion Durham Light Infantry, whose commanding officer – Lieutenant

Colonel RF Kirby – was responsible for the defence of the island, and the advance party of 1st LAA Regiment Royal Artillery whose 40mm Bofors guns were to be the main anti-aircraft defence of the island. RAF groundcrew added a further 100 airmen to the total British force.

As six Regiment squadrons[28] were earmarked for this operation, HQ 500 Wing was established at Hadera in Palestine on 21st September 1943 with Lieutenant Colonel GW Jones in command. However, it remained at Hadera throughout and played no part in the Cos operation, after which it was disbanded.

The island of Cos is about 30 miles long, with the town and harbour at the eastern end, separated by only a few miles of water from the Turkish coast. At that time, rough country tracks were the only links between the town and other parts of the island. The airfield at Antimachia, in the west, was small and sited on a plateau among broken and rocky terrain with rugged cliffs dropping down to the coast. It therefore proved difficult to defend against either air or ground attack.

The Germans concentrated a force of almost 400 fighter and bomber aircraft on airfields in Greece, Crete and Rhodes and began air strikes on Cos on 16th September. The Royal Artillery had only two LAA batteries on the island – one at Cos town and the other at Antimachia – and the infantry defences were equally widely spread. Bombers, with strong fighter escorts, delivered overwhelming attacks on the airstrips and the LAA gun positions. At Antimachia RAF aircraft, equipment, supplies and ammunition dumps (including the Regiment's reserves of 20mm HE ammunition) were destroyed. 2909 Squadron's gun detachments suffered casualties during these flak suppression raids because the rocky terrain made digging almost impossible and personnel had little protection against splinters from exploding German bombs. Despite this, the squadron was able to claim the destruction of four enemy aircraft, and damage to two more. The Royal Artillery's gunners, with their emplaced 40mm Bofors guns, referred to the RAF Regiment's exposed 20mm Hispanos as the "VC guns".[29]

The enemy air attacks continued until 20th September when RAF attacks on German airfields on Rhodes and Crete caused a lull which lasted until 26th September. In this period, further reinforcements were flown in to Cos from Palestine and Cyprus, including more of 2909 Squadron's personnel and guns. Three officers and 98 airmen of 2901 Squadron reached Cos by sea on 29th September but the balance of 2901 Squadron and a detachment of 2907 were still at Castelrosso when Cos was invaded. Other Regiment units provided reinforcements which reached Castelrosso in dribs and drabs, and a detachment from 2924 Squadron under the command of Flying Officer EG Hoddinott provided Hispano guns and crews for AA defence on the caiques which were carrying supplies from Castelrosso to Cos by sea.

The Air Commander landed at Antimachia on a brief visit to Cos on 24th September and subsequently reported that he was extremely impressed by the high morale of the RAF Regiment there, despite the casualties which they had suffered. He was, however, alarmed to discover that the RAF personnel on the island were armed only with Sten guns and he immediately ordered these to be replaced with rifles.

Unfortunately, it was to prove too late to implement this sensible decision. At the end of September the British force on Cos totalled 1,559 men: 1,100 soldiers (mainly infantry of 1st Bn DLI and gunners of 1st LAA Regt RA), 235 RAF personnel and 229 RAF Regiment officers and airmen.

German air attacks recommenced on 26th September and as well as continuing to inflict damage and casualties on the defenders, these succeeded in cutting the air and sea supply lines to Cos which was then effectively isolated from all outside support. By 1st October the airfield at Antimachia and the airstrips at Lambi, Salt Pans and Marmia were unusable and the few surviving Spitfires of No.7 Squadron SAAF were unable to take off.

Although German warships escorting a convoy of merchant ships had been seen off Naxos on 1st October, neither the Royal Navy nor the RAF had sufficient forces available to either shadow or intercept it and it was assumed that it was carrying reinforcements to Rhodes. It was therefore a complete surprise to the Cos garrison when, at dawn on 3rd October 1943 a battle group of brigade strength, drawn from the German 22nd Infantry Division in Crete, landed at three points on the island and, supported by a parachute assault on Antimachia mounted from Greece, while continuous close air support delivered co-ordinated attacks on the main airfield, the airstrips and the port and town of Cos. The 2901 Squadron detachments on the airstrips were soon overrun but at Antimachia 2909 Squadron continued to fight its guns in both the ground-to-air and ground-to-ground roles.[30]

The guns were redeployed to new positions as the enemy gained ground, but by 1700 all were out of action and the remnants of the defenders fell back to the port of Cos where Major HM Vaux[31] of the DLI had taken command of the defences after his commanding officer was wounded by a mortar bomb while giving orders to the company commanders.

Fighting continued until the early hours of the following day when the survivors surrendered. Isolated groups of the British garrison held out for a few days more while the SBS evacuated survivors, among whom were 17 RAF Regiment personnel, but the great majority of the British defenders became prisoners of war.[32] At a cost of 80 dead, the Germans had seized Cos in thirty-six hours of hard fighting and effectively demolished any further British ambitions in the Aegean.

With complete control of the air, it did not take the Germans long to recapture Leros and Samos from the British and on all three islands the German commander ordered the summary execution of the senior Italian officers for what he construed as their treachery in assisting the British – despite the fact that Italy had signed an armistice with the Allies, and left the German side, three weeks earlier.

This ill-starred venture is best summed up in the words of the official historians who wrote "This rash experiment had cost the lives of some hundreds of troops and airmen, a large quantity of valuable stores and equipment, a number of naval vessels and one hundred and fifteen aircraft. The German losses were as heavy, if not heavier, but they had regained lost ground and by so doing received much-needed encouragement. The operation, ill-judged from the beginning, had been the result of over-confidence, an unconscious flouting of a cardinal principle of modern warfare. Troops and ships in isolated positions without air support cannot long survive if their enemy, moving on interior lines, can bring his air power to bear at the crucial point."[33]

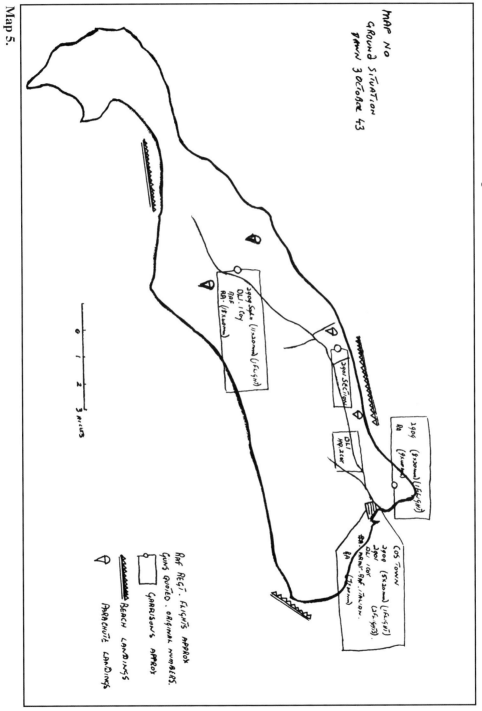

Map 5.

Sketch map of British defences and German attack on Cos – 3 October 1943

Training and Reorganisation

Operations in Sicily and Cos had absorbed all the RAF Regiment squadrons with any claim to operational efficiency; accordingly an RAF Regiment Depot was established at Hadera in October 1943 and the training school at Shallufa in Egypt was closed. Seven additional wing commander posts were established for training and supervisory duties and squadrons were ordered to concentrate at Aleppo for training. The first phase of the reorganisation was to form eight field and 12 AA (24 x 20mm guns) squadrons from the original six-flight squadrons. In December 1943 this plan was revised to produce eight field squadrons, 12 LAA squadrons, each of 6 x 40mm & 16 x 20mm guns, and eight AA squadrons with 24 x 20mm guns each. The remaining personnel were formed into two six-flight squadrons of the old pattern and a Depot squadron – a total of 31 squadrons of one type or another. With the introduction of the 40mm Bofors gun, Regiment officers and NCOs were trained on courses at No.2 Depot Royal Artillery before returning to their squadrons to carry out conversion training on the new weapons.

Once again, planning was overtaken by events and the reductions imposed in theatre manning levels led to the disbandment of ten RAF Regiment squadrons between January and March 1944.[34] This left 25 squadrons of various types but in April 1944 a further lowering of the Regiment manpower ceiling in the theatre – this time to 5,300 officers and men – led to reductions and reorganisation to make better use of men and equipment. The LAA squadron establishment was changed to two 40mm Bofors flights and one 20mm Hispano flight, resulting in further turbulence and retraining in order to regain operational status. This was, of course, achieved within the allotted time and the last RAF Regiment squadrons in the Middle East left for Italy in August 1944. From that time, until 1319 and 1321 Wings with seven squadrons under command, were deployed to Palestine in March 1945, there were no operational RAF Regiment units in the Middle East.

Operations Hardihood/Turpitude

As the Mediterranean campaign gathered momentum it was appreciated that if Turkey were to enter the war on the Allied side, land and air forces would have to be deployed to support the Turkish forces in Thrace. The original plan for this contingency was Operation Hardihood which, in August 1943, called for 90 RAF Regiment AA flights – or 15 AA squadrons – to protect the forward airfields. This was subsequently revised to a force of ten LAA and five field squadrons (although none was available at that time) and after the collapse of the Aegean operation in October 1943, RAF Regiment squadrons in Syria and Palestine were earmarked for this task until Operation Hardihood lapsed in March 1944.

In May 1944 Operation Turpitude was developed as a deception plan with the aim of encouraging the Turks to believe that substantial Allied forces were able to support them, should they enter the war, and to mislead the Germans into thinking that a major attack was being prepared against their forces in northern Greece. An Advanced Air Headquarters was formed at Aleppo and four RAF Regiment squadrons[35] together with 2 Armoured Car Company were deployed on exercises in northern Syria, close to the Turkish border. The success of the invasion of France in June 1944 made the deception plan in the Levant superfluous and Operation Turpitude was quietly run down, and its elements unobtrusively dispersed, in July 1944. The RAF Regiment squadrons returned to Egypt and Palestine prior to embarking for Italy but 2 Armoured Car Company remained in Syria to replace the 27th Lancers who were redeployed to Italy.

As an example of the flexibility with which RAF Regiment squadrons were deployed in this period, the movements of 2932 Squadron, commanded by Squadron Leader DA Pocock, between February 1943 – when it was formed as "C" Squadron RAF Regiment from six independent AA flights at Castel Benito in Libya – and March 1946 when it was disbanded at Moderndorf in Austria, are worth recording. Advancing from Libya towards Tunisia after its formation, it was ordered to return to Egypt – a road journey of some 1,500 miles – as the North African campaign was drawing to its close. Diverted to a maintenance unit between Alexandria and Cairo to assist in preventing the theft of 40-gallon drums of aircraft engine oil – which was successfully achieved by the ingenious, if unorthodox, use of No.36 hand grenades, the squadron moved on to Cairo West airfield to provide security for the international conference being held at the Mena Palace Hotel. Here the squadron mounted a guard of honour for the Prime Minister, Winston Churchill, before continuing its westward journey to Palestine where it was reorganised and partially re-equipped with 40mm Bofors guns.

It then became part of the Air Force presence in Syria under Operation Turpitude and deployed its guns at Minnick airfield outside Aleppo. In July 1944 the squadron moved to Egypt and went by sea to Italy where it joined other LAA squadrons in the defence of airfields on the Foggia plain. Detached to the Balkan Air Force as part of No.1328 Wing, the squadron moved to the Dalmatian island of Vis – where Tito, the Yugoslav partisan leader, had a refuge – to provide LAA defence for the British raiding forces based there. In May 1945 2932 Squadron left Vis and rejoined 1328 Wing in Austria at the former enemy airfields in the Moderndorf area before being disbanded in March 1946 as part of the post-war run-down of the British forces.[36]

Further east, detachments of 2926 and 2927 Squadrons were deployed in Persia at Ahvaz, the railhead for the mile-long supply trains which carried war material to Russia from America and Britain. Ships were unloaded at the port of Abadan and the trains were marshalled at Ahvaz for the 1,000-mile journey to southern Russia – and Regiment gunners from the two squadron detachments were used to protect the vital supplies carried on these long and lonely rail journeys.[37]

The RAF Regiment and Tactical Air Operations

The RAF in the Middle East became the Desert Air Force and developed tactical air operations in a Service which had been brought up to believe that its primary roles were air defence and the bomber offensive. The air war in North Africa became a university whose graduates were to achieve distinction in joint Army/Air operations in other theatres and among the subjects on the course were ground and low level air defence in mobile warfare. The inadequacies of both the ad hoc RAF ground and AA defence concept and the simplistic policy of relying on the Army to provide these in order to concentrate on flying tasks, were clearly revealed in the realities of war.

The introduction of a trained ground combat force as an integral part of the Air Force arrived just in time for the RAF in the Middle East to be able to perfect its tactical roles without being weakened by unco-ordinated measures for protection of its airfields and aircraft on the ground. From inauspicious beginnings, with inadequate resources and a shortage of time in which to achieve combat-readiness, the RAF Regiment units played an essential role in the final Air Force campaign from Alamein and Algeria to Tunis. At the same time, the operational squadrons of the Regiment were learning hard lessons in the unforgiving conditions of war and this undoubtedly provided valuable experience for those officers and airmen who were to serve subsequently in Italy, North-West Europe or the Far East.

Notes

1. Later Air Commodore AG Douglas CBE MC (1915-95), Director of Ground Defence 1966-70

2. *Morning Glory* (Somerset de Chair) Merlin 1988 p193

3. Operations in Iraq – AHB II J3/3

4. *Morning Glory* (Somerset de Chair) Merlin 1988 p194

5. Sqn Ldr MP Casano MC – interview 18 Apr 96

6. AHB II J1/12 para 381 (PRO)

7. ME File AAHQ WD/22/Air (PRO)

8. AM File DGD/TS 112 (Appendix) (PRO)

[9]   ME File S.46624 – 5 Jan 42 (PRO)

[10] ME File AAHQ.WD/22/Air – June 1942 (PRO)

[11] ME File S.53742/II – 4 Jun 42 (PRO)

[12] The first member of the RAF Regiment to be awarded the MM for gallantry was 1459700 AC1 Bullen, following operations in the Western Desert in Nov/Dec 1942

[13] Air Vice-Marshal DA Pocock CBE (Commandant-General RAF Regiment 1973-75) – letter 10 Feb 95

[14] Air Chief Marshal Sir Arthur Tedder, later MRAF The Lord Tedder GCB (1890-1967) Chief of Air Staff 1946-50

[15] ME File AAHQ WD/22/AirII 11 Sep 42 (PRO)

[16] AM File S.56366 – 21 Oct 42 (PRO)

[17] The AA batteries of the South African Artillery in South Africa had been transferred to the Air Force in 1942. In 1943 it was intended to form a SAAF airfield defence battalion as part of the SAAF (Airborne) Regiment which had already been established, but both these proposals failed due to manpower shortages. However, 56 LAA Battery SAAF had already been formed in the Middle East and further SAAF LAA units followed. The LAA regiments remained as part of the SAAF while the other components of the SAAF Regiment were amalgamated into an armoured reconnaissance regiment. By the end of the war, three LAA regiments, an armoured car regiment and two infantry battalions were operating as the SAAF Regiment .This was made easier by the fact that both the South African Army and Air Force used the same ranks and wore the same uniform – and were not unduly concerned about what cap badge they wore. However, as the war progressed and the ground and air threat to SAAF flying squadrons in Italy declined, the GOC of the 6th South African Armoured Division there succumbed to the universal military temptation to use the SAAF Regiment as reinforcements for the SA Army. See Martin & Orpen – The South African Forces in World war II

[18] Originally lettered "A", "B", "C" and "D" Squadrons, later numbered 2930, 2931, 2932 and 2933 Squadrons

[19] 2721, 2744, 2771, 2788 and 2825 Field Squadrons; Nos. 4088, 4089, 4090, 4091 and 4092 independent AA Flights.

[20] Colonel H Morrey Salmon CBE MC DL DSc (1892-1985). A pre-war territorial soldier who had been commissioned in 1915 and although returning to civilian life in 1919, remained on the Army Emergency Reserve in the inter-war years. Recalled to duty as an over-age captain in 1939, he became a station defence adviser to the RAF in 1940 as an acting major before moving to HQ Coastal Command as the Command Defence Officer, with the temporary rank of lieutenant-colonel in 1941. He was "Commander RAF Regiment", with the rank of colonel, in the Mediterranean Allied Air Forces from the invasion of North Africa to the occupation of Austria at the end of the war. He was one of the most able senior Army officers to serve with the RAF Regiment during the war and his leadership, energy and ability contributed much to the operational successes

of Regiment wings and squadrons in North Africa, Italy, the Balkans and Greece between 1943 and 1945.

[21] 322 Wing, Bone; 324 Wing, Souk el Arba & Souk el Khamis; 325 Wing, Maison Blanche; 326 Wing, Canrobert.

[22] 4337 to 4360 AA Flights, inclusive.

[23] Later Air Vice-Marshal DFW Atcherley CB CBE DSO DFC (1904-52). His Meteor aircraft disappeared on a solo flight from Egypt to Cyprus while he was AOC 205 Group MEAF.

[24] Tunis "A" Team: 2788 Squadron plus 4089 & 4337 Flights

Tunis "B" Team: 2721 Squadron

Bizerta Team: 2744 Squadron plus 4091 Flight

[25] Operation Accolade

[26] The 2nd Earl Jellicoe KBE PC DSO MC FRS. Born 1918. Commissioned into the Coldstream Guards and seconded to the Special Air Service and later to the Special Boat Squadron. Entered the Foreign Service, and then politics, after the war

[27] General Mueller was convicted of war crimes by a Greek military court after the war and executed by firing squad in Crete

[28] 2901, 2902, 2903 & 2908 Field; 2907 & 2909 LAA Squadrons

[29] Smith & Walker – *War in the Aegean* p95

[30] A military intelligence officer, Captain JF Clarke RA, wrote the following report after his escape from Cos:

"As one who took part in the recent fighting on Cos, I feel it is my duty to report on the magnificent work of the RAF Regiment on the island.

"I was on Antimachia airfield from the first day of our landing and saw the RAF Regiment arrive and go into action. For close on two weeks, through many ground strafing raids, their 20mm guns were our only defence. It was impossible to dig in the guns or protect them in any way so that in almost every raid the unprotected gun crews suffered casualties from fighters or tail gunners.

"All of us who saw the RAF Regiment in action were always impressed by the great spirit of the gun teams who were determined to fight their guns, no matter how easy a target they were for ground strafing 109s. There was a cheery and defiant courage about them, and a pride in their Regiment which impressed us all.

"Cos gave me, and most of the others on the airfield, our first chance of seeing the RAF Regiment in action and it was without doubt our common opinion that the Regiment put up an extremely fine show on the island. We will all remember them for their unfailing cheerfulness, their determination to fight their guns to the end and their great courage. We were all proud to know them."

[31] Major Vaux transferred to the RAF Regiment after the war and was killed in an aircraft accident while serving as a group captain with the RAF Levies Iraq. The

Vaux Trophy was presented to the Regiment in his memory

[32] Squadron Leader DJ Kilgallin, OC 2909 Sqn and the senior RAF Regiment officer on Cos, was released from a German POW camp in 1945 and returned to active duty. On 17 Jan 1946, when a staff officer at HQ 24 Group, he submitted his report on the RAF Regiment's operations in the defence of Cos to the senior RAF Regiment officer at HQ Technical Training Command, together with the names of the men in his squadron whom he recommended for gallantry awards. He stated that only five out of almost two hundred RAF Regiment personnel who were captured were unwounded. He received neither a reply or an acknowledgement of his report before he was demobilised later that year. He therefore raised the matter again – as a civilian – in 1947 as he was particularly disturbed at the absence of any recognition for three of his airmen – whom he named as Payne, Tucker and Oliver – in particular. In 1948 Military Medals wereawarded to Flight Sergeant (Acting Warrant Officer) DE Payne and LAC WW Tucker, both of 2909 Squadron, for gallantry on Cos five years earlier. Warrant Officer CAG Eyles provided a graphic description of the time when, as LAC Eyles of 2909 Sqn, he was a prisoner of war in Arbeit Kommando 107E, near Halle in Germany, from September 1943 to April 1945 (MS in the RAF Regiment Museum Archives)

[33] *The Royal Air Force 1939-45* Vol 2 (Richards & Saunders) HMSO 1975 p.345

[34] 2901, 2903, 2904, 2906, 2911, 2919, 2925, 2928, 2929 & 2934 Squadrons

[35] 2902, 2908 & 2924 Field Squadrons; 2932 LAA squadron

[36] Air Vice-Marshal DA Pocock CBE (Commandant-General RAF Regiment 1973-75) – letter 10 Feb 95

[37] I am grateful to Mr BT Reid for this information

6

Sicily, Italy, The Balkans and Greece

The soft under-belly of the Axis.
Winston Churchill, 11th November 1942

The Invasion of Sicily

The planned RAF Regiment component of the force for the invasion of Sicily (Operation Husky) consisted of fourteen squadrons: five LAA squadrons from the UK, three field and three LAA squadrons from North Africa and one LAA and two field squadrons from the Middle East. In the event, five of the North African squadrons were retained to follow-up the invasion while the sixth (2862 LAA) was deployed to Malta to defend the airfield on the adjacent island of Gozo.

As a prelude to the invasion of Sicily, massive air attacks were launched on the small islands of Pantelleria and Lampedusa which lay between Tunis and Sicily. On 18th June 1943 2744 Field and 2864 LAA Squadrons landed on Lampedusa to secure the airfield in preparation for the planned assault on Sicily. The importance of these islands diminished once Sicily had been successfully invaded, so 2864 Squadron returned to North Africa before being redeployed to Palermo on 15th August 1943. Squadron Leader AC Langham MC, the commander of 2864 Squadron, was not sorry to leave the former Italian convict island, which he described as "the most barren, rocky and inhospitable place I had ever seen".

His squadron's journey from Lampedusa to Sousse was not without incident when the engines of the Landing Craft Tank (LCT) on which they were embarked broke down while those on board watched a floating mine drifting closer and closer to their vessel. Fortunately, and to the great relief of all on board, the frantic repair work on the engines was completed in time to enable the vessel to

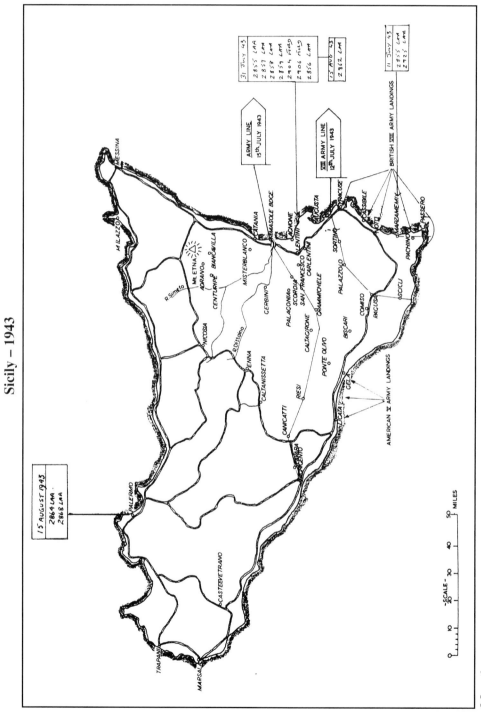

Sicily – 1943

Map 6.

get under way before disaster – and the mine – struck.

The airborne assault on Sicily began on the night of 9/10th July 1943 and was followed up the next day by landings from the sea. Personnel from the first two RAF Regiment LAA squadrons – 2855 from the UK and 2925 from the Middle East – went ashore on 10th July 1943 but unfortunately 2855 Squadron was without its guns and vehicles as the ship on which they had been loaded was sunk by enemy action before reaching the beaches. Once replacements had been received, 2855 joined 2925 at Pachino in providing AA defence for the airfield there. The second wave of RAF Regiment squadrons landed on 19th July; this consisted of 2857 LAA and three field squadrons – 2856, 2858 and 2859 – all from the UK. Once again, equipment was lost when the ships on which it had been separately loaded were sunk by air and submarine attack and it was some time before these additional losses could be replaced and the squadrons became fully operational.

2857 LAA Squadron, which had come from the UK, was deployed to reinforce AA defences in Sicily. An insight into the "them and us" attitudes, which coloured the relationships between Regiment and other Royal Air Force personnel at working level, was given by LAC Harrison, a clerk/general duties who was posted, with many other tradesmen, to the Headquarters Flight of 2857 Squadron when it was being formed at Kingscliffe, near Peterborough. There was considerable resentment among the RAF tradesmen – armourers, MT fitters, medical orderlies, clerks and cooks – at being posted to a Regiment squadron; in 1943 the Corps did not enjoy the respect of other branches and trades which it does today. Harrison's disillusionment was considerably increased when he learned that he had been posted to the squadron to replace an enterprising clerk who had taken advantage of the adjutant's absence to send a letter to Record Office – over the adjutant's forged signature – stating that the clerk in question was unfit to serve overseas and should be posted elsewhere in the UK immediately.

As the invasion force built up in Sicily, two ad hoc wing headquarters were formed to control the Regiment squadrons on the island. "A" Wing consisted of 2855 and 2858 LAA Squadrons with 2904 and 2906 Field Squadrons while "B" Wing comprised 2856, 2857, 2859 and 2925 LAA Squadrons, which were subsequently joined by 2862 LAA Squadron from Malta. As the advance continued, the RAF Regiment became the first British troops to occupy the airfield at Catania on the east coast of the island. Here, and at Palermo, the LAA squadrons were in action against enemy aircraft and suffered losses of 16 men killed and 13 wounded by enemy action.

However, once 2857 LAA Squadron had landed in Sicily, LAC Harrison was able to write home that "we are in Sicily at last…living in an olive grove which has been converted into a village of bamboo and straw huts. Lentini was attacked by Ju 88s at night but being deployed nearby at Scordia our guns remained silent so as not to give away the position of our own airfield.The next day we heard that 20mm rounds had landed on parked aircraft at Lentini and we received instructions about not using ball ammunition in the AA role."[1] Harrison stayed with the squadron as it moved northwards through Italy until early in 1944 when he was posted back to the Middle East for aircrew training. He returned to Italy at the beginning of 1945 as an air gunner in a Liberator squadron.

In fact, there had been other occurrences – notably when General Montgomery and Air Marshal Coningham had been visiting another airfield in Sicily – when 20mm rounds, including high explosive shells, from Naval Oerlikon guns had impacted on or near personnel and aircraft. Restrictions were therefore placed on all 20mm weapons used in the anti-aircraft role which limited their arcs of fire and engagement patterns so as to avoid a recurrence of these problems.[2] In addition, a high incidence of mechanical failures occurred at this time in the Hispanos used by the RAF Regiment which meant that guns fired only a few rounds before stopping. Incidents such as these added weight to the case for replacing the Regiment's elderly 20mm Hispanos with the more effective 40mm Bofors – and its self-destructing ammunition – as soon these could be made available.

Once the eviction of the Germans from Sicily had been completed, ten of the eleven Regiment squadrons on the island prepared for the move into Italy, leaving only 2868 LAA Squadron behind to defend the airfield at Palermo.

The Invasion of Italy

The Allied armies crossed the Straits of Messina and landed in southern Italy on 3rd September 1943.[3] The first Regiment unit to land in Italy was 2856 LAA Squadron which arrived at Reggio on 10 September. 2906 Field Squadron landed on the beachhead at Salerno on 11th September and between 17th and 30th September another ten RAF Regiment squadrons arrived in Italy.[4]

In September 1943, as the Allied armies advanced northwards, the flat plain which stretches to the north and east of Foggia became available for air bases from which bomber aircraft could strike at industrial targets in north Italy and Austria – and at the Ploesti oilfields in Romania. The deployment of Regiment LAA squadrons to the Foggia plain reflected the importance of these airfields on the east to the bomber offensive while the Naples airfields on the west were used for fighter and ground attack aircraft on the axis of advance to Rome. In order to release the solitary field squadron on the west coast for a more active role, a USAAF defence battalion[5] took over the security of Capodichino airfield, outside Naples, from 2906 Field Squadron which then moved forward to provide ground navigation markers for aircraft operating in the New Zealand and Canadian divisional areas. The field squadron on the east coast – 2904 – carried out reconnaissances for forward landing grounds between Termoli and the front line before being deployed in the V Corps area to defend the forward RAF radar units – 873, 6042 and 6043 AMES.

In December 1943 2856 LAA and 2925 LAA Squadrons moved from the Foggia plain to join 2904 Field Squadron on the line of the Trigno river while 2858 LAA Squadron deployed to defend Campomarino landing ground south of Termoli. On the west coast, reinforcements from the Middle East in the shape of four field squadrons – 2721, 2744, 2788 and 2825 – landed at Naples in the same month.

By October 1943 the front line ran across Italy from the Volturno river on the west to the Trigno river on the east. Now there were 13 RAF Regiment squadrons on the Italian mainland: three LAA and one field in the Naples area, one field at Termoli, six LAA on the Foggia plain and two more LAA at Taranto.[6] The German evacuation of Sardinia, and their forced withdrawal from Corsica, led to 2869 LAA Squadron being sent to Sardinia on 1st November 1943; it remained on the island until 17th May 1944. 2866 LAA Squadron deployed to Corsica on 27th November 1943 and remained there until 12th October 1944. It was briefly reinforced by 2861 Squadron, which arrived on 9th February 1944 and left on 21st July 1944. Both squadrons were heavily engaged against enemy bombing raids on the airfield at Poretta in May 1944. At the end of 1943 the RAF Regiment force level in Italy amounted to 20 squadrons: seven field and 13 LAA. A further three squadrons were in Sicily, Sardinia and Corsica respectively while two more remained in reserve in North Africa.

In the preparations for the advance to Rome, the USAAF asked for an escorting force for their technical intelligence teams and 2721 Squadron landed at Anzio on 30th May 1944 to carry out this task. During the advance from Naples the squadron occupied Ciampino airfield, ten miles south-east of Rome, before becoming the first Allied troops to enter Ostia and Fiumicino. Then, with their American companions, they entered Rome on 6th June 1944 and were thus among the first British units to reach the Eternal City.

As the Allied armies continued their advance, some bombing attacks on German forces in the forward battle zone had fallen short of the Allied front line and hit friendly troops instead. Following a

Support Weapons Flight 2906 Field Squadron at Salerno.

review of ways in which attacks on Allied ground forces might be avoided in future, RAF Regiment squadrons were tasked to co-operate with flying squadrons by laying out navigation aids on the ground to mark the forward line held by the Army.

In November 1943 2906 Field Squadron began this task, using marker panels by day and flares by night to indicate the bomb line. In January 1944 they were relieved of this task at Montenero Petaciato and St Vito Chiento by 2857 LAA Squadron, who were themselves replaced in this role by 2856 LAA Squadron at Castel Frentano. Within a few days, 2856 Squadron were the victims of a USAAF bombing attack by Flying Fortresses which had mistaken the navigation aid markers for target indicators. Fortunately, there were no casualties on that occasion.

However, the single incident which caused the largest loss of life in a Regiment unit in Italy had occurred in August 1943 when a USAAF aircraft with an engine on fire attempted a crash landing on the airfield at Tortorella and slewed off the runway into tents occupied by No.2933 LAA Squadron. The ensuing fireball killed 15 squadron personnel, as well as the pilot, and injured many more Regiment NCOs and airmen.

On 1st January 1944 the Air Ministry ordered the reduction of the RAF Regiment force level in the Middle East and Central Mediterranean theatres to 8,500 officers and men. This was apportioned between the Middle East (5,000) and the Mediterranean (3,500) – which limited the Regiment combat units in Italy to five field and 15 LAA squadrons. This was achieved by disbanding 2904 and 2906 Field Squadrons and 2925 LAA Squadron.

The landings at Anzio on 22nd January 1944 threw immense strain on the Allied armies and Regiment units were diverted to a variety of non-RAF tasks in this period. Some field squadrons were used in the infantry role and placed under Army command: 2771 and 2788 Squadrons operated on the Cassino front under command of the 2nd New Zealand Division and 4th British Division respectively from 24th April to 27th May 1944.

In September 1944 2721 Squadron was attached to the Household Cavalry Regiment in the Sant'Archangelo area before accompanying Skinner's Horse (an Indian Army regiment) from San Piero to San Sofia. There the squadron went into the front line and

3" Mortar flight in action near Monte Cassino.

carried out patrols with the Lovat Scouts, whose commanding officer had to ask the squadron commander to "produce a less dashing level of activity as your patrolling is causing the enemy to increase his strength in this area." A month later 2721 Squadron was heading for Ravenna with the 27th Lancers and after an assault crossing of the river Uniti, entered the town. From there the squadron advanced to the north-west to hold the line of the river Lamone between two Canadian regiments – Lord Strathcona's Horse and the Governor-General's Horse Guards – until relieved by 2788 Field Squadron. By this stage in the campaign 2721 Squadron had become the most decorated unit in the RAF Regiment, its awards including one Military Cross, five Military Medals and numerous mentions in despatches. Among the flight commanders in this squadron were two – Flying Officers JT O'Sullivan[7] and RH Millhouse[8] – who were to play prominent roles in the post-war Regiment.

In the battle for the Gothic Line in September 1944, 2744 Field

Squadron Observation Post near Cassino, 1944.

Squadron was employed in providing navigation aids (which were now called Ground/Air Landmarks or GALs) for friendly aircraft. These had to be positioned as far forward as possible and it was while engaged on these tasks near Cattolica that Flying Officer SW Harris and his team of one junior NCO and one aircraftman driver encountered an enemy patrol. In the fire fight which followed both he and his driver were hit by enemy small arms fire. Having extricated his men from the engagement, although wounded in the chest and back, Harris went forward to recover the jeep in which he and his men had been travelling and drove them to safety. He was subsequently awarded the Military Cross.

Wing Commander Downes and Squadron Leader Allen planning the next move.

In addition to those tasks in the forward area, the armoured flight of 2744 Squadron was used to provide Rover tentacles which relayed requests for close air support from Army units to the cab rank of ground attack aircraft keeping station above the front line. Flying Officer HH Wood-Glover[9] and his armoured cars carried out this task with speed and accuracy and the squadron's success in this joint-service role received much favourable comment from both Army

and Air Force commanders. Towards the end of the campaign one of the squadron officers – Flying Officer JF Ringer – was awarded the Military Cross and one of the squadron NCOs – Corporal RR Hope – received the Military Medal.

The first RAF Regiment wing headquarters had been formed – unofficially – by Colonel Morrey Salmon in the final stages of the North African campaign in 1943. Two more ad hoc wing HQs had existed temporarily in Sicily to meet the needs of the moment, and the justification for such controlling formations became even more obvious as the Italian campaign progressed. In February 1944, 1, 2 and 3 Wing Headquarters were formed in Italy and in April, as 1319, 1320 and 1321 Wing HQs, were deployed to Vasto, Naples and Foggia respectively to command the Regiment squadrons in those areas. In May 1944, as the advance moved beyond Rome, 1320 Wing moved to Orvieto while on the east coast 1319 Wing reached Pescara.

In July 1944 No.2788 Field Squadron was detached from 1320 Wing to take part in Operation Dragoon and subsequently landed on the beaches at St Raphael in the south of France. In the same month, 1322 Wing Headquarters and four LAA squadrons – 2907, 2914, 2932 and 2933 – arrived at Taranto from the Middle East and were deployed to the airfields in the Foggia plain.

As part of the planned force level reductions in the Middle East and Mediterranean, 2858, 2860, 2863, 2869 and 2905 LAA Squadrons were withdrawn from Italy and embarked at Naples on 17th May 1944 for the United Kingdom. Ten days later, three LAA squadrons – 2900, 2913 and 2916 – disembarked at Taranto from the Middle East.

On 22 August 1944 three field squadrons – 2902, 2908 and 2924 – arrived at Taranto from the Middle East and were promptly allocated to 1321 Wing and placed under command of the Balkan Air Force for operations on the Dalmatian coast under the control of Land Forces Adriatic. In September the decision was taken to remove all LAA squadrons from Italy; of the 14 squadrons in this category, two were retained in 1321 Wing as part of the Balkan Air Force, two were allotted to 1322 Wing as part of Air Headquarters "X" for operations in Greece and the remaining ten squadrons were earmarked for redeployment to the United Kingdom or for disbandment.

Thus by December 1944, as the Italian campaign approached

its end, only five RAF Regiment squadrons remained in Italy: two rifle and three field, together with the RAF Regiment reinforcement depot at Acerra, near Naples. 1319 Wing was at Rimini, on the Adriatic, with 2864 and 2866 Rifle Squadrons while the three field squadrons of 1320 Wing – 2721, 2744 and 2788 – were either being used in the infantry role alongside Army units or were carrying out ground/air landmarking tasks for the Air Force. In April 2866 Squadron was in action at Ravenna against a raiding force of pro-German Italian troops and in the same month 2744 Squadron was placed under the command of 15 Army Group at Ferrara for Army reinforcement tasks.

During the period of the Italian campaign, companies of the Iraq Levies had been stationed in Palestine and Cyprus in order to deploy RAF Regiment squadrons to operational theatres but by 1945 it became necessary to return the Levy companies to their homeland. Consequently those RAF Regiment squadrons which were not earmarked for immediate disbandment at the end of the war were redeployed from Italy, Greece and Austria to Palestine where terrorist action aimed at driving out the British administration was gathering momentum.

The Regiment and the Mediterranean Experience

The Italian campaign had given the RAF Regiment the opportunity to consolidate the lessons which had been learned in the Middle East campaigns and to develop its organisation and combat efficiency in a variety of roles in extremes of terrain and climate. Regiment squadrons confirmed their importance to air operations, not only in securing and defending airfields, but also in working with aircraft operating in the forward areas.

The introduction of wing headquarters was a successful step forward in co-ordinating command and control of two or more squadrons, as well as providing a much-needed intermediate level between squadrons and group headquarters. In addition, the flexibility of Regiment units, and the adaptability of their officers and airmen, enabled them to reinforce Army units when required – and to acquit themselves in accordance with the highest traditions of the Royal Air Force.

Operations in The Balkans

In January 1944 the Germans were in possession of all the islands off the Dalmatian coast, with the exception of Vis and Lagosta. The Yugoslav partisans led by Josip Broz, or Tito as he called himself, held these islands and had fortified Vis as an alternative partisan headquarters should Tito and his staff be forced to leave the mainland to avoid German attack. As far as the Royal Air Force was concerned, the short airstrip on Vis made it a useful forward base for fighter aircraft.

The Balkan Air Force had been formed, from the Mediterranean Allied Air Forces, in January 1944 and established its headquarters at Bari, on the Adriatic coast. Its role was to operate directly with Land Forces Adriatic and to give support to the Yugoslav partisans. A flight of 2867 LAA Squadron, equipped with 20mm Hispanos, arrived on Vis in January 1944 to provide anti-aircraft defence for both the airstrip and the partisan headquarters but the Yugoslavs were concerned that the guns would give away the position of their HQ and insisted that they should be sited well away from it.

The defences of the airstrip were, however, subsequently improved by the arrival of 2932 LAA Squadron with its 40mm Bofors guns. In September 1944 the 2867 Squadron detachment handed its Hispanos over to the partisans, and departed, leaving 2932 Squadron to continue providing LAA cover until the squadron was withdrawn to Austria in May 1945.

In July 1944 1321 Wing Headquarters, with 2825 Field and 2923 LAA Squadrons under command joined the Balkan Air Force presence on the Adriatic coast. 2825 Squadron became part of the coastal raiding force of Army and Royal Marine Commandos which operated, as part of Land Forces Adriatic, against German positions on the mainland. When, in October 1944, 2825 Squadron was redeployed to the mainland, 2932 Squadron replaced it in the tri-Service raiding group operating from Vis. An RAF Regiment parachute unit, known as "Celyforce" and commanded by Squadron Leader H Cely-Trevilian, had been formed to support RAF air operations liaison teams with Tito's partisans but when this requirement lapsed, Celyforce became a Special Duties detachment in the SBS organisation in the Adriatic and took part in long-range coastal raiding, which included landings on enemy-held islands, manning the guns on small naval vessels and – from time to time – acting as a section of the Special Boat Squadron.

From Vis 2825 Field Squadron had been deployed to Dubrovnik from where it operated against the German lines of communication from October 1944 to January 1945. It was eventually withdrawn as the result of pressure from Tito who considered that its continuing success was giving British forces too much influence in his country.

In September 1944 1321 Wing HQ was transferred to AHQ Greece to control the RAF Regiment squadrons which were being sent there and 1328 Wing HQ arrived from Italy to take its place in the Balkan Air Force. In February 1945, 1328 Wing moved to Zara, on the Yugoslav mainland, with 2914 LAA and 2825 Field Squadrons and the armoured flight of 2771 Field Squadron to secure the airfield at Prkos. With detachments of Royal Engineers to maintain the runway and USAAF ground crews to service the aircraft, the airfield at Prkos became an emergency landing ground for aircraft returning to their bases in Italy from bombing operations. As the war in the Balkans drew to a close, Yugoslav pressure for Allied forces to leave their territory increased and the remaining Regiment units were redeployed to Greece and Italy – and after VE Day – to Austria.

Greece

The RAF component of the British forces tasked to liberate Greece from German occupation was Force 276, commanded by Air Commodore Harcourt-Smith, in which the RAF Regiment component consisted of 1321 Wing HQ with two field and two LAA squadrons under command.

In September 1944 a composite force drawn from Land Forces Adriatic and the Balkan Air Force was assembled with the aim of seizing the airfield at Araxos in the Peleponnese to enable air support to be provided for future operations in Salonika. This was code-named "Bucketforce" and comprised elements of the Special Boat Squadron and the Long Range Desert Group, a troop of Royal Marine Commandos, a company of Highland Light Infantry – and 2908 Squadron RAF Regiment – totalling some 450 all ranks, under the command of Lieutenant Colonel the Lord Jellicoe.

Following a parachute drop on Araxos airfield, the main force landed at Katakolon on the west coast of the Peleponnese. The RAF

Greece – 1944/45

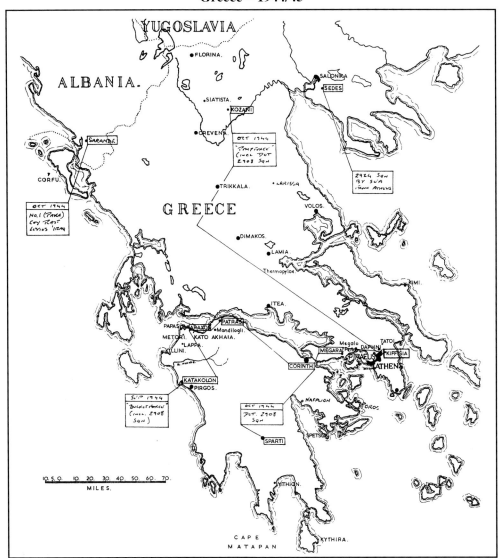

Map 7.

Regiment component included a specially-trained mine clearance
party of two officers and 39 airmen drawn from various Regiment
squadrons other than 2908. One of the many unusual features of this
force was that 2908 Squadron had its own chaplain – The Reverend
(Squadron Leader) GH Church – who made an outstanding
contribution in the many and varied situations which the squadron
encountered during its service in Greece.

From Katakolon Jellicoe's force advanced northwards to seize Patras, the third largest port in the country and the principal harbour of the Peleponnese. Here they found the German rearguard preparing demolitions before withdrawing to the mainland and a brisk fire fight – in which the six-pounder anti-tank guns of 2908's support flight played a notable part, including the sinking of a German E boat – ensued and the Germans left hurriedly before they could cause much damage. Continuing the advance eastwards to the Corinth Canal, 2908 Squadron crossed into mainland Greece and reached Megara on 10th October, and after an engagement at Megalo Pekvo, entered Athens four days later. From there the squadron divided into two groups – one returned to the Peloponnese to pacify Sparta and the other went north as part of another composite force to harass the Germans as they retreated towards Yugoslavia.

In an attack on the German rearguard at Kozani, just inside Yugoslavia, "Pompforce" – consisting of two companies of 4th Battalion Parachute Regiment, a detachment of the SBS and the 2908 Squadron detachment – scaled an almost perpendicular rock face in order to attack the enemy position from the rear. On the road below, an enemy anti-tank gun scored a hit on an armoured car of 2908 Squadron, mortally wounding the flight commander. The driver, Corporal GH Wingate, although wounded himself, brought the vehicle back to safety – and was awarded the Military Medal for gallantry under fire.

In October 1944 Land Forces Adriatic launched an attack to seize the port of Sarande – on the Albanian mainland opposite Corfu – to deprive the German forces retreating northwards from Greece of an evacuation port. It was decided to reinforce the formation ("Houndforce") tasked for this operation with a mountain warfare/ paratroop company in order to seize the high ground which overlooked, and dominated, the harbour.

1 (Parachute) Company of the RAF Levies Iraq duly went ashore and stormed up Hill 246 with such speed that the enemy garrison was taken by surprise and 96 German soldiers were captured, without any casualties being incurred by the Levies. The company commander, Major Guy Hudson, then sent one of his Levy officers – Ram Khamshi (Second Lieutenant) Shliman Bukho – to inform the brigadier that the objective had been taken by his men. Unfortunately,

Corporal GH Wingate MM after the action at Kozani.

as Bukho approached the Commandos holding the beach head, they failed to recognise him as one of the British force and opened fire, wounding him. Despite his cries – albeit in broken English – that he was British, the firing continued and he was unable to deliver his message.

Believing that Hill 246 was still in German hands, Royal Navy warships shelled the position and RAF Spitfires joined in the attack. The twenty or so Levy casualties (including British officers) caused by this friendly fire did not inhibit the Levy sense of humour when they later claimed that being attacked by all three British Services in the course of a single day qualified them as experts in combined operations.[10]

The liberation of Greece produced a struggle for power between the two largest political factions – the Greek government in exile, which returned with units of the Greek regular army which had been fighting with the Allied forces, and the communist party which had been organising the resistance within occupied Greece. The military wing (ELAS) of the communist party (EAM) began to seize key points and attack police and military units loyal to the government with the aim of taking control of the country. EAM regarded this as a civil war and avoided any confrontation with the British forces until the British government, alarmed at the prospect of yet another communist state in the eastern Mediterranean, ordered British troops to intervene on the side of the Greek government by disarming the ELAS forces. The result was to produce confrontation – which led to open warfare – between the British Army and RAF on one side and EAM and ELAS on the other.

Air Headquarters Greece, commanded by Air Commodore GW Tuttle,[11] established its headquarters near an airstrip in the town of Kifissia, fifteen miles north-east of Athens, where sufficient accommodation of the right quality was available and where communications with its subordinate units could be easily maintained. No prior thought had been given to the security of the AHQ site as at that stage no one had foreseen that fighting would break out between the British forces and left-wing Greek partisans.

The RAF Regiment squadrons in Greece were deployed on various routine tasks, either with Army units or securing airfields in Salonika for occupation by RAF aircraft – as 2924 Squadron was

Map 8.

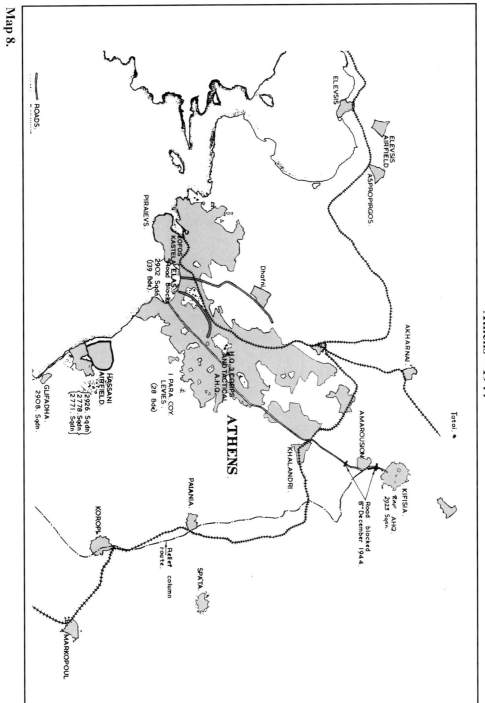

Athens – 1944

ROADS.

doing at Sedes, where they had been sent by sea from Piraeus. The LAA squadrons were at Hassani airfield, four miles south-east of Athens, and when the internal situation began to deteriorate in mid-November 1321 Wing HQ, (Wing Commander J Simpson) with 2923 LAA Squadron under command, was moved to Kifissia to provide defence for the AHQ complex. On 5th December 1944 the British began to engage ELAS forces and although the Regiment commander at Kifissia recommended that AHQ be moved to a more defensible location, his advice was not taken. Instead, a hastily-assembled group of surplus RAF personnel was sent from the Middle East to increase the number of combatants at Kifissia.[12]

Hassani airfield, now held only by 2926 LAA Squadron, was reinforced by 1 (Parachute) Company of the RAF Levies Iraq, fresh from their action at Sarande. When Hassani was attacked by ELAS forces, 2908 Field squadron was made available as a further reinforcement for the airfield, which was successfully defended. Later, in Athens 2902 Field Squadron used six-pounder guns to provide close support for its field flights and the infantry operating alongside them, while the Iraq Levies parachute company operated with other Airborne forces, in the street fighting which finally cleared the ELAS partisans from the city.

Meanwhile, at Kifissia Wing Commander Simpson was doing what he could, with the 183 Regiment officers and airmen under his command, to put the sprawling AHQ complex in an adequate state of defence. Unfortunately, the various buildings occupied by the RAF were scattered in the built-up area of the town and the perimeter was too great for the total complement of 589 officers and airmen to defend effectively. This resulted in the nine 40mm guns available having to be deployed singly on the streets leading to the AHQ area while the four 20mm guns were used to strengthen the defences of the Hotel Cecil – which was the AHQ building used as the command post.

ELAS road blocks, effectively isolating Kifissia from Athens, had been in place since 10th December. In the early hours of 18th December over 1,000 ELAS partisans – supported by mortars and artillery – began their attack on the AHQ. Fighting continued throughout the night and into the following day, when the attackers used mortars and artillery against the defending force which had to rely on small arms once the 2923 Squadron Bofors and Hispano guns, sited in the ground-to-ground role and without mutual support, had been put out of action and casualties inflicted on their detachments by small arms fire. Expectations of prolonging the resistance faded when a parachute drop of ammunition and food by a Wellington aircraft drifted outside the defence perimeter and fell in the enemy lines. Under cover of darkness the partisans began to make inroads into the defended area by dynamiting buildings and infiltrating through the shattered walls.[13]

The urgency of the situation at Kifissia was not appreciated by the Army HQ in Athens and the joint Army/RAF Regiment relief force which had been assembled postponed its departure for 24 hours in the expectation that it would not be required. On the 19th December, however, led by two troops of 46th Royal Tank Regiment and the armoured car flights of 2771 and 2908 Field Squadrons, the column began a circuitous advance from Glifadha, south of Hassani, to Kifissia – only to be delayed by destroyed bridges and mines along the road. Progress was painfully slow and when the column reached Kifissia later the same day, it was to find that the defenders, having exhausted their ammunition, had surrendered about four hours earlier before being promptly spirited away into the hills by their captors. Only the dead, wounded and a few survivors, who had successfully evaded the attackers, were found in the wrecked headquarters by the relief column. The RAF prisoners of the victorious ELAS force were to experience hardship, abuse and ill-treatment at the hands of their captors[14] before they were released at the end of January 1945,[15] when the civil war in Greece finally ended.

Once the situation in Greece had stabilised, most of the RAF Regiment units there were withdrawn in March 1945. 2771 and 2788 Field and 2914 and 2926 LAA Squadrons returned to Italy, and 1 (Parachute) Company went home to Iraq.

The Regiment units which were lost at Kifissia were speedily reformed: 1321 Wing in Greece, under Wing Commander WH Chapman, in January 1945 and 2923 Squadron in Italy, as a rifle squadron, in February 1945. 2908 Field Squadron remained in Athens – with detachments elsewhere in Greece and in Crete – until October 1945 when it joined 1328 Wing in Austria.

The RAF Regiment – and Army – units ordered, in May 1945, to what was to become the British Zone of Occupation in Austria

The Battle for AHQ Kifissia – December 1944

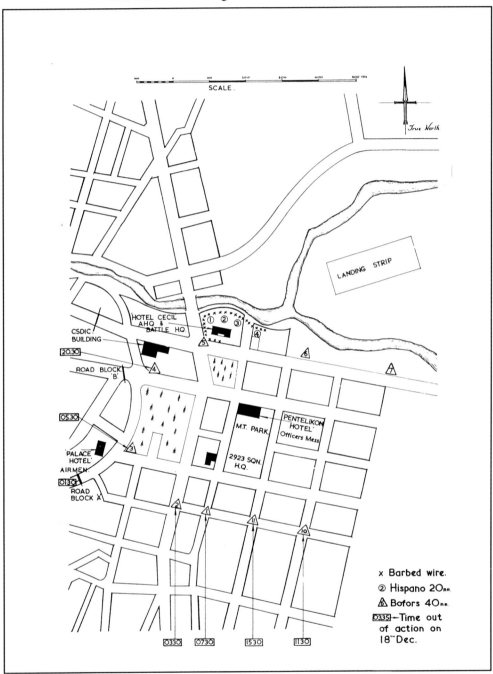

Map 9.

were initially delayed at the Austrian frontier by the Soviet Army, but once they reached their assigned locations[16] they were able to balance their air disarmament tasks with excellent recreational facilities. Celyforce organised a Regiment ski-ing centre, a sailing club was established on the Worthersee and there were ample facilities for riding and game shooting. The Army had already established strings of captured racehorses, and opened three race courses (including one in Vienna), when the Chief of the Air Division of the Control Commission in Austria[17] ordered 2932 Squadron – based at Graz – to find sufficient racehorses to run RAF race meetings. This order was promptly carried out by the Regiment, which added yet another unestablished task to its record of successes.[18] More important, perhaps – particularly for those who had been away from the UK for three or more years – was the introduction of home leave, made possible by the Medloc military train services which ran from Trieste, through Austria and Germany, to the Channel ports on the French coast.

1321 Wing, with two field squadrons – 2902 and 2924 – was redeployed to Palestine in March 1945, as did 1319 Wing with 2721 and 2788 Field and 2864, 2923 and 2969 Rifle Squadrons from Italy. In March 1946, 1320 Wing HQ, with 2771 Field and 2908 Rifle Squadrons, left Austria for Palestine, where they were joined by 2742 Armoured Car Squadron from the United Kingdom.

The RAF Regiment, having fought through the Western Desert and North Africa to Sicily, Italy, the Aegean, the Balkans and Greece, had – by the end of 1945 been reduced in strength in the Middle East to barely a dozen squadrons, concentrated in the increasingly unstable mandated territory of Palestine. Although the Second World War had ended, peace was still a long way away for the officers and airmen of the RAF Regiment – whose future existence was still undecided.

Notes

[1]   LAC R Harrison (Clk/GD in 2857 Sqn) – letter 25 Jul 43

[2]   AM file TAC 2/55 (PRO)

[3]   Operation Baytown. The Army's air defence component for the invasion included six LAA regiments (18 LAA batteries = 324 40mm guns) against the assessed threat from the estimated 320 Luftwaffe aircraft in Italy

[4]   2904 Field & 2858 LAA (Reggio), 2867 LAA (Salerno), 2859 & 2925 LAA (Gioa del Colle), 2904 Field, 2856 & 2857 LAA (Bari), 2904 Field (Foggia), 2860 LAA (Naples)

[5]   Prompted by the lessons of Crete – and the formation of the RAF Regiment – the USAAF formed its own airbase defence units from 1942 onwards. These were disbanded at the end of the war and, with the establishment of the USAF as an independent Service, this task was subsequently added to the roles of the USAF Security Police. See *Vick*, Ch3 p21 n1

[6]   Naples: 2860 LAA, 2859 LAA, 2867 LAA, 2906 Field

Taranto: 2864 LAA, 2865 LAA

Foggia: 2855 LAA, 2856 LAA, 2857 LAA, 2858 LAA, 2862 LAA, 2925 LAA

Termoli: 2904 Field

[7]   Later Group Captain JT O'Sullivan OBE, Commandant RAF Regiment Depot 1963-66

[8]   Later Wing Commander RH Millhouse MBE

[9]   Later Group Captain HH Wood-Glover MBE

[10] Gp Capt JT O'Sullivan – letter 26 Mar 96

[11] Later Air Marshal Sir Geoffrey Tuttle KBE CB DFC FRAeS (1906-1989). Deputy Chief of Air Staff 1956-59

[12] Mr HF Williams – letter of 26 Oct 95

[13] Flt Lt R Hart (2923 Sqn) – report dated 5 Nov 47

[14] Mr HF Williams – letter of 26 Oct 95

[15] Flt Lt R Hart (2923 Sqn) – report dated 5 Nov 47.

[16] 1320 Wing (Nos.2744, 2825, 2866 & 2926 Squadrons) to Klagenfurt

1328 Wing (Nos.2771, 2914 & 2932 Squadrons) to Vienna, Bruck and Graz

[17] Air Vice-Marshal R Foster – later Air Chief Marshal Sir Robert Foster KCB CBE DFC (1898-1973) C-in-C 2 ATAF 1951-53

[18] Air Vice-Marshal DA Pocock CBE (Commandant-General RAF Regiment 1973-75) – letter 18 Mar 96

7
_____

The Return to North-West Europe

The land battle will be a terrific party and we will require the full support of the air all the time.
General Sir Bernard Montgomery, 15th May 1944

Planning and Preparation

From 1943 onwards the planning for the invasion of Europe by American, British and Canadian armies gathered momentum until the skeleton planning staff expanded and became a key element in Supreme Headquarters Allied Expeditionary Force Europe (SHAEF) under General Dwight D Eisenhower of the United States Army. An RAF Regiment officer, Wing Commander CW Mayhew, was a member of the planning team from its inception and he subsequently became head of the RAF Regiment staff within SHAEF itself.

The concept of operations for the British and Canadian armies was that they would advance north-west from the landing beaches in Normandy, through the Low Countries and into the north German plain. Throughout this, they would be supported by the RAF's Second Tactical Air Force (2 TAF) in much the same way as the Army had been supported in North Africa by the First Tactical Air Force. It was therefore unthinkable that 2 TAF would contemplate operating in Europe without RAF Regiment wings and squadrons to provide ground and LAA defence for the airfields which would have to be captured – and defended against ground and air attack.

On 19th March 1944 the Vice-Chief of Air Staff approved a Regiment force level of 19 Wings, each containing one field and one LAA squadron, for 2 TAF. There was a problem in that the LAA squadrons were still, partially at least, equipped with the 20mm Hispano gun and the memories of the day in Sicily when an airfield had been sprayed with 20mm shells from Naval Oerlikons was fresh in the mind of the AOC-in-C 2 TAF.[1] He accordingly demanded that the Regiment LAA squadrons assigned to him should be re-equipped with 40mm Bofors guns – or he would go into Europe without LAA defences. The only source of these weapons was the Army but the War Office suggested that the RAF problem could be solved by replacing the 20mm Hispanos with 20mm Polstens – which used self-destructing ammunition and would not therefore damage aircraft on the ground. This was not well received by the RAF and the Army eventually agreed to supply the required number of Bofors guns to bring each LAA squadron up to an establishment of 12 40mm guns.

HQ 2 TAF then expressed the view that the prevailing composition of the Regiment wings would lead to inflexibility in operations with differing tasks; furthermore the field squadrons were not suited to carrying out the many and varied roles which might be expected of them in mobile operations in NW Europe. After due consideration, it was agreed that Wing Headquarters would be used to control whatever mix of two or more squadrons was deemed appropriate for operations at any one time and would not become rigidly standardised formations. Again, the establishment of the field squadrons was reviewed and it was decided to reallocate their armoured cars into separate armoured car squadrons.

The reorganisation of the field squadrons produced a force of seven rifle squadrons (each with a squadron headquarters, three rifle flights and a support flight of 3" mortars) and six armoured car squadrons, with four flights of six armoured cars in each. This provided the RAF Regiment element of 2 TAF with a much more effective and flexible organisation. The LAA squadrons now had, in the 40mm Bofors, a gun with greater range and hitting power both in the ground-to-air and ground-to-ground roles than the 20mm Hispano. The rifle squadrons, with four 3" mortars each, had the necessary firepower to seize and hold forward airfields and dominate the surrounding areas while the armoured car squadrons could provide long-range reconnaissance, convoy escorts and rapid reinforcement with mobile firepower.

However, even as the plans for RAF Regiment involvement in Operation Overlord were being finalised in May 1944, the War Office – this time with the support of the Prime Minister – was renewing its demands for more men for the infantry from the RAF Regiment. This was despite the fact that the deployment of RAF Regiment LAA squadrons on airfields in the UK had already released over 13,000 soldiers back to the field army and that there were less than 4,000 RAF Regiment gunners deployed on ground defence tasks at home. The Secretary of State for Air advised the Prime Minister that "there is not one man more in the RAF Regiment than is necessary to meet existing war requirements; in any event, most of those in the RAF Regiment are LAA gunners, not infantrymen."[2] This made no impact at all on Churchill, who responded "the Army has already culled its AA gunners – now it is the turn of the RAF Regiment. I want 25,000 men transferred, including 2,000 immediately for the Guards as replacements. They will be much better employed there than loafing around already overcrowded airfields."

The Air Ministry answer was to offer the equivalent of 15 LAA squadrons – some 3,000 men – out of a total UK-based strength of 38,000. Faced with these unassailable facts, Churchill reluctantly amended his original demand to 10,000 men – of whom 2,000 were required immediately to bring the Guards up to strength. A call for volunteers from the Regiment and other Group V trades was made, but as the conditions included the requirement for all NCOs to forfeit their rank on transfer, there were few sergeants or corporals among the 691 volunteers. As, even in the midst of war, there was no legal method of forcibly transferring men from one Service to another against their will, the shortfall of 1,309 men had to be made up by discharging selected RAF Regiment airmen and immediately calling them up for Army service. Of the 2,000 transfers obtained in this underhand way, 1,539 went to the Guards and 461 to infantry regiments.[3]

An eminent historian has made the point that the value-system of one society is a closed book to a member of another culture[4] and the various micro-cultures which flourish in the British Army are classic examples of a form of this phenomenon. The 2nd Battalion of the Scots Guards had returned to the UK from the Middle East in 1944. Grievously under-strength after several years of hard fighting, the battalion needed some 400 reinforcements before being able to participate in the campaign in North-West Europe. These were to come from the RAF Regiment and – justifiably aggrieved at the ministerial sleight-of-hand which had forced them out of the RAF against their will – the Regiment contingent marched towards the Scots Guards camp outside Hawick dressed in No.1 RAF blue uniform (and not in their No.2 khaki battledress) defiantly chanting "we are the RAF, RAF, RAF".

In the disparaging manner often adopted by tribal groups towards outsiders, the Scots Guards regarded the men of the "disbanded RAF Regiment" merely as aerodrome guards who had received an extra 6d a day more than the infantry for "the so-called skilled work of guarding aerodromes against German parachutists who never appeared" and treated them as raw recruits to be moulded into the standard pattern of guardsmen.[5]

In reality, of course, the RAF Regiment gunners were trained and disciplined airmen from LAA squadrons whose personnel were as professionally competent in that role as the LAA gunners of the Royal Artillery who had already been rebadged as infantrymen. And the higher rate of pay was one which the LAA gunners of the RAF Regiment and the Royal Regiment of Artillery shared in recognition of the higher skill standards of artillerymen vis-a-vis infantrymen. Fact and legend are uneasy bedfellows and it suited the Army to ignore the origins and qualities of its new intakes and attribute their subsequent attainments to the indoctrination received in their Army environments. The 2nd Bn Scots Guards certainly did this successfully, and went on to fight with distinction, from the Rhine to the Baltic between February and May 1945, albeit that the battalion's achievements were based on the fighting qualities of the former RAF Regiment gunners who made up the greater part of the unit.

The Vice-Chief of Air Staff complained that "reductions in RAF Regiment LAA squadrons are being updated every time a new Joint Intelligence Committee estimate of the threat of air attack is produced – and each re-estimate constantly produces a lower threat." The Commandant-General RAF Regiment had made his own enquiries into the Army's claims for more infantrymen and these revealed that of the 17,500 artillerymen taken from AA Command, only 4,100 had gone to the infantry. The other 13,400 had been transferred to other arms and services – a fact which may have weakened the War Office's arguments, but did not deter a renewed attack on the RAF Regiment's manpower.

Consequently, at a meeting chaired by Clement Attlee, as Lord President of the Council, in London a week before D-Day, the objections raised by VCAS (Air Marshal Sir Douglas Evill) and the Commandant-General RAF Regiment (Major-General Liardet) were rejected. The War Office's argument that "we can no longer afford to maintain a special body of troops purely for the defence of airfields...the time has now come to consider whether the greater part of it should not be taken to reinforce the field formations of the Army" was heard sympathetically by the politicians and civil servants who were obviously so impressed by the Army's reasoning that they summarily dismissed the Air Force's case for retaining the means for its own defence.[6] The Cabinet subsequently decided that the 140,000 young men who were due to be called up in the first half of 1945 would all be directed to the Army. In addition, both the Royal Navy and the Royal Air Force were required to find 20,000 men each who would agree to transfer to the Army.

Thus in 1945 the RAF Regiment had to surrender a further 5,000 men (including 300 sergeants and 500 corporals who were allowed to retain their rank) as their share of the RAF's manpower contribution to the Army. The net result was that a further 36 RAF Regiment squadrons were disbanded and the level of support for the RAF's post-war disarmament teams was reduced by ten RAF Regiment squadrons. Another result was that medical employment standards for home service had to be reduced so that the UK-based squadrons could be manned by men who had been medically downgraded, thus releasing fully-fit gunners for overseas service.[7]

It was clear that, at this stage in the war, the prospect of victory and the return to conditions of peace had alerted the War Office to the long-term dangers of a post-war Royal Air Force which could be self-sufficient in those roles which the Army had deemed to be its own in pre-war days.

Despite its repeated inability to provide the Air Force with the necessary ground and low-level air defence in war-time which it had promised to do in peace-time, the War Office was obviously determined to assert the Army's case for control of all aspects of land-based operations in the post-war era, regardless of whether the resources to achieve this were there or not.

The Invasion of Europe

D-Day was 6th June 1944 and the British and Canadian landings were made on the Normandy beaches code-named, from west to east, Gold, Juno and Sword. The first RAF Regiment units arrived off Juno beach on D-Day itself but because of the congestion caused by the assault landing of over 25,000 men on Juno beach alone, were not able to disembark until D+1. On that morning Colonel RL Preston, the senior Regiment staff officer of HQ 83 Group, went ashore with his team, followed by 1304 and 1305 Wing Headquarters and 2809, 2819 and 2834 LAA Squadrons.

By D+12 there were ten Regiment squadrons deployed on forward airfields, although not all had reached France without mishap. Nos.2817 and 2876 LAA Squadrons had embarked in Landing Craft Tank (LCT) at Gosport and were heading for the invasion beaches where they were due to land at dawn on D+2 when they were intercepted by German naval forces. LAC Derrick Dean of 2876 Squadron described the scene: "at about 0400 a German aircraft dropped flares over the convoy which illuminated the vessels for patrolling German E Boats. Although the convoy scattered on the orders of the commander, the enemy boats were successful in attacking some of the LCTs. The one carrying 2817 Squadron received direct hits which smashed the ramps and pierced the hull. Our craft manoeuvred alongside to take off the dead and wounded and to tow the damaged LCT towards the beaches. Despite our efforts, she began to sink and we took the remaining personnel – RAF Regiment and Royal Navy – on board while the guns, vehicles and equipment of 2817 Squadron went down with the LCT. Our squadron went ashore on Juno beach and, despite stiff enemy resistance, reached the airstrip at Coulombes before midday where we immediately went into action against German aircraft. That night we mounted patrols to clear the surrounding area of the snipers who had been bothering us during the day".[8]

By the end of August 1944 the Regiment component of 2 TAF was 19 wing headquarters, 18 LAA squadrons, eight rifle squadrons and four armoured squadrons. In order to exercise control of the LAA defences in the combat zone, HQ 106th Anti-Aircraft Brigade Royal Artillery was placed in overall command of both Army and RAF Regiment LAA units. In an attack on the airfield at Martragny in

Map 10.

The first RAF Regiment units to land in Normandy – 7 June 1944

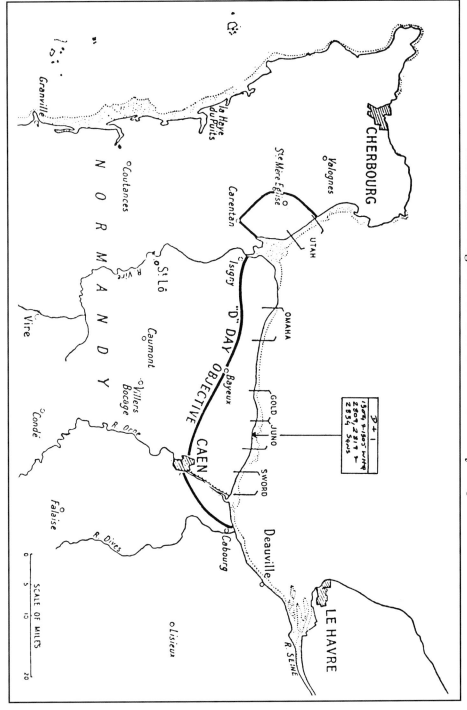

July 1944 2703 LAA Squadron and an Army LAA battery shot down fourteen of the attacking aircraft. Unfortunately, in the general melee one of the Army guns opened fire on RAF aircraft as well – for which the entire gun detachment was placed in close arrest by the battery commander and charged with "irresponsibly opening fire on friendly aircraft"!

The success which Regiment squadrons had achieved in escorting Air Technical Intelligence (ATI) teams in the Mediterranean theatre resulted in their employment in similar roles in Europe. With armoured car and rifle flights to escort them, ATI teams went ahead of the Army to secure German radars at Mount Pincon and Houlgate and to examine the major rocket site in the quarries at Hautmesnils. On 25th August 2798 Rifle Squadron, which had been protecting RAF radar sites in one of the American corps areas, was ordered to secure Longchamps racecourse in Paris as a possible landing site. With guides from the French Maquis the squadron took a devious route into the city to reach its objective – thus becoming one of the first Allied units to enter the French capital. On 31st August 1944 another RAF ATI team, designated "R" Force, entered Rouen escorted

RAF Regiment LAA gun detachment in Normandy – Summer 1944.

by 1315 Wing HQ, 2717 Rifle Squadron and 2757 Armoured Car Squadron.

Air Defence in the United Kingdom

At this point in time a serious threat was posed to the UK base by the first of the German V weapons – the flying bomb which was launched from North-West Europe and had intended to be used to disrupt preparations for the Allied invasion. However, even after the Allied armies were advancing from Normandy, the V1 attacks were an unwelcome response from the Germans.

Intelligence information about the V weapons was being collated from 1943 onwards and plans had been made to redeploy heavy and light AA guns to the South Coast to counter the flying bomb threat, should it materialise. Consequently a large number of AA units had to be retained in Britain against this threat, instead of being sent to North-West Europe where they would have improved the AA defences of 21 Army Group and 2 TAF.

When the first flying bombs were launched in June 1944, Operation Diver was implemented by deploying 528 HAA guns, 804 LAA guns and 400 searchlights in a belt between Folkestone and Beachy Head between 28th June and 3rd July. The RAF Regiment contribution to this amounted to 31 LAA squadrons and as the V-1 launching sites in France were forced northwards by the advancing British forces, the flying bomb flight lines were forced towards the Thames estuary. The AA defences were accordingly extended eastwards and a further 21 LAA squadrons were deployed in Kent to cover the open flank which had existed until then. Thus the RAF Regiment contribution to the Diver gun boxes totalled 52 LAA squadrons and over 600 guns. As the Allied armies overran more and more of the V1 launching sites, the threat diminished until it finally disappeared in October 1944, when Operation Diver was terminated and the last guns withdrawn.

Land and Air Battles in North-West Europe

As 21st Army Group advanced into Belgium and Holland, RAF Regiment squadrons were operating as part of 2, 83, 84 and 85 Groups of 2 TAF. The 83 and 85 Group squadrons were engaged in a variety of tasks, ranging from clearing the enemy – and the mines which they left behind – from newly-captured airstrips to ferrying aircraft fuel from supply depots to airfields and re-arming aircraft on airstrips in the forward areas. The liberation of Brussels on 3rd September 1944 saw 2781 Armoured Car Squadron enter the city ahead of the leading Army units and to be welcomed by thousands of deliriously happy Belgians. Stopping only briefly to enjoy the kisses, flowers, wine and champagne which were pressed upon them, the squadron eventually reached its destination – the airfield north of the city.[9]

As the advance rolled forward towards Beauvais, Antwerp, Eindhoven and Volkel there was little enemy air activity and the LAA squadrons were used in their secondary role to assist in maintaining the momentum of the advance. Close behind the Guards Armoured Division, 2781 Squadron entered Eindhoven and cleared the airfield for occupation by two fighter wings of 83 Group. At this stage, the German front line was on the line of the Wilhelmina Canal, six kilometres to the north, and 2781 and 2726 Squadrons were deployed to hold the south bank of the canal nearest the airfield, from where they were in daily contact with the enemy.[10]

In 84 Group, however, the Regiment squadrons were mainly employed in escorting the Air Technical Intelligence teams which were busy examining the aircraft, weapons and equipment which the Luftwaffe had left behind.

Although enemy air activity had steadily decreased since the early days of the invasion, it had not disappeared and on 28th November 1944 2875 LAA Squadron became the first AA unit to destroy a German jet fighter when an Me 262 fell to one of the squadron's 40mm guns deployed on the airfield at Helmond in Holland. The entry in the squadron's operations record book reads "Weather very cold indeed and rather overcast. Another Me 262 very unwisely visited the airfield – with fatal results. Squadron guns opened up and the crew of B11 gun was successful in shooting it down. During the evening a personal message of congratulations was received by the squadron commander from the AOC 83 Group."

From September 1944 onwards the approach of winter slowed down the advance as the weather favoured the defenders in the flat terrain of the Low Countries. In periods of positional warfare along the Leopold Canal, the Waal and Maas Rivers some of the Rifle and Armoured Car squadrons were deployed alongside British and

Canadian Army units in direct contact with the enemy. During one such operation, when 1313 Wing (2757 Armoured Car and 2816 Rifle Squadrons) was holding part of the line of the Leopold Canal with the Canadians, the 3" mortar flight of the rifle squadron fired over 2,000 high explosive bombs, and 200 smoke rounds, against German positions. This was done so effectively that one of the support flight NCOs – Flight Sergeant Greening – was awarded the Military Medal for maintaining mortar observation posts in areas exposed to enemy fire.

In another incident, a flight of the same squadron went to the rescue of men of 40 LAA Regiment Royal Artillery whose escape route had been cut by the enemy. The flight commander, Flying Officer NJ Page, was awarded the Military Cross for his conduct in this action. 1313 Wing was subsequently relieved in the line by 1315 Wing (2777 Armoured Car and 2717 Rifle Squadrons). Other Regiment units which were placed under Canadian Army command in this period were 2713 and 2798 Rifle and 2809 and 2742 Armoured Car Squadrons.

It was at this time that AC Cook of 2742 Squadron was ordered to "brew up" for his flight, which was bivouacked in a farmhouse. The staple means of field cooking in the British service were the Soyer stove (invented during the Crimean War) and the somewhat more modern hydraburner. The latter used pressurised kerosene to produce fearsome jets of roaring flame which generated sufficient heat to cook enough food for 50 men. Unfamiliar with the finer points of field cooking, AC Cook, a "B" Flight gunner, dutifully refilled the tank of the hydraburner – but mistakenly with petrol instead of kerosene – before lighting it. The resulting explosion, fortunately, did no more damage than to dislodge the soot of ages from every chimney in the farmhouse, rendering it uninhabitable by its civilian owners and Regiment lodgers alike. The flight sergeant made life so unpleasant for the unfortunate perpetrator of this disaster that AC Cook positively welcomed his posting to India after VE Day.[11]

In the British sector, 2781 Armoured Car and 2827 Rifle Squadrons were attached to 1st Battalion Oxfordshire & Buckinghamshire Light Infantry. During this detachment, Flying Officer JRB Wild of 2781 Squadron distinguished himself while carrying out reconnaissances and was awarded a Military Cross. 2726

Rifle Squadron came under the command of 2nd Battalion Irish Guards (then an armoured regiment) with whom they held the line on the east bank of the River Maas.

In the advance to the River Waal 2798 Rifle Squadron was redeployed from the Canadian sector to join the Reconnaissance Regiment of 43 (British) Division and in the subsequent fighting, while under Army command, LAC TG Davies earned a Military Medal.

The German Army's last attempt at a counter-stroke began on

RAF Regiment LAA gun detachment in Holland – winter 1945.

16th December 1944 when they launched an all-out offensive through the Ardennes, close to the boundary between the British and American sectors. In the British sector the RAF's forward radar and wireless observation units of 72 Wing were deployed well forward – and protected by 2742 and 2804 Armoured Car Squadrons with 2811 Rifle Squadron in support. The surprise which the Germans achieved, and the speed of their advance, made it both difficult and dangerous to withdraw the 72 Wing units, with their cumbersome equipment and heavy vehicles, from an area in which there were more poor tracks than good roads. Nevertheless, the Regiment squadrons – usually operating as individual flights – acted as pathfinders, escorts and rearguards for the technical units and their highly-classified equipment and brought them back to safety in the British lines.

On 31st December 1944 83 Group had six RAF Regiment wing headquarters, with nine LAA, two rifle and two armoured car squadrons under command. In No.84 Group the count was eight wing headquarters with ten LAA, five rifle and two armoured car squadrons while 85 Group had two wing headquarters with five rifle and two armoured car squadrons. 2 Group contained one wing headquarters and seven rifle squadrons. One rifle squadron was retained as the defence force for HQ Allied Expeditionary Air Forces.[12]

On New Year's Day 1945 the Luftwaffe, emulating the Wehrmacht in the Ardennes a fortnight or so earlier, unleashed an all-out dawn attack on Allied airfields. In the space of one and a half hours over 750 German aircraft, in waves of between ten and 50 aircraft, attacked numerous airfields and – having achieved almost total surprise – succeeded in destroying numbers of Allied aircraft on the ground.

Ten of the airfields which were attacked were defended by RAF Regiment LAA squadrons[13] which destroyed 41 of the 335 attackers and damaged a further 28, incurring losses of two killed and ten wounded among the gun detachments. As a result of these actions, Military Medals were awarded to LAC H Adair of 2876 Squadron and Sergeant GD Toye of 2701 Squadron. The airfield at Grimbergen – which was unoccupied by aircraft and therefore had no resident LAA squadron – was the temporary home of 2777 Armoured Car Squadron and a flight of 2719 Rifle Squadron. However, when enemy aircraft attacked the airfield, personnel of these two squadrons responded with rifle and machine gun fire, damaging two and shooting down three aircraft – and capturing the pilots who had parachuted to safety. This brought the RAF Regiment's tally for the day to 44 Luftwaffe aircraft destroyed and 30 damaged.

Shortly before this unexpected attack it had been decided that the LAA squadrons would be more useful in the rifle role, but after 1st January 1945 the planned conversion of LAA squadrons to rifle squadrons was halted, and more LAA squadrons were called forward from the United Kingdom. By the 18th February 1945 the number of RAF Regiment squadrons in 2 TAF had risen to a total of 65: 28 LAA, 31 rifle and six armoured car squadrons.

There were, of course, many former members of the Regiment – who had been compulsorily transferred to the Army – serving in North-West Europe at this time. In 1944 the Brigade of Guards had been particularly short of men and, in addition to the low manning level in 2nd Battalion Scots Guards, neither the Grenadiers nor the Coldstream were able to raise their planned 6th battalions. Lieutenant RP Laurie[14] of the 5th Battalion Coldstream Guards recalls a draft of RAF Regiment gunners, most of whom elected – and were selected – to join the battalion. When 5th Coldstream fought their way across NW Europe to the Rhine and beyond, there were in their ranks – and in Lt Laurie's platoon – former RAF Regiment gunners among the guardsmen.

The Closing Stages

As the end of the war in Europe approached, HQ 2 TAF selected the small German spa town of Bad Eilsen as its post-war base and formed a task force to seize it before the Army could reach it. Operation Woolworth (so named because two squadron leaders named Marks and Spencer respectively were among the officers in the force) was formed around elements of 2804 Armoured Car Squadron and 2729 and 2807 Rifle Squadrons. The task force received permission to pass through the Army's front line, although fighting was still taking place around Buckeburg and Bad Oeynhausen – not far from Bad Eilsen – and on 8th April 1945 the town of Bad Eilsen was taken by the Regiment.

The largest hotel in the town was occupied by the Focke Wolf aircraft design and development teams, headed by the distinguished

Professor Kurt Tank. He and his colleagues were arrested by the Regiment force commander and taken back for interrogation by an ATI team. For his part in this operation, Flight Lieutenant WR Jay of 2804 Squadron was awarded the Military Cross. On 17th April 2862 Rifle Squadron arrived to reinforce the garrison and preparations were made for the arrival of Headquarters Second Tactical Air Force.

At about this time, 2781 Squadron was involved in clearing the enemy from the airfield at Achmer, near Osnabruck, and Flying Officer JS Millar's dash in leading the attack, and rescuing wounded RAF personnel under fire, was rewarded with the Military Cross.

The successful use of Regiment squadrons to escort ATI teams and to secure enemy assets in the closing stages of a campaign had not gone unnoticed – indeed one officer of the technical intelligence branch (AI 2) at the Air Ministry went so far as to say that their task would have been impossible without the Regiment.[15] The success of these RAF Regiment operations resulted in the prevention of looting and the destruction of Luftwaffe assets by British units as well as by the defeated enemy forces.

Aware of the need to secure important German Air Force materiel against both these threats[16] the AOC 83 Group ordered his Regiment units to pass through the Army's forward positions on 4th May 1945 and occupy all enemy airfields and installations in the Schleswig-Holstein peninsula pending the arrival of the Air Disarmament Teams. In fact, the RAF Regiment forces were to do far more than that: by disarming all German forces in the peninsula, collecting and securing weapons and ammunition, arresting senior Nazi officials, guarding prisoners, and feeding starving prisoners of war, they played an important role in establishing the conditions for the subsequent British administration of the territory.

Nine RAF Regiment task forces went forward to seize Luftwaffe bases from the line Hamburg-Lubeck northwards through Kiel, Husum and Schleswig to Flensburg on the Danish border, with a tenth flying into Kastrup, outside Copenhagen.[17] Despite encountering units of the German Army and Air Force – including SS and Parachute Divisions – and the German Navy at Kiel who had still to be convinced that the war was nearing its end, 16 airfields were occupied without incident and over 50,000 German troops, including a number of general and flag officers, were disarmed and taken prisoner.

As an example of the confused conditions which existed at this time, Squadron Leader Mark Hobden's task force from 2726 Squadron first encountered Soviet forces east of Travemunde before being held up at the Kiel Canal by an SS brigade whose commander refused to accept that the end of the war was at hand. After an hour or so of delicate negotiations the RAF Regiment force was able to resume its advance to Flensburg where it secured the airfield. On the following morning, RAF Regiment officers were in the group which arrested Grand Admiral Doenitz (Hitler's successor as Fuhrer of the German Reich) in Flensburg and escorted him and his staff to the airfield from where they were flown to Supreme Headquarters Allied Powers Europe for interrogation.

The Regiment task forces then turned to the task of feeding and rehabilitating the large number of Russian prisoners of war who were found living in appalling conditions in prison camps in the peninsula. German conjecture on the reasons for the RAF's occupation of the Schleswig-Holstein peninsula included the assumption that the RAF Regiment were either the shock troops of the combined British Army and RAF or the RAF's own counterpart of the Waffen-SS.[18] In any event, the official view was that "there is no doubt that the satisfactory occupation of Schleswig-Holstein was almost entirely due to the firm and very prompt action taken by the Regiment."[19]

On 5th May a representative detachment from 2819 Squadron was flown into Denmark to occupy Kastrup airfield and represent the RAF in the liberation ceremonies in Copenhagen. Corporal EF Westrope, who became a Ground Gunner at RAF Warmwell in 1940 and was a founder member of 819 Squadron at Chelveston in 1941 – renumbered 2819 in 1942 – waded ashore with the squadron in Normandy on D+1. He described arriving at Kastrup in Denmark three days before VE Day with Luftwaffe ground crews marshalling the RAF aircraft as they landed.[20] Once the 2819 detachment had taken over the airfield, a continual stream of German aircraft arrived loaded with senior officers who preferred surrendering to the British rather than the Russians. The squadron airmen found taking prisoners as they deplaned an unwelcome and boring diversion from the hospitality which the Danish people were lavishing on other members of the RAF in Copenhagen!

Meanwhile, RAF Regiment squadrons formed part of the British

force which landed in Norway. 2737 and 2949 Rifle Squadrons, which
had been trained in mountain warfare techniques in Scotland,
embarked with the 3rd and 52nd Infantry Divisions for the liberation
of Norway in order to occupy German airfields there. They were
joined by 1318 Wing HQ – and also by 2875 Squadron which was
moved by air from Schleswig to Oslo in Halifax bombers instead of
the Dakota transport aircraft which they had expected. Although all
the squadron personnel and equipment were squeezed into the
cramped interiors of the Halifaxes, there was no room for the second-
in-command's most treasured possession – the squadron piano –
which had been acquired in Normandy and provided music for the
squadron as it moved through NW Europe. It was left, standing alone
and forlorn, in a field in Germany as 2875 Squadron lifted off for
Norway.[21]

On VE Day (8th May 1945) there were 19 wing headquarters
and 75 RAF Regiment squadrons in 2 TAF.[22] Most were to be
disbanded within 12 months as their personnel were demobilised,
but a number remained in Germany and Austria as part of the British
Air Forces of Occupation, to secure the RAF's new bases on former
Luftwaffe airfields and to support the work of the RAF's disarmament
teams.

The Campaign in Retrospect

The importance of the Regiment contribution to the maintenance
of offensive air operations had been proved in the Middle East and
Mediterranean theatres and the inclusion of Regiment officers as
specialist advisers in the planning for the campaign in North-West
Europe clearly demonstrated the acceptance of this fact by those
responsible for what was to be the decisive theatre of operations in
the war against Germany. From an initial force level of 19 field and
19 LAA squadrons, the Regiment almost doubled in size to a total of
75 squadrons by the end of the war 11 months later. This growth was
not driven by RAF Regiment commanders or staff officers but was
the response to the continuing demands by RAF commanders at all
levels for more RAF Regiment units to enable air operations to
continue despite enemy air and ground action against RAF airfields
and installations in the combat zone.

The versatility of the Regiment squadrons enabled them to

RAF Regiment armoured cars formed part of the British Air Forces of Occupation.

contribute to air operations in many ways – from ferrying aircraft fuel to forward airstrips and rearming fighter and fighter/bomber aircraft between sorties to clearing mines and booby-traps and securing airfields as well as escorting convoys and air intelligence teams. All this was in addition to their primary roles of LAA and ground defence for RAF airfields, installations and forward units as well as the important tasks of reconnoitring and clearing likely airstrips and operating bases for flying squadrons.

Ironically – in view of the ponderous inter-Service politics which gave the Army total responsibility for the protection of RAF airfields and installations, and for which the Army seldom had the forces to spare in war – RAF Regiment squadrons were frequently called upon by Army commanders to reinforce units under their command. This was a recurring feature of the war in South-East Asia and the Mediterranean theatres as well as in North-West Europe.

The flexibility of the Regiment's organisation – with the ability to concentrate several squadrons in wing strength or to disperse its squadrons in detachments of flight strength, in a variety of roles as the situation demanded – enabled it to meet whatever tasks the RAF required of it, within the limitations of its strictly-controlled manpower resources. Just as important was the familiarity which Regiment officers and airmen had with other RAF personnel, RAF operational and administrative procedures, the environment of airfields and the handling of aircraft, all of which ensured that no time was wasted in integrating their tasks with those of the Royal Air Force in general. And – as was proved on many occasions – aircrew preferred to have RAF Regiment LAA defences around their airfields, if only for their confidence in the Regiment's ability to distinguish friendly from hostile aircraft!

Without the presence of Regiment wings and squadrons in 2 TAF, it is doubtful whether the quantity and quality of the tactical air support given to the land battle in NW Europe would have been as great – which would have been to the grave disadvantage of 21st Army Group. Indeed, when the former commander of that formation addressed the Royal United Services Institute ten years later on the subject of "Organisation for War in Modern Times", he stressed the need for "air forces...(to have) units of ground airmen to defend their own bases".[23]

As one of the outstanding military commanders of the Second World War, Lord Montgomery made it clear that generals had no wish to look over their shoulders and divert important – and often scarce resources – to the protection of assets which were the responsibility of air marshals. The Army's task was to fight – and win – the land battle while the Air Force was responsible for creating a favourable air situation and providing the necessary air support. Confusion about inter-Service responsibilities at lower levels only served to divert activity from the maintenance of the aim – which was to defeat the enemy by the deployment of superior ground and air forces at the critical points.

Notes

[1] Air Marshal Sir Arthur Coningham KCB KBE DSO MC DFC (1895-1948). AOC-in-C 2 TAF 1943-45

[2] 32 field squadrons & 202 LAA squadrons

[3] LAC Frank Conn of 2772 Squadron was one of the gunners compulsorily transferred to the Army and was demobilised from the Royal Army Pay Corps in 1946. Almost fifty years later he stated "I have never forgiven the RAF for what they did to me in March 1945." (*RAF Regiment Comrades Association Journal*, Summer 1994)

[4] Oswald Spengler, quoted by Hughes in *Consciousness & Society* p377

[5] Elliott – Esprit de Corps – A Scots Guards Officer on Active Service 1943-1945 pp104/106

6   A228427/T10d/1(PRO)

7   Air Historical Branch Narrative. The forced transfer of 200,000 Luftwaffe personnel to the Wehrmacht in the winter of 1942-43 had resulted in considerable deterioration in the technical efficiency and morale of the German air force (Tedder – *Air Power in War* pp46-47)

8   Mr DE Dean – letter 23 Aug 95

9   Group Captain MF Hobden OBE – letter 20 May 1996

10   ib.

11   Mr A Cook – letter 5 Sep 95

12   83 Gp: 1300, 1301, 1302, 1303, 1304 & 1305 Wing Headquarters

     2703, 2734, 2774, 2809, 2817, 2834, 2875, 2876 & 2879 LAA Squadrons

     2726 & 2827 Rifle Squadrons 2781 & 2806 Armoured Car Squadrons

     84 Gp: 1310, 1311, 1312, 1313, 1314, 1315, 1316 & 1317 Wing Headquarters

     2701, 2736, 2773, 2800, 2845, 2872, 2873, 2874, 2880 & 2881 LAA Squadrons 2717, 2719, 2724, 2816 & 2843 Rifle Squadrons 2757 & 2777 Armoured Car Squadrons

     85 Gp: 1306 & 1309 Wing Headquarters 2713, 2750, 2770, 2798 & 2811 Rifle Squadrons

     2804 & 2742 Armoured Car Squadrons

     2 Gp: 1318 Wing Headquarters 2729, 2776, 2831, 2848, 2863, 2871 & 2879 Rifle Squadrons

     HQ AEAF: 2897 Rifle Squadron

13   Ophoven – 2876 & 2794 LAA: 4 EA destroyed

     Eindhoven – 2703, 2773 & 2817 LAA: 6 EA destroyed

     Volkel – 2784, 2809 & 2834 LAA: 5 EA destroyed

     Helmond – 2873, 2875 & 2881 LAA: 6 EA destroyed

     Heesch – 2734 & 2819 LAA: 7 EA destroyed

     Deurne – 2880 LAA (1 Flt): 1 EA destroyed

     Gilze Rijen – 2895 & 1 Flt No.2736 LAA: 3 EA destroyed

     Woernsdrechte – 2872 LAA: 2 EA destroyed

     Brussels – 2800 LAA: 3 EA destroyed

     Melsbroek – 2701 LAA: 4 EA destroyed

14   RP Laurie Esq OBE JP DL – letter 21 Jul 95

15   Wing Commander GR Shillitoe RAFVR – letter 9 May 94

16   *The Dissolution of the Luftwaffe* (HMSO) p52

[17] Lt Col Casey + 2809 LAA to Lutjenholm

Lt Col Crabbe + 2856 Rifle & Flts from 2765 Rifle, 2875 LAA, 2781 & 2806 Armd Car to Leck & Flensburg

Wg Cdr Godfrey + 2881 LAA & 1 Flt 2806 Armd Car to Neumunster

Lt Col Lindsay + 2 Flts 2726 Rifle & 1 Flt 2806 Armd Car to Hohn

Flt Lt Fisher + 1 Flt 2819 LAA to Kaltenkirchen

Wg Cdr Gould + 2794 LAA, 2827 Rifle & Flts from 2781 & 2806 Armd Car and 2726 Rifle to Eegebek, Schleswig & Husum

Lt Col Lockwood + 3 Flts 2765 Rifle & 1 Flt 2806 Armd Car to Kiel

Wg Cdr Flemming + 1 Flt each from 2765 Rifle & 2806 Armd Car to Fuhlsbuttel & Uetersen (Hamburg)

Sqn Ldr Hobden + 1 Flt 2762 Rifle to Travemunde (Lubeck)

Sqn Ldr Hamer + 1 Flt 2819 LAA to Kastrup (by air)

[18] *The Dissolution of the Luftwaffe* (HMSO) 1995 p64

[19] ib.

[20] Mr EF Westrope – author of No.2819 Squadron History – letter 15 Nov 95

[21] Mr DAW Stewart – author of No.2875 Squadron History

[22] 28 LAA Squadrons, 41 Rifle Squadrons & 6 Armoured Car Squadrons = 75 total. There were also 19 Wing HQs, controlling two or more squadrons each, in NW Europe at the end of the war

[23] Field Marshal Viscount Montgomery of Alamein KG GCB DSO (1887-1976)

8

The War in South-East Asia

The enemy had, by mid-March, dug in so close to the airstrip that by night our troops disputed with his patrols in the no-man's-land of the actual runway. At dawn each day, before aircraft could land, a sweep had to be carried out to drive back enemy infiltration and to clear the ground of mines.

Field Marshal Lord Slim[1]

Britain's military position in the Far East in 1941 was very close to a nightmare scenario, mainly because the battle fleet on which the concept of British power in the region had been based was committed to the Atlantic and the Mediterranean. As it happened, the great naval base which had been built for it was defended not by the land, sea and air forces considered to be necessary to meet the threat, but by whatever forces could be spared from other, more pressing, tasks in other theatres.

Although the RAF had some medium bombers, flying boats and torpedo bombers based in Singapore in peace, there were no fighter aircraft there,[2] and the total number of aircraft was well below the force of 336 aircraft which had been decided as essential in 1931, when the threat was of a far lower level. In order to extend the range of the aircraft operating from Malaya, the forward airfields had been sited without regard to the Army's tactical dispositions, despite the fact that the RAF had neither ground nor anti-aircraft defences of its own to protect its aircraft and installations.

Regardless of the efforts of the Commander-in-Chief Far East[3] to overcome the failings of pre-war planning, when the Japanese attack came the British Army and the RAF fought the land and air battles separately with the inevitable result: two months after the enemy landed in Malaya, Singapore fell to the Japanese Army's divisions which had advanced from the north – and not to an enemy fleet from the east, as had been the assumed threat when the Singapore base had been conceived and built.

It was not until a desperate attempt was being made to organise a joint British/Dutch force in the Dutch East Indies that a defence force of three officers and 72 airmen arrived on the airfield at Palembang in Sumatra late in February 1942.[4] Other reinforcements which arrived there included 258 Squadron with Hurricanes – and their defence officer, Flying Officer Taute. Although commissioned into the Administrative & Special Duties Branch, as a defence officer Matthys Taute had automatically become an RAF Regiment officer on the 1st of that month. He took command of the airfield defences and conducted them so energetically before being taken prisoner that he was awarded the Military Cross when released from captivity at the end of the war.

In his post-war report,[5] Air Vice-Marshal PC Maltby made it clear that the strategic dispersal of the 15 airfields in Malaya had made them tactically difficult for the Army to defend and the subsequent loss of the airfields – for which the RAF had no defensive resources of its own – deprived the Army of the air support which it needed to counter the Japanese attack. He concluded that "the issue of a modern war largely depends on the struggle for secure air bases…the side which is successful, and denies its opponent the advantage of secure air bases, dominates the whole theatre of war."

More fortunate was LAC Mabbett and the 70 or so Ground Gunners who sailed with him from Liverpool for Singapore in December 1941. The voyage, via the Cape, took so long that while still on board ship they were told by their flight commander – Pilot Officer Kennedy – that they had become part of the RAF Regiment. Singapore having fallen, they disembarked in India and eventually reached what was to become the RAF Regiment Depot (India) near Secunderabad, in Hyderabad State, where LAC Mabbett subsequently became the sergeant in charge of the Demonstration Flight. His previous flight commander had also gained rapid promotion and as Squadron Leader Kennedy was commanding officer of the Depot.

Sergeant Mabbett later joined 2959 Squadron at the RAF Regiment Battle School at Argatala, near the Burmese border, as a flight sergeant and went with the squadron to Cox's Bazaar, Ramree

Island, Elephant Point and Rangoon before returning to India and the United Kingdom. He recalled being ordered to mount a guard of honour at Chittagong airfield for the Supreme Allied Commander, South-East Asia who, when he heard of it, specified that it should be a "very small guard of honour". And so it was – only eight men – but it met with the approval of Admiral Lord Louis Mountbatten.[6]

After Malaya, Singapore and the Dutch East Indies, the focus of the war in South-East Asia moved to Burma, where the invading Japanese 15th Army began its drive towards eastern India. Here, in an area of some 250,000 square miles of mountains, jungles, plains, swamps and vast rivers, the British 14th Army and 3rd Tactical Air Force were to fight, often in appalling climatic conditions, for more than three years until the Japanese had been driven out of Burma. From there, preparations for the recapture of Singapore and Malaya were completed and only the Japanese surrender, after the atomic bomb attacks on Hiroshima and Nagasaki, obviated the need for the planned large-scale invasion to take place.

The organisation of airfield defence in India remained dormant until October 1942 when the RAF Regiment Training Centre – subsequently the RAF Regiment Depot (India) – was established on the airfield at Begampet, west of Secunderabad, with a staff of seven officers and 46 NCOs and airmen. It was soon running three-week long defence courses with intakes of 90 trainees a week and in November the first RAF Regiment AA Flights were formed and given numbers in the block 4351 to 4500. Staff posts were established: a group captain at Air Headquarters and a squadron leader at each of the seven group headquarters – 221 to 227. Wing Commander JH Harris[7] arrived in Delhi in December 1942 to become the Command Defence Officer with the acting rank of group captain.

Almost immediately, he found himself involved in a three-sided struggle over manpower levels. Requests to London for RAF Regiment reinforcements were met with the counter-proposal that this problem should be resolved by transferring Indian soldiers from the Army to form a ground and LAA defence force of 185 British officers and 5,765 Indian other ranks. This suggestion fell on deaf ears at GHQ India, as did the subsequent idea that the RAF might enlist and train its own Indian recruits. After much time had been wasted in such unproductive arguments, the Air Ministry gave way and reluctantly agreed to an establishment of 162 officers and 4,092 airmen for the RAF Regiment in South-East Asia.

Even at such an early stage of the campaign in Burma it was clear that this could not produce sufficient flights and squadrons to take over the responsibility for the defence of forward airfields. The only solution was to rely on what troops the Army could provide for that task and use the limited number of trained RAF Regiment personnel to supplement station personnel in the defence of their airfields. Relying on RAF tradesmen, who had to abandon their aircraft servicing tasks to take up arms when attack threatened, inevitably reduced the intensity of flying operations – to the detriment of the Army's tasks.

By March 1943 the Training Centre at Secunderabad had become the RAF Regiment Depot (India) and soon developed a fearsome reputation for the rigorous discipline and training which transformed ground gunners into gunners. Called forward from sedentary AA duties on an airfield in Bengal for RAF Regiment conversion training at Secunderabad, LAC Jewitt viewed the prospect with some apprehension. When he arrived, he found an atmosphere of super-discipline and high achievement which combined to produce a spirit of total dedication. The Burma Star magazine Dekho reported that "the assault course at Secunderabad gained the reputation of being the most exacting in the Far East". Surviving the rigours of the course, LAC Jewitt joined Sergeant Mabbett in the Demonstration Flight which, when issued with Australian-type bush hats, became known as "Kennedy's Cowboys".[8] The Depot became the centre for training the field squadrons (6 officers, 158 airmen) and AA flights (2 officers, 37 airmen) which were destined for Burma. These units were at the extreme end of the supply chain and were not as well equipped as their counterparts in the Middle East and the United Kingdom. The field squadron – with three rifle flights – had two support flights, each armed only with six LMGs. The AA flights each had 18 .303" LMGs – and little prospect of receiving more suitable and effective weapons. Nevertheless, by the middle of 1943 nine field squadrons and 29 AA flights were available to 3 TAF and its operational groups.

In July 1943 the long arm of the Air Ministry reached out to South-East Asia to order a reduction in the RAF Regiment strength,

Map 11.

Eastern India and Burma

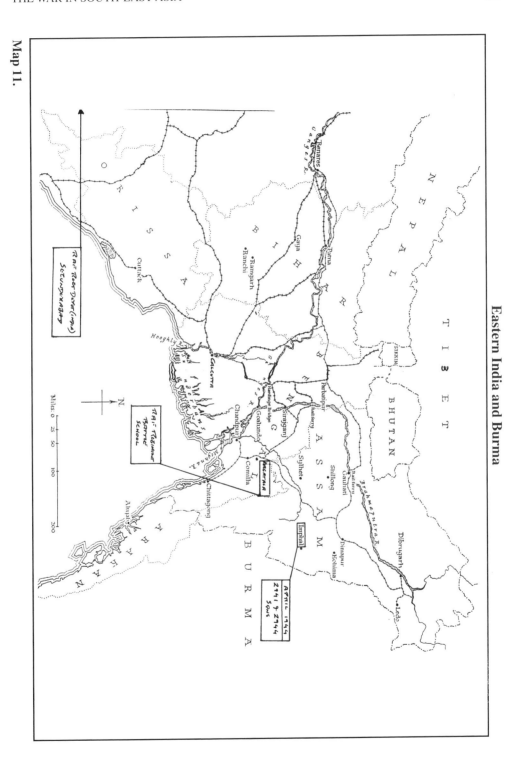

commensurate with similar reductions being made in other theatres. The statement that the 141 officers and 4,549 airmen in the theatre were to be reduced to a maximum of 2,000 all ranks was too much for AHQ India which responded with a firm statement that any reduction below 2,500 was unacceptable. After further exchanges, a compromise proposal for a strength of 152 officers and 2,358 airmen – to be deferred until June 1944 – was agreed.

Faced with this manpower crisis, the RAF looked for other ways of improving station defences and acquired 189 surplus armoured cars which were then allocated among the eight Groups in 3 TAF. The intention was that these vehicles would be distributed to forward airfields, where they would be manned by station personnel in the event of a ground attack. The implementation of this policy was, not surprisingly, found to be impracticable and most of the armoured vehicles were subsequently transferred to Regiment field squadrons, where they were found to be of limited use in the difficult Burmese terrain.

In February 1944, as part of the reorganisation due to the planned run-down of Regiment manpower, 12 LAA squadrons, each of eight officers and 156 airmen, equipped with 24 20mm Hispano guns were formed from the 62 AA flights, and the personnel left over from this reorganisation were remustered to other trades. These LAA squadrons were assigned to 221 and 224 Groups only; airfields in the other six groups had to provide their own AA defence by using station personnel to man AA machine guns when air attack threatened.

Early in March 1944 the Japanese began their advance towards the railhead at Dimapur, which would have been their gateway to India. The British plan depended on holding Kohima and Imphal at all costs and in doing so to wear down the enemy who were operating at the end of a long supply line. The total RAF Regiment force level in the whole of the Imphal plain at this time was one field squadron (2946) and 11 AA flights, of which a detachment of the field squadron and three AA flights were at Imphal airfield itself.

As the Japanese advanced towards the Imphal plain, the airfields there – for which the Army were unable to provide defence forces – came under increasing threat from ground attack. As a result of the reductions which had been imposed by the Air Ministry, there were not enough RAF Regiment units available for these tasks and RAF technicians again had to be diverted from servicing aircraft to static defence tasks.[9] On 26th March the GOC IV Corps complained of the reduction in the flying effort which resulted from this and AOC 3 TAF reported that of his 53 airfields only seven were defended by Army units and the RAF Regiment had barely sufficient strength to protect a further four.

In view of the overriding importance of the airfield at Imphal, the small Regiment detachment there was reinforced by 2941 and 2944 Field Squadrons, and four AA flights, flown in from Chittagong in USAAF DC-3s.[10] LAC Henry Kirk was an armourer in 2944 Squadron and in addition to carrying out his share of defence duties every night, was in charge of the squadron mule train which carried supplies to the Regiment positions on the surrounding hills by day. Once he had become a seasoned muleteer, he came to respect the many good qualities of these much-maligned animals on which so much depended in terrain impassable to motor vehicles.[11]

At the beginning of May AHQ India reported to VCAS in London that seven of the eight flying squadrons in the Imphal plain had been withdrawn as there were not sufficient forces – either Army or RAF Regiment – to defend the airfields on which they had been based.[12] Despite these hard facts, the Air Ministry approved the transfer of a further 1,500 Regiment gunners to the Army in June 1944 and advised AHQ India that no RAF Regiment reinforcements would be sent to South-East Asia. The AOC-in-C immediately ordered a halt to the run-down of RAF Regiment manpower – now down to a strength of 3,300 all ranks – and the AOC 3 TAF[13] sent his Command Defence Officer back to London to press the case for more RAF Regiment reinforcements for the theatre. His assessment was that 3 TAF required a minimum of 12 field and 18 LAA squadrons to support its operations from forward airfields. Meanwhile, the first of the new LAA squadrons – 2958 with its three flights of eight 20mm Hispanos each – was deployed to defend the airfield at Chittagong.

In July 1944 it was decided to form five Wing headquarters[14] and a further five LAA squadrons[15] from the resources which existed within Air Command South-East Asia and the necessary re-training was carried out at the Forward Training Centre at Argatala. With nine field and five LAA squadrons to defend its airfields, the AOC 221 Group wrote "I consider it probable that the Group could not have occupied airstrips as far forward as we did, with consequently better close air support for the Army, had I not been confident that the RAF Regiment could have maintained the necessary security."[16]

As the British advance eastwards against the retreating Japanese gathered momentum, a flight of 2944 Squadron became the first RAF Regiment force to cross the Chindwin in August 1944 and in the following month a flight of 2942 Squadron was attached to 6 Bn Oxfordshire & Buckinghamshire Light Infantry at Maungdaw. LAC Tom Collier was member of a joint RAF Regiment/Ox & Bucks LI patrol of two officers and 18 men which set out at 0200 one morning to establish a base on a hilltop about four hours march away.

Before reaching the objective the patrol was ambushed by a larger Japanese force and was pinned down in the resulting fire fight. By 1030 the situation had worsened and it became obvious that the patrol would not be able to withdraw without covering fire. Flying Officer Al Mitchell was successful in eluding the enemy and reaching a British base, from which he was able to call for artillery fire to be directed on the Japanese while the remnants of the patrol withdrew. Flying Officer Mitchell was awarded the Military Cross but LAC Collier, who had been wounded, was separated from the remainder of the patrol and only reached safety some three days later, thanks to the assistance he received from Burmese villagers.[17]

In October 1944 a change of heart in London was indicated by the receipt of Air Ministry authority to add three more wing headquarters and eight field squadrons to the RAF Regiment establishment in 3 TAF. This brought the approved force level up to thirty squadrons – now to be 20 field and ten LAA. Another refreshing sign was the numerical increase in the Regiment establishment in ACSEA, which was to rise to 4,800 officers and airmen in January 1945 and to 6,500 by July 1945. But once again, the gap between establishments and strength was bedevilled by inadequate reinforcement levels – and poor standards of medical fitness in the reinforcement drafts. As an example, in one draft of 241 airmen, 101 men were found to be below the minimum medical standard for RAF Regiment units.

In January 1945 a welcome reinforcement of six field squadrons and two LAA squadrons[18] arrived at Secunderabad from the UK and in the following month it was decided to emulate the 2 TAF example

Map 12.

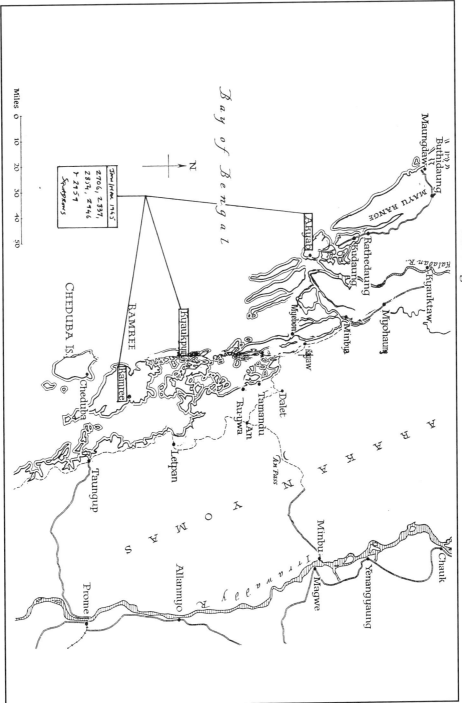

Landings on the coast of Burma – 1945

RAF Regiment personnel going ashore at Akyab.

by removing the armoured flights from the field squadrons to form three armoured car squadrons at Argatala.[19] RAF Regiment squadrons, including 2706, 2837, 2854, 2946 and 2959, were deployed to Akyab, Ramree and Cox's Bazaar to secure airfields and 2962 LAA Squadron was detached to the Cocos Islands to defend the airfield which was an important staging post for transport aircraft as well as an operational base for bomber and fighter aircraft.

The Battle for Meiktila Airfield

The town of Meiktila was the main administrative centre for the Japanese 15th and 33rd Armies. Its supply bases, ammunition depots, airfields and hospitals were essential to the Japanese forces in Burma and its capture would open the way for the British advance to Mandalay and Rangoon. Following an elaborate deception scheme, which misled the Japanese commanders as to the British intentions, Meiktila was seized at the beginning of March 1945 and the adjacent airfields – of which Meiktila East was the most important – were brought into use for resupply by transport aircraft.

When they realised that Meiktila had become as important to the British as it had been to them, the Japanese launched a series of ferocious counter-attacks, using every available unit which could be thrown into the battle. General Kimura, the Japanese commander, succumbed to the same temptation which his British counterparts had faced on other occasions and withdrew the army battalions and LAA artillery which had been assigned to defend the Japanese air force's airfields in order to strengthen his forces in the land battle. What the Japanese air force commanders thought of this is not known, but it left their airfields at the mercy of the RAF at the critical time when the Japanese army needed all the support which its air force could provide; without it, defeat for the Japanese ground forces proved inevitable.

The immediate result of the Japanese counter-attack was to cut the British supply routes and make air supply the only link with the encircled British and Indian forces holding Meiktila. Consequently, the airfield at Meiktila East became the vital ground for both sides and it changed hands daily in a battle which raged for three weeks. By day the airfield was in British hands, by night the defenders

The painting, by Michael Turner, PGAvA, illustrates one of the dawn counter-attacks by No.1307 Wing RAF Regiment that were a daily feature of the siege at Meiktila Airfield which lasted for over three weeks.[20]

withdrew into their defensive boxes and the Japanese occupied the broken ground around the runway. Each morning the battle to regain control of the airfield so that food and ammunition could be flown in, and wounded flown out, began again. On one such morning, the Regiment defenders drove back two companies of Japanese infantry, killing 48 of the enemy for the loss of seven airmen.[21]

1307 Wing Headquarters RAF Regiment (Wing Commander CM Lander) with 2708 Field and 2963 LAA Squadrons, reinforced by detachments of 2941 and 2968 Field Squadrons, played a major role in the defence of "D" box, which was on the edge of the main runway. Sharing the task with the Regiment were detachments from the British and Indian Armies, although every man on the airfield was involved in its defence in one way or another.

Wing Commander Lander's diary of events – which runs from

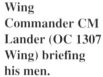

Wing Commander CM Lander (OC 1307 Wing) briefing his men.

1st to 16th March gives a graphic description of the almost continuous close-quarter fighting which characterised the struggle for the vital airfield.[22] His leadership and bravery inspired everyone under his command, but when leading the dawn assault on 23rd March he was among those killed. He had carried the attack so far into the Japanese defended area that it was several days before his body could be recovered for burial. There were, undoubtedly, many other examples of gallantry by Regiment officers and airmen in the fierce fighting which characterised the battle for Meiktila and its airfield but the courage of Sergeant Norman Gerrish, at least, was recognised by the award of a Military Medal.

Nevertheless, a heavy price had to be paid and Colonel Alasdair Tuck, who was present throughout the battle, commented that too much had been asked of the RAF Regiment at Meiktila: "the Japanese sent endless patrols in on the RAF Regiment Commando (*sic*) at night and by the end the commander and all his officers had been killed and morale was at rock bottom."[23] The pilot of one of the L-5 light aircraft of 194 Squadron, which were often the only aircraft able to land with vital supplies and evacuate casualties, reported that the airfield had been cleared for him to land by a bayonet charge led by the medical officer of 1307 Wing, who was the last officer left alive in the Regiment force at Meiktila.[24]

As the 14th Army drove forward on its narrow axes of advance, large numbers of Japanese troops were cut off and by-passed in the areas in which the airfields used by aircraft supporting the Army were sited. As these were obviously vulnerable to hostile ground attack, 1307 and 1330 Wings, with seven squadrons under command, were tasked with holding these vital links in the chain of air operations upon which the Army depended.

Apart from carrying out routine Regiment tasks – such as clearing the airfield at Thabutkon of Japanese snipers and infiltrators[25], the Regiment showed its versatility in other ways – such as 2967 Squadron's work in repairing the damage to the airfield at Kyaukpu, on Ramree Island, so that Spitfires could operate from it.[26]

As the advance from Meiktila to Rangoon continued on the axis Toungoo-Pegu, 2759 Squadron was tasked with clearing Japanese troops who had been by-passed by the advance of 19th Indian Division and were operating in the vicinity of Tabetgwe, some twenty miles west of the fighter airfield which the squadron was defending. Because of the difficult terrain, the OC 2759 Squadron – Squadron Leader Charles Killeen – arranged for elephants to be procured from the local Burmese and the fighting patrol set off with its personnel and equipment mounted on this unusual form of animal transport. The week-long patrol was successful in accounting for over twenty Japanese soldiers and recovering a large amount of arms, ammunition and explosives. The squadron then continued its advance southwards as the fighter aircraft for which it was responsible moved nearer to Rangoon.

The capture of Rangoon was based on an advance by 17th Indian Division from the north and an amphibious operation, Operation Dracula, from the south in which 1327 Wing HQ with 2959 and 2967 Squadrons were included. The fall of Rangoon isolated large numbers of Japanese troops in the Pegu Yomas mountain range, between the Sittang River and the sea. Their presence threatened the security of the complex of airfields around Toungoo and 1307 Wing, with five squadrons under command, was diverted to reinforce the Army units which were clearing the enemy from that area.

In July 1945 the RAF Regiment order of battle in ACSEA consisted of ten wing headquarters, 18 field squadrons, 12 LAA squadrons and one armoured car squadron.[27]

With the defeat of the Japanese in Burma, preparations were made for the invasion of Singapore and Malaya in September 1945. The RAF Regiment element of Operation Zipper comprised five Wing headquarters, nine field squadrons and five LAA squadrons – some 2,500 men. In addition, 2810 Squadron, commanded by Squadron Leader H Sullivan,[28] was selected to man Visual Control Posts (VCPs) as part of the Airborne Control Unit in the assault and in order to carry out these duties all squadron personnel were trained as parachutists. In the event, the Japanese surrender in August 1945 forestalled the implementation of the invasion plan and the return to Malaya was carried out unopposed, albeit in the somewhat unstable post-war situation in which various local groups were contending for power.

2896 Field Squadron sailed from India to Singapore on board MV Derbyshire in August/September 1945, manning the ship's guns during the voyage. 1324 Wing HQ and 2748, 2846, 2852 and 2941

Burma

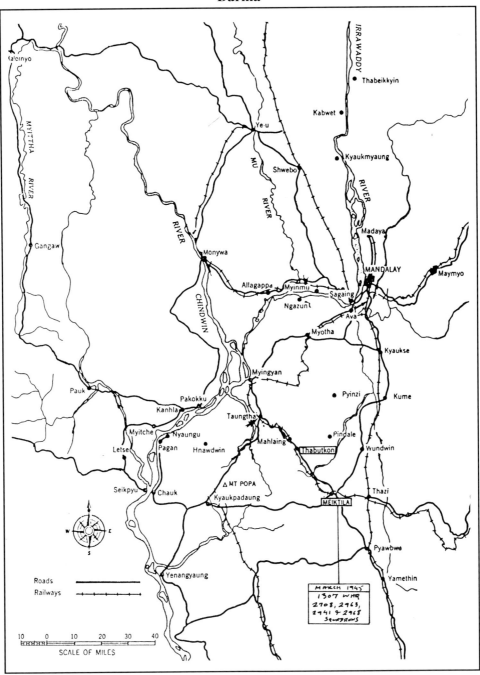

Map 13.

**An RAF
Regiment patrol
crossing a river
in Central
Burma while
seeking out
Japanese cut off
from their
retreating
armies.**

Squadrons landed on the designated invasion beaches at Morib in
Malaya. The Wing HQ and two squadrons occupied the airfield at
Kuala Lumpur and the other two squadrons motored to Singapore
via Muar to RAF Seletar and RAF Tengah, becoming the first British
units to cross the causeway linking Malaya and Singapore since 1942.
1329 Wing HQ, with four squadrons, took over the garrison of Penang
from the Royal Marines and re-established local government on the
island – even to the extent of opening, and operating, the local radio
station. 1331 Wing HQ and two squadrons landed in Hong Kong and
secured the airfield at Kai Tak before detaching a flight to join the
RAF element of the British occupation force in Japan. Meanwhile,
2945 Squadron moved to Don Muang airfield, outside Bangkok, to
provide security – in a somewhat turbulent environment – for the
RAF aircraft which were operating from there.

At the formal surrender of all Japanese land, sea and air forces
in South-East Asia, which was held in Singapore on 11th September
1945, 2896 Field Squadron provided the RAF guard of honour for
Admiral Lord Mountbatten who invited Corporal W Vance of that
squadron to witness the actual signing ceremony. When the newly-

appointed Governor of Burma arrived at Rangoon in October 1945, the guard of honour which received him was mounted by 2942 Squadron.

In the absence of French forces to reoccupy their former colonies in Indo-China (now Vietnam, Laos and Cambodia), British forces moved in to disarm the Japanese and restore law and order. In the early hours of 1st October 1945, 1307 Wing HQ and 2963 LAA Squadron left Hmawbi in Burma by air and landed at Tan Son Nhut airfield, outside Saigon, later the same day. They were joined ten days later by 2967 Field Squadron which arrived in Saigon by sea from Rangoon. In order to control the very large area allocated to the RAF Regiment, a disarmed Japanese infantry battalion, over one thousand strong, was placed under command of 1307 Wing for internal security duties – which they carried out in an exemplary fashion, even though only armed with cudgels and pickhelves. 2967 Squadron subsequently provided the RAF representation at the ceremonial surrender of Japanese commanders' swords in Saigon in December 1945 and Lord Louis Mountbatten commended the OC

Men of the RAF Regiment loaded into a landing craft (infantry), ready to go ashore at Georgetown, near Penang.

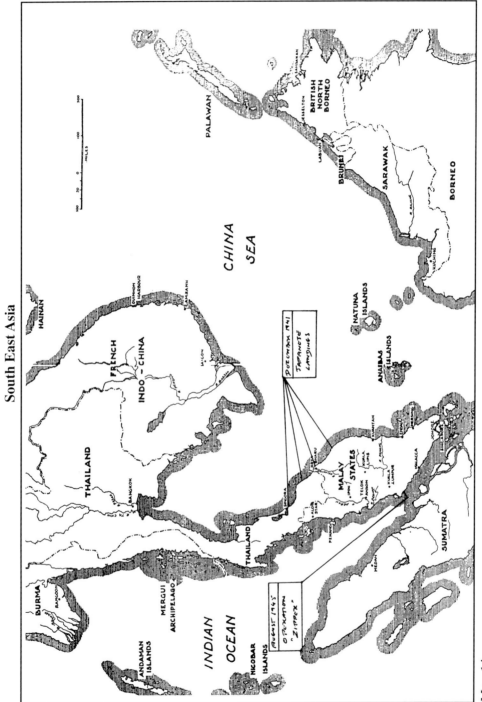

Map 14.

1307 Wing for the arrangements which he had made to ensure the success of the ceremony.

Operation Mastiff was the plan to establish contact with prisoners of war and civilian internees in Japanese camps immediately after the surrender and a number of 2810 Squadron personnel were in the teams which were parachuted into remote areas of the Dutch East Indies to carry out these tasks. The unstable situation which developed when nationalist groups began terrorist attacks on Allied personnel resulted in 1308 Wing HQ, with 2943 and 2962 Squadrons, being deployed to Kemajoran in Java and 1323 Wing HQ, with 2944, 2961 and 2968 Squadrons, to Medan in Sumatra in October 1945.

In November 1945, during an RAF funeral in a cemetery in Batavia, the escort party from 2962 Squadron was ambushed by Indonesian terrorists. The NCO in charge, Sergeant AC Haines, dealt promptly with the situation and drove the attackers off without loss to the funeral party. He was subsequently awarded the Military Medal for his actions.

In June 1946 a party of some 40 Indonesians attacked a post of seven Regiment airmen at Medan airfield. Despite the gallantry and initiative of the guard commander – LAC Holbrook – who was killed leading his men against the attackers, the detachment was overrun with casualties of two airmen killed and two seriously wounded. The squadron commander – Squadron Leader Williams – took charge of the reserve flight and restored the situation, killing a number of the enemy and driving off the remainder. Corporal LE Hyde gave a graphic description of the incident, including photographs of the military funerals of his colleagues which followed.[29]

The official history records that "the vigilance and courage of the Regiment gunners throughout this difficult period was beyond praise and they suffered a number of casualties as a result of enemy action."[30] This was to be a foretaste of the hostile situations in which the Regiment was to be involved almost continually from the end of the Second World War onwards.

The Campaign in Retrospect

Although tanks had been used to good effect by the Army, armoured cars had not been able to cope with the rugged terrain and the poor roads in Burma. This was probably why the Army had been

RAF Regiment armoured cars in the Dutch East Indies, 1945.

so ready to supply the RAF with almost 200 of these vehicles for airfield defence in 1943. Their limitations, when used as armoured car flights in the field squadrons, led to the decision in 1945 to concentrate these vehicles in three independent armoured car squadrons – but, in the event, only one of these was operational by the end of the war.

Air mobility placed greater demands upon RAF Regiment flights and squadrons than in any other theatre – no fewer than 21 units, and their weapons and equipment, were involved in air-transported operations on no less than 36 occasions. Consequently, RAF Regiment squadrons reached a high standard in preparing their own air movement and loading tables and were frequently deployed operationally immediately after deplaning at their destinations.

Anti-aircraft defences were, however, infrequently employed against enemy aircraft, due largely to the effectiveness of RAF counter air operations. In Burma, Regiment AA units opened fire on only 25 occasions, destroying four enemy aircraft and damaging a further seven. Nevertheless, their 20mm Hispano guns were used very effectively in the ground-to-ground role on numerous occasions.

Not surprisingly, the supply of up-to-date weapons and equipment for Regiment units in ACSEA lagged behind other theatres as a result of the priority given to operations in North-West Europe and Italy; for example, 20mm Hispanos were only issued to the LAA squadrons in 1944, and 3" mortars were not supplied to field squadrons until early in 1945.

However, early in 1943 the Command Defence Officer at AHQ India had been given the authority to direct the administration and resupply of all RAF Regiment units in the theatre, and the policy paid considerable dividends. This was proved when the Deputy Air Commander visited RAF units in Indo-China in October 1945 and reported "The RAF Regiment are doing extremely well and are very smart. Obviously the stock of the RAF is high as a result. Unfortunately, apart from the RAF Regiment, the dress of RAF officers and airmen is disgraceful but commanding officers explained that their demands for clothing had not been answered."

In his final despatches on the campaign in South-East Asia, the Air Officer Commanding-in-Chief Air Command South-East Asia[31] wrote:

"In the various campaign stages of the war in South East Asia I have been left in no doubt whatsoever about the usefulness, efficiency and fine example of that most junior of all our forces – the RAF Regiment.

"In South East Asia the RAF Regiment proved itself a force capable of carrying out more than the tasks which its originators claimed the Regiment could accomplish. It was not a force of men dressed up as guards and picqueted around some airfield or supply dump with guns propped in their hands. These men were so trained in the art and strategy of ground defence and jungle warfare that they were able to undertake with success counter measures against Japanese infiltration parties who might set themselves up near the perimeter of some airfield and constitute a menace until hunted down and destroyed.

"The most outstanding episode of the RAF Regiment's service in this theatre was the assistance they gave in the defence of Meiktila airfield. It was essential to comb the airfield and its environs every

RAF Regiment 20mm Hispano detachment in Burma, 1945.

morning for snipers before permitting aircraft to land. Every gully, foxhole or other feasible hiding place for a sniper had to be examined. The patrols started just after daybreak and took almost two hours to complete. It was thorough and effective, but the only sure way of clearing the area of the enemy to ensure the safety of our aircraft.

"If the RAF Regiment in South-East Asia had done nothing more than provide vital protection for our airfields, the record of its achievements would still read with commendable credit. That it was able to perform further additional services and maintain a smartness and discipline which called forth praise from Army and Navy alike, demonstrates the value of the Regiment as an adjunct to the Royal Air Force. In my many tours and inspections throughout this Theatre I have noticed the almost "jealous-like" pride which the Regiment squadrons have in their own service."

From inauspicious beginnings, the RAF Regiment developed to make an important contribution to the war against the Japanese in Burma. The combination of sound administration by RAF Regiment staff at Command and Group HQs, hard training and good discipline in the training machine, crowned by leadership in the field, produced units whose high morale and esprit de corps enabled them to overcome the many problems inherent in fighting a skilled and resolute enemy in unfamiliar conditions.

Without the RAF Regiment in South-East Asia, 3 TAF would either have had to operate from airfields further back from the combat zone, or the Army would have had to detach troops from the land battle to defend forward airfields against enemy attack. In the first case, this would have resulted in a reduction in the amount of air support to the Army and in the second, a reduction in the Army's forces available for the land battle. The official reports of the air commanders involved show how fully the contribution made by the Regiment squadrons and flights was valued by the flying squadrons of the Royal Air Force in enabling air operations to continue in an hostile environment without enemy interference.

Notes

[1]   Slim – *Defeat Into Victory* p442

[2]   Probert – *The Forgotten Air Force* p12

[3]   Air Chief Marshal Sir Robert Brooke-Popham GCVO KCB CMG DSO AFC (1878-1953). Reverted to retired list 1942

[4]   Probert – op cit p69

[5]   London Gazette No.38216 20 Feb 1948. Air Vice-Marshal Maltby was briefly AOC Java in 1942 and a prisoner of war in Japan 1942-45. Later Air Vice-Marshal Sir Paul Maltby KCVO KBE CB DSO AFC (1892-1971)

[6]   Mr H Mabbett – letter 20 Aug 1995

[7]   Later Air Vice-Marshal Jack Harris CB CBE (1903-63) – the first RAF Regiment officer to become Commandant-General of the RAF Regiment (1959-61)

[8]   Mr L Jewitt – letter 21 May 1995

[9]   "The RAF Regiment, trained in infantry work, were insufficient in numbers and in this grave emergency the Army commanders could not spare the soldiers to guard the fighters." Wings of the Phoenix p.77

[10] Probert – op cit p189

[11] Mr H Kirk MBE (President RAF Regiment SEAC Association) – letter 24 Feb 96

[12] CS15602/1 ACC.905 (PRO)

[13] Air Marshal Sir John Baldwin KBE CB DSO (1892-1975). Report on Air Operations in South-East Asia 16th November 1943 to 31st May 1944 published in the Third Supplement to the London Gazette N.39173 dated 13th March 1951.

      "Units of the RAF Regiment have proved themselves of the greatest value in the campaign, of which the insecurity of airfields and warning establishments in forward areas has been a feature. When radar stations were established well in advance of the front line and within range of the enemy's guns and patrols, it says much for the RAF Regiment that the radar crews enjoyed undisturbed conditions in which to carry out their work. It has proved to be quite unsound to rely on the Army providing troops for local defence in times of crisis when the land situation deteriorates. This is the time when they are really needed by us, but this is the time when they are invariably withdrawn to take part in the land battle. As a result, air operations have been seriously prejudiced, and I have fully reported this matter, protesting against the cut in field squadrons of the RAF Regiment."

[14] 1323, 1324, 1325, 1326 & 1327 Wing Headquarters

[15] 2964, 2965, 2966, 2967 & 2968 LAA Squadrons

[16] Probert op cit p239 (AVM F S Vincent)

[17] Mr T Collier – letter 10 Aug 1995

[18] 2708, 2743, 2748, 2802, 2810 & 2896 Field; 2846 & 2852 LAA Squadrons

[19] 2970, 2971 & 2972 Armoured Car Squadrons

[20] The painting, by Michael Turner, PGAvA, was commissioned to mark the Regiment's 50th Anniversary and hangs in the Depot Officers' Mess.

      The overturned steamroller in the foreground and the collapsed rattan control tower, built by the Japanese, in the middle distance were significant reference points for fire-control orders during the battle. The wrecked Dakota, a victim of the previous day's enemy artillery fire, is still to be cleared away and the Hurricane IIc flying overhead is from one of the thirteen Hurricane Fighter/Recce squadrons in the Command at the time.

The significance of the pagoda was that the tinkling of the bells still hanging from it signalled the arrival of a cooling breeze to dispel the stifling heat which enveloped the airfield. Because of the heat, many men discarded their steel helmets in favour of Australian-type bush hats, despite the risks from shell splinters which caused numerous casualties.

I am indebted to Air Commodore MS Witherow for the detailed description of the scene which he researched for the artist when the painting was commissioned

[21] *Wings of the Phoenix* p128

[22] DGGD/74 – Confidential Report No.33

[23] Allen – *The Longest War* p449

[24] Probert op cit p266 (John Dunbar)

[25] Probert op cit p263

[26] ib. p256

[27] 1307, 1308, 1323, 1324, 1325, 1326, 1327, 1329, 1330 & 1331 Wing Headquarters

2708, 2739, 2743, 2748, 2759, 2802, 2810, 2896, 2941, 2942, 2943, 2944, 2945, 2946, 2964, 2966, 2967 & 2968 Field Squadrons

2706, 2837, 2846, 2852, 2854, 2958, 2959, 2960, 2961, 2962, 2963, & 2965 LAA Squadrons 2970 Armoured Car Squadron

[28] Later Group Captain H Sullivan CBE, Commandant RAF Regiment Depot 1961-63

[29] Mr HE Hyde – letter 14 Sep 95

[30] Lee – Eastward: *The RAF in the Far East 1945-72* p62

[31] Air Chief Marshal Sir Keith Park GCB KBE MC DFC MA (1892-1975). Air operations in South East Asia 3 May to 12 Sep 1945. Published in the Supplement to the *London Gazette* No.39202 dated 13 Apr 1951

9

Reorganisation and Redeployment

Soldiers in peace are like chimneys in summer, but what wise man pulls down his chimney when his almanac tells him summer is at hand?

William Cecil, Lord Burghley, 1555

As in 1918-19, all three Services entered into a period of retrenchment and reorganisation in 1945-46. This was characterised by rapid demobilisation and redeployments in the United Kingdom and overseas as British forces readjusted to their post-war garrison duties. In North-West Europe, the Second Tactical Air Force changed its role and became the British Air Forces of Occupation in the British Zone of Germany. In the Mediterranean, the RAF withdrew from Italy and North Africa to the Suez Canal Zone and the pre-war air bases in Palestine, Iraq and Aden.

The RAF Regiment wings and squadrons which had been deployed to Sumatra and Java after VJ Day to assist in taking over from the defeated Japanese until the return of the Dutch authorities were inevitably drawn into the conflicts which formed part of the political struggle between the militant local factions and the former colonial power – in this case the Dutch.

It was an unhappy period for the British, caught as they were in the crossfire of insurgency which was no concern of theirs, but in 1946 the last RAF Regiment units in Java were – with other British forces – withdrawn and disbanded.

In the Far East, the RAF handed over to the Armee de l'Air in French Indo-China and the Royal Netherlands Air Force in the Dutch East Indies and began preparing to leave the Indian sub-continent where independence was obviously not far off. Elsewhere in the Far East, the Royal Air Force re-established its peace-time presence by

returning to its former bases in Singapore, Malaya, Hong Kong and
Ceylon.

The Post-War Status of the Regiment

Meanwhile, back in London, the continued existence of the RAF
Regiment and, indeed, the Royal Air Force's view of the need for
ground and low-level air defence in the future had yet to be
determined. The Directorate of Ground Defence had been established
with a limited period of life in 1940 but it had survived, and expanded,
to meet the demands of its parent Service throughout the war. Major-
General Sir Claude Liardet relinquished his appointment as
Commandant of the RAF Regiment and Director-General of Ground
Defence in 1945 and the Air Ministry had to appoint his successor –
Major-General AE Robinson, late of the Green Howards, who had
served with the Iraq Levies before the war – on an interim basis.

The RAF Regiment had not been promised a long-term
existence when it was formed in 1942 under the pressures of war,
and its retention in the post-war Air Force was not assured. Early in
1945 Air Marshal Sir Edgar Ludlow-Hewitt[1] had carried out an
independent study into the future of the RAF Regiment and had
concluded that there would be a requirement for it in the RAF in
peace.

In August 1945 the Air Council invited his successor as
Inspector-General of the RAF, Air Chief Marshal Sir Arthur Barratt[2],
to re-examine his predecessor's recommendations on the future of
the RAF Regiment, the inference being that the Air Council was not
completely convinced by the content of the Ludlow-Hewitt report.
He was joined in this study by, among others, Air Commodore D A
Boyle, then AOC 11 Group, who had been the secretary to the
Findlater Stewart Committee in 1941.

The Barratt Committee reported in December 1945, and its
findings were considered by the Post War Planning Committee at a
special meeting held in the Air Ministry on 8th January 1946.[3] Apart
from the principal recommendation that all RAF personnel should
achieve higher standards of ground defence training in the future,
the report proposed that the majority of the airmen in Group V trades
should form a greatly enlarged RAF Regiment, since their presence
on stations would enable Regiment squadrons to be formed on an ad

hoc basis when required. This would have had the advantage of requiring a much smaller establishment of full-time Regiment personnel than the alternative of retaining the war-time organisation of the Regiment, even on a lesser scale.

Air Chief Marshal Sir Douglas Evill, Vice-Chief of Air Staff,[4] who had personal experience of the unpreparedness of the RAF for major war in 1940, dissented from this approach. He insisted on the retention of the Regiment structure on the grounds that only this would meet the RAF's requirements for full-time ground and low-level air defence at home and overseas. He stressed that the training of all RAF officers and airmen in ground defence skills, and the provision of officers and NCOs for locally-enlisted forces abroad, required a permanent and combat-ready force which could maintain the necessary cadre of trained officers and NCOs. His arguments – and determination – resulted in the Air Council's approval for the continuation of the RAF Regiment as part of the post-war RAF, with an interim establishment of 3,300 all ranks within the total RAF ceiling of 200,000.

Following further studies within the Air Staff, firm decisions were made regarding the future size and shape of the post-war Regiment. The title of Commandant RAF Regiment & Director-General of Ground Defence was changed to Commandant-General RAF Regiment and Inspector of Ground Combat Training.. After a more detailed analysis of the roles and responsibilities of the Regiment in the United Kingdom, Germany, the Middle East and the Far East, the peace-time establishment of the RAF Regiment was set at 667 officers and 5,191 warrant officers, NCOs and aircraftmen. The final seal of approval for the continuation of the Regiment's existence was given by HM King George VI in 1947 when he accepted the appointment of Air Commodore-in-Chief of the Corps whose foundation he had authorised in 1942.

The Post-War Training Pattern

In the United Kingdom the RAF Regiment Depot moved from its requisitioned war-time home at Belton Park in Lincolnshire to one of the original Royal Flying Corps stations – RAF Catterick in North Yorkshire – in August 1946. The LAA Gunnery School, which had moved from Butlin's holiday camp at Filey to Nethertown in

August 1945, settled at the Army's pre-war anti-aircraft gunnery range at Watchet in Somerset.

The Depot was the centre for the initial and further training of all RAF Regiment officers, NCOs and airmen but due to pressures on accommodation and training areas a disused bomber station at Wombleton, on the edge of the North Yorkshire moors, was used for both basic and battle training courses. The feelings of isolation and desolation which Wombleton engendered in the unsuspecting National Servicemen who found the reception party – usually in the charge of Warrant Officer "Danny" Gourd – waiting when their train reached the end of the branch line at Nawton, were such that no subsequent posting held any terrors for them.

Warrant Officer DA Gourd was to become one of the RAF Regiment's legends; impeccably turned out and the paragon of a British warrant officer, he never accepted anything less than perfection from those under training and his sharp eyes and quick tongue ensured an immediate conformity by officers, NCOs and airmen alike. He allowed nothing to deflect him from his task of imposing the highest standards of drill, discipline and dress on all ranks at all times. Few of those involved could forget participating in a parade on an ice-covered runway in sleeting weather when the band – unwisely – failed to appear and WO Gourd ordered the shivering ranks to whistle the RAF March Past so that the parade could be held with accompanying music. A subsequent consolation for the gunners on that parade was to see – in even worse weather – Mr Gourd mercilessly drilling the band as a punishment for their absence from his parade.

The author Keith Waterhouse was posted to Wombleton as a Clerk/GD during his National Service but – due to confusion with another Waterhouse (u/t Gunner) – found himself on a basic gunner course until the misunderstanding had been resolved. He, too, lived in fear of WO Gourd but discovered that his bark was worse than his bite. Returning to camp with some friends after spending the evening in a pub in Helmsley, the revellers found a horse wandering down the road. They led it to the guardroom and tethered it while one of the braver members of the party went in to rouse WO Gourd to tell him that a horse had been posted in to the unit. Without a moment's hesitation Mr Gourd replied "we have no billets for horses. Send it on fourteen days leave with hay" and went back to sleep.[5]

Towards the end of 1947 Wombleton became untenable and was abandoned by the RAF when the gunner training courses were moved to another disused airfield in the more populated area of Skipton-on-Swale, not far from Thirsk in North Yorkshire. It was also a more efficient training base, being located on a single site, rather than several dispersed sites each some distance apart. In addition, the accommodation at Skipton was in Nissen huts which actually kept out the rain and the snow – unlike those at Wombleton. However, as the training intakes reduced, and more accommodation became available at Catterick, Skipton was closed and the land returned to civilian ownership and agricultural use.

Deployments in Overseas Commands

In Germany the sixteen wing headquarters and seventy-five squadrons which had formed the RAF Regiment component of 2 TAF on VE Day were rapidly run down in 1945/46 to leave four wing headquarters[6] and 12 squadrons[7] in the British Air Forces of Occupation (BAFO) by August 1947.

In the Middle East, 1 and 2 Armoured Car Companies were incorporated into the RAF Regiment in October 1946 as 2701 and 2702 Squadrons respectively before resuming their former single figure numbers in 1947. During 1945 and 1946 three wing headquarters and nine squadrons had been redeployed from Greece, Italy and Austria to Palestine, where they were joined by a tenth squadron from the United Kingdom. However, by 1947 the Regiment force level had reduced to two wing headquarters[8] and eight squadrons[9] with an independent armoured car flight[10] in Aden where it operated in support of the Aden Protectorate Levies, whose British Army officers were in the course of being replaced by RAF Regiment officers.

In the Far East, the ten wing headquarters[11] and 35 of the 36 squadrons[12] which had formed part of Air Command South-East Asia had all been disbanded by the end of 1946. The fact that only one squadron (2700) was left in the United Kingdom at that time made it abundantly clear to the Air Ministry that there was already an impossible home/overseas tour ratio for officers and airmen in the post-war deployment pattern of the RAF Regiment. It was therefore decided not to base Regiment squadrons in the Far East but to meet the ground defence commitment there with a locally-raised force, which would be trained, organised and equipped to the same establishment as RAF Regiment rifle squadrons. This solution appealed to the Treasury as well, as it was likely to prove to be a less costly one. Thus the sole surviving squadron (2810) in the Far East was retained until April 1947, when it was disbanded at RAF Changi, and its remaining officers and NCOs used to raise the RAF Regiment (Malaya). After serving with distinction in jungle operations against the Communist terrorists in the Emergency which began in 1948 and did not officially end until 1960, the last squadron of the RAF Regiment (Malaya) was disbanded in July 1961.

The Royal Auxiliary Air Force Regiment

An attempt had been made to resolve the deficiency in UK-based RAF Regiment squadrons by forming Royal Auxiliary Air Force Regiment LAA squadrons alongside the flying squadrons of the Royal Auxiliary Air Force. Although the formation of 20 such squadrons had been approved in 1946, only 12 were actually raised.[13] In common with all reserve forces, the ability of these squadrons to fulfil their war roles was directly related to their success in recruiting and retaining their auxiliary personnel. In this, some squadrons were inevitably more successful than others, but the overall picture was patchy and it was always clear that the RAF could not rely on having twelve fully-operational LAA squadrons, ready for war, from an embodied RAuxAF Regiment. On the other hand, these units served to establish a territorial link with the civil population and local authorities, creating an awareness of the role of the regular force. When the war-time 40mm L60 Bofors gun was to be replaced by the more complex 40mm L70 version, it was decided that the new weapon posed too great a training task for the undermanned Auxiliary squadrons. As a result, the RAuxAF Regiment squadrons were converted to the field role in 1955 and this proved to be a more attractive option for recruiting than the LAA role had been.

The Rationalisation of Wing and Squadron Numbers

The decision to abandon the four-figure wartime numbers of squadrons and wings was implemented in 1947, probably without adequate forethought. In the rapid and large-scale disbandment of squadrons, the long-term value of retaining the heritage of some of the most distinguished wartime squadrons was not always appreciated. In this way the RAF Regiment lost any subsequent entitlement to many of the battle honours which had been earned by its squadrons during the war. This was particularly so in the case of the squadrons which had fought in South-East Asia and which were disbanded without retaining any links with the post-war Regiment. In fact, over one hundred squadrons with distinguished operational records disappeared without trace in 1945 and 1946, and none of the fifteen or so which survived to become part of the post-war Regiment had fought in South East Asia – so none of the potential battle honours such as "Imphal", "Meiktila", "Arakan" and "Rangoon" can ever be borne on Regiment squadron Standards.

This unfortunate situation was subsequently exacerbated by the indiscriminate re-numbering of post-war squadrons which, wittingly or unwittingly, has cast another six of the foundation squadrons into limbo. This is because squadrons whose numbers have been taken by other squadrons cannot be re-formed in the future with the result that the links with the squadrons of 1st February 1942 have been progressively reduced as a proportion of the total Regiment front line.

Furthermore, the choice of new squadron numbers was made without any consideration of the problems which might arise from duplicating the numbers already in use by flying squadrons. Admittedly, 1 and 2 Armoured Car Companies – formed in 1921 and 1922 respectively – had an irrefutable claim to become 1 and 2 Squadrons of the RAF Regiment, but they already had their own badges and traditions reaching back to the earliest days of the Royal Air Force. One course might have been to follow that example and choose numbers for the post-war Regiment squadrons from among those which had been used by those disbanded flying squadrons which would never be reformed. This would have been a positive move to demonstrate that the existence of the RAF Regiment was inextricably linked to the Royal Air Force, so emphasising that the Corps would always be "an integral part of the Royal Air Force".

It was a situation which produced opposing views within the Corps but an independently-based pattern of numbers for RAF Regiment squadrons was introduced, despite the inevitability of confusion with flying squadrons past or present. This was to lead to the situation which was to arise in the Gulf War of 1990/91, when a large number of flying and Regiment squadrons – with numbers which did not immediately indicate their role – were deployed together in Saudi Arabia.

Thus while the history and traditions of some RAF Regiment squadrons go back as far as 1942, the remainder have their origins in the post-war years. 1 and 2 Squadrons alone can look back to the earliest days of the Royal Air Force when the foundations were laid for the development of the independent air service which has served – and continues to serve – the nation so well.

Experiments in the Airborne Role

In 1947 HQ 38 Group – which had carried the Airborne Forces to Normandy, Arnhem and the Rhine – was tasked to develop an air-portable capability for an RAF Regiment wing which could then be flown into overseas areas to secure an airfield for transport operations. 2 Wing Headquarters, with 15 and 16 LAA Squadrons and 63 Rifle Squadron, assembled at RAF Upavon in 1948 to carry out unit air-portability trials. The two LAA squadrons worked on methods of loading their 24 Bofors guns, and associated equipment, into four-engined Hastings aircraft while the Rifle squadron developed loading tables for its move by smaller two-engined Valetta aircraft. 63 Squadron completed its task sooner than the two LAA squadrons – which were finding a number of problems in dismantling their 40mm Bofors guns so that they could enter the side-loading doors of the Hastings in several pieces, secure them adequately for flight, unload them on arrival and assemble the guns for action. To fill in time which the Rifle squadron had at its disposal, the officers and airmen of 63 Squadron were trained as parachutists in order to give the wing an all-round airborne role.

However, it all turned to ashes as the task was one for which the aircraft available at that time were unsuited and even if the LAA squadrons could have been deployed to a distant airhead, there was no airlift capacity for their vehicles, which would have been left behind. Apart from the fact that the problems of loading and unloading Bofors guns in and out of Hastings aircraft proved to be insuperable, the Air Ministry refused to recognise the parachutist qualifications of the 63 Squadron personnel, despite the fact that they had completed the course at the RAF's No.1 Parachute Training School and were carrying out parachuting duties. Although RAF Regiment parachute units had been raised in both the Middle East and Far East during the war and had been authorised to wear parachute wings and receive parachutist pay, the official response in 1949 was "the RAF gives wings and pay to people for staying in aircraft, not for jumping out of them".

The project was abandoned, and the squadrons remained at Upavon in their normal roles until 1950 when they were deployed at very short notice to Sculthorpe, Lakenheath and Mildenhall to protect the USAF heavy bomber force, with its weapons, which was deployed to those airfields from the continental USA in response to Russian hostility in Europe.

The Last Days of the Palestine Mandate

In Palestine the pre-war violence between Arab and Jew inevitably returned in another form – this time in acts of terrorism against the British by Zionist activists determined to establish an independent Jewish state in place of the mandated territory of Palestine, for which Great Britain had assumed responsibility after the first world war. Unfortunately, pre-war British governments had not been successful in meeting the aspirations of either the indigenous Arab population or the growing number of Jewish settlers. The result was that the British forces stationed in Palestine received little support – and even less goodwill – from the population, and bore the brunt of local dissatisfaction and antagonism towards the policies which emanated from Westminster and Whitehall. Despite the sometimes extreme provocation directed against them, the British forces acted with restraint and employed minimum force in attempting to maintain law and order – a rather different pattern of behaviour from that which has prevailed in the area since the British departed in 1948.

In 1946 the six rifle squadrons in Palestine were spread widely in an attempt to protect every possible RAF installation: hospitals and medical units, maintenance units, signals installations, radar sites – and airfields. The result was, of course, that the policy of trying to defend everything with the limited resources available ensured that nothing was defended adequately. This indiscriminate and piece-meal deployment of under-strength Regiment units produced a posture which was, predictably, quite incapable of meeting the threat posed by experienced and skilled saboteurs, many of whom had learned their trade by operating against the Germans in occupied Europe.

Attacks on the Royal Air Force by Jewish terrorist organisations began in January 1946 and in the following month the radar station at Mount Carmel was demolished by a thoroughly professional attack. A week later, simultaneous raids were made on the RAF stations at Qastina, Peta Tiqua and Lydda, in which twenty aircraft were destroyed. At Peta Tiqua, outside Tel Aviv, Flying Officer HEG Price took his section of 2 Armoured Car Company to the Spitfire dispersals where he personally removed an explosive charge from one of the aircraft radiators. From then onwards, attacks on RAF installations continued unabated and the British government's inflexible policies were successful only in unifying its opponents – and international public opinion – against the actions of British forces in Palestine.

From the Regiment's point of view, the situation could not have arisen at a worse time. Experienced officers and NCOs were being demobilised steadily and without regard to the requirements of the operational situation. The effectiveness of the squadrons in Palestine suffered because "the majority of airmen, having done all that was asked of them in nearly six years of war, were now desperately anxious for repatriation and while they had risked their lives during the war, were not always willing to do so merely in order to safeguard an aircraft or equipment store against an attack by a Jewish gangster."[14] Furthermore, "reinforcements for those repatriated were often raw and untrained boys who were not of the usual RAF calibre and no match for the ex-members of the European underground movements who were largely responsible for the attacks on RAF installations."[15]

Pilot Officer Ferrey, having completed his OCTU training at Catterick, and subsequent armoured car training at Wombleton, arrived in Palestine in 1947 to join 2 Armoured Car Squadron at Ramleh. Detached to support the Palestine Police in Jerusalem, his section was heavily involved in escorting convoys and in anti-terrorist patrols which frequently resulted in exchanges of fire with terrorists and dealing with the human and material damage caused by bomb attacks. Following an incident in which he and the crew of his armoured car caught a terrorist red-handed, he appeared as the principal witness for the prosecution at the trial, after which he was posted to the Canal Zone to avoid possible reprisals by the Irgun Zvai Leumi – the terrorist group involved. Ferrey then enjoyed a very pleasant month in command of the RAF Regiment flight responsible for the security of the houseboats on Lake Timsah, which formed the residence of the AOC Middle East Air Force, before returning to 2 Squadron which had, by then, redeployed to Amman.[16]

Lacking in experience and combat skills, those reinforcement drafts which were sent to Palestine further diluted the Regiment squadrons' operational capabilities, which were already exacerbated by the low manning levels which remained unrectified, despite the urgency of the situation. Although the total RAF Regiment strength in Palestine on 1st July 1947 was 1,183 all ranks, by the end of that year there was only sufficient manpower available to keep four of the six rifle squadrons – 52, 58, 62 and 66 – at an operational level: 53 and 65 Squadrons having been reduced to mere number-plates, without officers or airmen. The two armoured car squadrons, also below strength, were fully employed in protecting RAF road convoys moving between stations.

Pilot Officer Wilcock reported that on joining his squadron – with three other young officers fresh from OCTU – he took command of a flight which had only one NCO – an equally inexperienced corporal – in it. He was at least fortunate in that his squadron was commanded by a flight lieutenant as it was not unusual for quite junior flying officers to be in command of the undermanned squadrons. On a lighter note, he was given the task of escorting an ENSA concert party – which included the young Tommy Cooper – from Haifa to RAF Ein Shemer. Arriving earlier than expected at the hotel in Haifa, he entered the bedrooms to rouse the members of the concert party – and was extremely embarrassed to discover that the accommodation was being happily shared by the male and female entertainers.[17]

As political indecision continued in London, the situation went from bad to worse in Palestine and by mid-1947 most RAF aircraft were concentrated on the single airfield at Ein Shemer together with 20 Wing Headquarters, 58 and 66 Rifle Squadrons and a flight of 1 Armoured Car Squadron. Other RAF Regiment units were deployed to the RAF stations at Ras-el-Ain, Kolundia, and Ramleh, as well as to protect Air Headquarters Levant in Jerusalem itself. Eventually, the remaining RAF units withdrew to the airfield at Ramat David in the Haifa enclave in May 1948, leaving Ein Shemer in the hands of a RAF care and maintenance party – and two Regiment squadrons. Towards the end of May, a surprise attack on Ramat David airfield by Egyptian Spitfires destroyed two RAF aircraft. When the attackers returned for a second strike they were all shot down – one falling to the light machine guns of 52 Squadron RAF Regiment.

The British evacuation in June 1948 ended almost thirty unrewarding years of fulfilling a League of Nations mandate and the two Regiment wing headquarters, with the five surviving squadrons,[18] were transferred to Transjordan, the Canal Zone and Aden. The Regiment squadrons deployed to Transjordan and Egypt moved by road and apart from the logistic problems inherent in such long journeys over poor desert roads, there was a shortage of trained HGV drivers. LAC Brett of 66 Squadron recalled that any airman who would admit to some sort of driving experience was given a few hours of local training before setting off to drive a three-ton truck in convoy to Egypt – a journey which was, not surprisingly, more hazardous than it might otherwise have been.[19]

In his final report, the AOC Levant[20] praised the contribution which the RAF Regiment had made to the security of RAF installations and he was particularly appreciative of the work of the armoured car squadrons in protecting RAF road convoys from ambushes and terrorist attacks.

A Regiment squadron had been temporarily deployed to British Somaliland in 1949 for internal security tasks, and the withdrawal from Palestine did not produce a respite for the Regiment squadrons in the Middle East. It was not long before the Aden-based squadrons were carrying out roulement tasks on forward airstrips in Kenya – where suppression of the Mau Mau rebellion required the deployment of already overstretched British forces from 1952 to 1955 – as well as in the Aden Protectorate and the Gulf. The Malayan Emergency, the Abadan oil refinery crisis in Iran and the Korean War, although not directly impinging on the RAF Regiment, were all unwelcome additions to the main threat posed by the Cold War and it is to the credit of the British armed forces that they so often succeeded in holding the ring despite the level of over-commitment which they had to endure as British foreign policy objectives were pursued with inadequate military resources to underwrite them.

Egypt and the Suez Canal Base

In Egypt tensions grew over the British failure to produce an acceptable Anglo-Egyptian Treaty to replace the pre-war one which had expired and required renegotiation. Anti-British demonstrations took place in Cairo and the threat to British installations in the Canal Zone jeopardised the effectiveness of the main British base in the Middle East. Among the many contingency plans which were developed at this time was Operation Rodeo Flail which was designed to protect British interests in Cairo and Alexandria by deploying an Army brigade to each city from the Canal Zone. The plan was that the first brigade would move to Cairo by road while the second brigade would emplane in RAF transport aircraft and be landed on the airfield at Alexandria.

Not unreasonably, the Army commander considered the prospect of flying his troops into an airfield defended by hostile LAA guns to be an unacceptable risk and he invited the Air Force to produce a more realistic solution to the problem. The RAF commander concerned was Air Vice-Marshal David Atcherley, who had initiated the operation to seize Cap Serrat by RAF Regiment squadrons in 1943, and he had no difficulty in devising a plan to neutralise the airfield before the Army arrived.

His solution was for a Regiment force to be flown into the airfield in three Valetta aircraft under cover of darkness. On landing, the RAF Regiment assault force was to attack and disable the LAA defences, after which the main Regiment force would be flown in to secure the airfield perimeter prior to the arrival of the Army brigade. The plan was practised intensively on the RAF airfields in the Canal Zone, but political approval for the operation never materialised.[21]

The Redeployment to Cyprus

When the Anglo-Egyptian dispute was eventually settled in 1954, it was decided to relocate the British base in Cyprus. The concept was that this would preserve a British military presence in the eastern Mediterranean, which could be expanded by a return to the Canal Zone in an emergency under the terms agreed between

Egypt and Britain. Three Regiment wing headquarters[22] and five squadrons[23] were redeployed from the Canal Zone to Cyprus where Akrotiri and Nicosia were developed as the major RAF stations from which British support could be given to the Baghdad Pact nations. Unfortunately, it was at this point in time that the activists for the union of Cyprus and Greece began their campaign of anti-British terrorism aimed at driving out the colonial power and establishing Greek Cypriot control, and union with Greece, on an island which had been Turkish for over three hundred years, retained a substantial Turkish population, and had never belonged to Greece.

The EOKA campaign developed on much the same lines as the Jewish campaign had in Palestine, and the British forces suffered similar disadvantages. The workforce on Army bases and RAF stations was provided by the indigenous population, many of whom were Greek Cypriots who provided both active and passive support for the EOKA terrorists by hampering activity and by supplying intelligence information about British operations. Once again, British forces were set impossible goals in the cause of political geography – in this case the maintenance of a national operational base in the eastern Mediterranean under conditions which became increasingly more difficult and unstable. The security of the RAF stations at Nicosia and Akrotiri, as well as the small RAF units scattered throughout the island, became an extremely demanding commitment which absorbed large amounts of manpower.

One attempt to resolve the problem was the formation of Security Flights, composed of RAF Regiment and RAF Police personnel, but in most cases the role of the RAF Regiment squadrons in the theatre was to provide VIP escorts, guards and sentries – a task which placed considerable responsibility on junior airmen who were often operating on their own. AC DR Walker of 34 Squadron described the difficult situations which often faced the lone armed sentry when harassed by the locally-employed Greek Cypriot workforce on isolated parts of the stations, and the feelings aroused in his fellow RAF Regiment airmen by the cold-blooded murder of unarmed Servicemen in the crowded streets of Nicosia.[24] Apart from the routine of station defence and security tasks, RAF Regiment personnel were employed on anti-terrorist patrols, convoy escorts and the personal protection of VIPs. There were, inevitably, several occasions on which Regiment personnel became involved in fire-fights with EOKA terrorists and in one such encounter Sergeant Hyson, of 63 Squadron, earned a mention in despatches for his leadership.

The Brief Return to Suez

The Anglo-Egyptian treaty which provided for a British return to Egypt in the event of an external threat to the Suez Canal was, in British eyes, seriously compromised by the nationalisation of the Suez Canal Company by the Egyptian government. The subsequent Anglo-French attempt to regain control of the Canal involved a hastily-planned military intervention based on the contrived claim that this was necessary to prevent the Canal from being seized by the Israeli army. Apart from the fact that the British military operation had to be improvised with whatever resources could be found, regardless of their suitability, the length of time needed to prepare the assault gave ample scope for the mobilisation of hostile international opinion by Egypt and its allies. In the event, the combination of American and Soviet opposition to the Anglo-French adventure brought it to a halt before most of the military objectives had been gained.

Operation Musketeer was launched in November 1956 and 48 Squadron RAF Regiment went ashore from HMS Ocean by helicopter to secure Gamil airfield from which RAF aircraft were to operate. "Had it not been for the presence of 48 Squadron RAF Regiment, which did invaluable work in securing Gamil airfield, the task might well have been beyond the slender resources of 215 Wing."[25]

No.48 Squadron had, in fact, been bombarded with conflicting orders while it was preparing for the operation at its Rudloe Manor base. Initially a field squadron, it had been ordered to convert to the LAA role for Musketeer but no sooner had this been completed than it was re-roled as a field squadron and embarked as such for Suez. The final touch was an order to leave its support weapons (3" mortars) behind and deploy as four rifle flights. 63 and 194 Squadrons were tasked to follow-up 48 Squadron, but neither had reached further east than Malta when the Suez cease-fire came into effect, leaving 194 Squadron to move on to Cyprus while 63 Squadron remained in Malta. Meanwhile, in Cyprus the Regiment's LAA squadrons were deployed at the main airfields, where they were reinforced by Army LAA batteries placed under the operational command of the respective RAF Regiment wing headquarters. It is of interest to note that the Army report on this part of the operation stressed the unfamiliar aspects of the airfield defence role for the Royal Artillery batteries involved and complimented the LAA squadrons of the RAF Regiment[26] on the high standards of efficiency and aircraft recognition which they had displayed.

For the RAF Regiment it seemed that the certainties inherent in real war against the Germans and their allies had merely changed into the uncertainties of attacks by any groups which happened to dislike the British; a situation which required vigilance against enemies who caused casualties by stealth while avoiding battle. What came to be called low-intensity operations were here to stay.

This trying and unsatisfying period in the Regiment's activities was summed up in the official history by the terse comment that "since 1946 the RAF Regiment had little respite in the eastern Mediterranean and their high standards of competence had been displayed in numerous dangerous situations."[27]

The RAF Levies Iraq

Wartime expansion had increased the Iraq Levies to a force level of some 12,000 men in independent companies, deployed both in Iraq and in Iran, the Persian Gulf, Palestine and Cyprus, in addition to the infrastructure of the force headquarters, depot and training schools. It was an ethnically mixed force which contained Assyrians, Kurds, Arabs, and even Baluchis, with British officers and NCOs in addition to the indigenous officers and NCOs. By the end of 1943 the deployment of 84 Levy companies, including an independent parachute company, had released over 8,000 British personnel for combatant duties in other theatres.

At the end of the war the Iraq Levies were reduced in strength to 60 British (mainly RAF Regiment) officers and 1,672 locally-enlisted officers and men in a force headquarters and two operational wings, each of four squadrons. 1 Wing comprised Christian Assyrians and Kurdish Muslims and was deployed in Habbaniya, Mosul and Ser Amadia while 2 Wing was entirely Arab in composition and was divided between Shaibah and Basra.

Boxing Day meet of the Royal Exodus Hunt, outside the Officers' Mess at RAF Habbaniya.

The Iraq and Aden Levies retained some of the ethos of the Indian and British Armies which had influenced their formative years. Both, for example, retained horses as "officers' chargers" – although there were no longer any mounted troopers to lead in cavalry charges. In Aden the chargers were used as polo ponies but in Iraq there was the Royal Exodus Hunt as well. The first hounds used to hunt the jackal in Iraq had been introduced by 110 Company of the Indian Army Service Corps at the end of the First World War. The idea spread, and in 1924 the Iraq Levies began hunting the jackal with English foxhounds at Mosul and Kirkuk. Legend has it that such was the enthusiasm among the tribesmen for this strange English sport, that even when the tribes were in rebellion against the government, a truce was declared on one day each week so that the Hunt could meet – and the tribesmen could join in the chase!

In 1928 the Hunt moved to Hinaidi – then the RAF's main station – and was formally established as the Exodus Hunt. The name had nothing to do with the Children of Israel – it was, more prosaically, the Urdu for the numbers one hundred and ten (ek sau das) and was used as a tribute to the founders of hunting in Iraq. It did not acquire its Royal prefix until 1935 when the King of Iraq became its patron. The Hunt country lay to the south-east of Baghdad and the posts of Master, Huntsman, Whippers-in and Secretary were, more often than not, filled by Regiment officers in the post-war period.

Unfamiliarity with the peculiarities of Levy life sometimes resulted in unfortunate situations. The Animal Transport Company, of 26 horses and 96 mules, was commanded by a pilot officer who had little previous experience of handling equines. The AOC Iraq from 1948 to 1950 was Air Marshal Sir John Boothman – a winner of the Schneider Trophy before the war – who regularly rode the two Arab ponies allocated for his use and stabled at Air House. He occasionally allowed others to stable their horses in the spare stalls there and one of the beneficiaries of his generosity was the female representative of St John Ambulance at the nearby RAF Hospital. Unfortunately, her pony was elderly and nearing the end of its days and the Force veterinary officer ruled that it should be "cast" – the military terminology for being put down. The owner tearfully asked for permission to take a last ride, promising to leave her horse tied up outside the stables to be dealt with after she had left.

The OC AT Company duly arrived at the AOC's stables, led away the grey pony standing outside and dispatched it with a single shot from his service revolver. He was subsequently dismayed to be summoned by the air marshal who enquired why his favourite pony had been cast. It transpired that the AOC's groom, unaware of the arrangements, had stabled the elderly pony he found tied to the rail outside, leaving in its place the AOC's horse to cool down after the air marshal's early morning ride. It took some ingenuity on the part of the Force veterinary officer and the OC AT Company to resolve the situation to the satisfaction of Air Marshal Boothman and the Force accountant officer.[28]

When the British mandate ended in 1948, and Iraq achieved full independence, it became necessary to formalise the new relationship between Britain and Iraq. The Treaty of Portsmouth gave Britain the right to retain air bases in Iraq, but the legal situation regarding the enlistment of Iraqi citizens (Assyrians, Kurds and

Arabs) in the armed forces of a foreign power with bases in Iraq produced some problems.

The prevailing atmosphere in the Middle East was not conducive to the maintenance of privileges which had overtones of pre-war colonialism and by 1955 Britain had agreed to withdraw its forces from Iraq. Once the decision had been taken for the RAF to leave, the RAF Levies Iraq had no further role and the force was disbanded at Habbaniya following the handover of the station to the Royal Iraqi Air Force in May 1955. Although both the Colonial Office and the Air Ministry developed a comprehensive system of compensation and resettlement for the officers and men of the ethnic minorities – Assyrians and Kurds in particular – who had served the British crown so loyally, the responsibility for their ultimate well-being lay with the Iraqi government which, despite the assurances it gave, had little affection for either Muslim rebels or the Christian minority within Iraq.

There were also two RAF Regiment squadrons in Iraq at this time: 2 Field – which was redeployed to Nicosia – and 21 LAA – which was disbanded – when the RAF finally withdrew from Iraq after 33 years of peace and war.

The Aden Protectorate Levies

RAF Regiment officers and NCOs replaced the British Army component of the APL at the end of the war and the force was reduced to a peace-time establishment of 1,347 all ranks. Colonial Office policy in the post-war period was for the Government of Aden to take a more active part in the development of the tribal states which formed the Western Aden Protectorate. This involved supporting the tribal rulers against instability in their own areas as well as safeguarding the Protectorate against intervention by the potentially hostile ruler of the Yemen. Accordingly, APL garrisons were established on the frontier, near major Yemeni towns, alongside airstrips at Dhala, Mukeiras and Beihan. Smaller posts were occupied by Levy forces in troubled tribal areas – such as Ataq, Lodar, Mafidh, Nisab, Rabat and the Jebel Jihaf – as the situation required.

This deployment pattern inevitably resulted in frequent small-scale operations which resembled Mr Jorrocks's description of fox-hunting as "the image of war.... with only five and twenty percent of

its danger". Nonetheless, such skirmishes often involved battle casualties and demanded courageous leadership by officers and NCOs of the Levies. Between 1949 and 1960 six RAF Regiment officers and four Arab officers were awarded Military Crosses and three Arab NCOs and one RAF Regiment NCO received Military Medals, for gallantry in actions against hostile tribesmen – both in the Western Aden Protectorate and in Trucial Oman. These awards provoked some opposition on technical grounds in Whitehall as the issue of the General Service Medal for the Arabian Peninsula was not authorised until January 1961 and the regulations for gallantry awards were such that these could only be awarded once a state of "active service" had been declared in an "operational area".

That the recommendations for these awards were approved, despite the lengthy correspondence which they generated within Whitehall as the result of inter-Service rivalries and Treasury concerns at the costs which might result from a state of active service, was a victory for common sense – and for those at the sharp end of colonial government policies.[29]

The Commandant-General inspecting a quarter-guard of the APL at Dhala in the Western Aden Protectorate.

In 1953 a difference of opinion arose between the British and Saudi Arabian governments over the borders between the Gulf states (which were under British protection) and Saudi Arabia, which claimed the Buraimi Oasis. It was, in fact, the first step towards reasserting the Saudi claim to the coast of the Persian Gulf and it was therefore essential – from the British point of view – to show firmness in maintaining the status quo. A wing of the APL was detached to Sharjah, from where it maintained the integrity of the borders until the dispute was settled by political negotiation, and 2 Squadron was deployed in support from Habbaniya. However, the immediate effect was to put an excessive workload on the remaining APL squadrons in Aden

The emergency of a growing insurgency within the Western Aden Protectorate, which was supported by the supply of arms and money from Saudi Arabia, the Yemen and Egypt, produced a situation which was beyond the capability of the inter-war policy of imperial

A Squadron of the Aden Protectorate Levies setting out for operations in the Western Aden Protectorate.

policing by aircraft supported by small ground forces.

The first indication of the changing situation occurred in 1954 when continual incursions were made from the Yemen into the Audhali Sultanate. Encouraged by their success, the dissident tribesmen laid siege to the isolated APL fort at Rabat in the Wadi Hatib. Although a large-scale expedition to relieve the garrison was successful, the forts at Nisab and Marwaha were besieged subsequently and air and ground operations continued throughout the year. The APL was neither organised nor equipped for widespread and sustained military operations – it lacked, for example, supporting artillery and engineers which were essential for successful infantry work – and this was demonstrated the following year when another relief column was ambushed en route to Rabat with the loss of two RAF Regiment officers, one Arab officer and five Arab soldiers killed and a larger number wounded.

This was a situation which was exacerbated by the declining morale of the APL, due to inadequate pay, over-commitment on sustained operations and continual subversion by the Yemeni authorities who were offering substantial sums to Levy soldiers who defected to them, with a large bonus for any who killed a British officer before deserting. Unfortunately, it took some time for these facts to be understood by HQ Middle East Air Force and the Air Ministry and the remedial action, when it was eventually taken, was too little and too late.[30]

In the face of such large-scale opposition, which was absorbing almost all of the Colony's weakened military resources, the Aden government decided to withdraw from the Wadi Hatib and a mixed force of British infantry and armoured cars was flown in to join an RAF Regiment squadron and an APL wing which had moved to Ataq. This force was the largest which had ever been assembled for an operation in the WAP and its role was to achieve the evacuation of the garrison and the destruction of the abandoned fort at Rabat. With every aircraft at RAF Khormaksar giving support – including a heavy bomber squadron of Lincolns and 198 sorties by the Venoms and Vampires of 8 Squadron – the operation was successfully completed.[31]

Following the escalation in the political and military scenes in the Aden Protectorate, it was decided to give the Army responsibility for dealing with the external and internal threats which had arisen

An RAF Regiment-manned armoured car of the APL.

and British battalions and their supporting arms were deployed to Aden. As the junior partner in this new situation, the APL passed to the control of the Army on 1st February 1957 when Group Captain AG Douglas CBE MC handed over his command to Colonel DW Lister DSO MC.[32]

Although the APL was promptly increased in size and reorganised into battalions, a number of company commander posts were retained for RAF Regiment officers who thus continued to serve with the APL. As events progressed, the APL subsequently changed its name to the Federal Regular Army (FRA) before becoming the fully independent South Arabian Army (SAA).

With these organisational changes, and the British Army's deployment to Aden, 20 Wing (58 and 66 Squadrons) of the RAF Regiment, based at RAF Khormaksar, was disbanded in 1957. It was not until the terrorist threat emerged in the State of Aden in the 1960s that the RAF Regiment was to return to Aden where it remained until the final British withdrawal in 1967.

The Royal Air Force Regiment (Malaya)

The decision to form a third locally-enlisted ground defence force in the Far East was based on the unbalanced home/overseas tour ratios which resulted from the post-war deployment pattern of RAF Regiment units – and the economic advantages which accrued from using cheaper locally-enlisted personnel to replace British personnel who cost more to maintain on overseas tours of duty. The imbalance between home and overseas service for Regiment airmen elsewhere was, nevertheless, to be a continuing problem for many years as roulement tasks regularly arose to disrupt almost every attempt to redress the balance between time spent in the UK and overseas.

An Order-in-Council, signed by HM King George VI, established the RAF Regiment (Malaya) in April 1947 as a part of the Royal Air Force. In this, it differed fundamentally from the other two locally-enlisted forces which had been established, originally by the British Army, in Iraq and Aden as supplementary military units on the model of the Indian Army, and adapted to the policy of air control. For example, the native officers and NCOs in Iraq and Aden ranked below their British counterparts, messed and lived separately from them and spoke their own languages on duty.

Conversely, the RAF Regiment (Malaya) was established to provide locally-raised RAF Regiment squadrons to fulfil the Regiment's airfield defence roles in the Far East. The Malay officers and senior NCOs of the RAF Regiment (Malaya) had equal status with their British counterparts and were full members of the RAF officers' and sergeants' messes on the stations on which their units were based. English was the daily language of the RAF Regiment (Malaya) – although attached British officers were expected to be proficient in Malay as part of their understanding of the culture of the officers and airmen under their command – and Malay officers and NCOs attended training and qualification courses in the UK – where they received a local overseas allowance to compensate them for their lower rates of pay!

The other main difference was that only ethnic Malays were recruited into the RAF Regiment (Malaya), despite the fact that there was a large Chinese element – and a less numerous Indian one – in the overall population. There were, at that time, overwhelming military advantages in maintaining this policy – for which the British Army's Malay Regiment (later the Royal Malay Regiment) had set the precedent both before and after the war.

The RAF Regiment (Malaya) was established with an authorised strength of 1,054 all ranks and its Depot (including the training school) was formed at Kuala Lumpur in 1947. The first two squadrons – 91 and 92 Rifle – were declared operational there in January and April 1948 respectively. The Depot moved to Sembawang, on Singapore Island, in May 1948 where the remaining three squadrons – 93, 94 and 95 Rifle – achieved operational status between May 1948 and January 1949. The Depot moved again in August 1949 – this time to Changi – and was joined by the RAF Regiment (Malaya) Wing Headquarters in April 1952.

The outbreak of the communist insurgency inspired by the (almost entirely Chinese) Malayan People's Liberation Army in 1948 drew the RAF Regiment (Malaya) into the military operations of the "Emergency" from its beginning until it ended in 1960. 91 Squadron set the pattern in June 1948 when it began anti-terrorist operations in Johore as part of the Army brigade responsible for that area, and it was succeeded by the other squadrons in turn – until its own turn came round again. The Brigade of Gurkhas and the Royal Malay Regiment were the only other units to establish an unending sequence of operations in the jungles of Malaya over the

A sergeant of the RAF Regiment (Malaya) in ceremonial uniform.

12-year period and the RAF Regiment (Malaya) was recognised, with them, as having the greatest accumulated experience of this gruelling type of warfare. Although the deep jungle afforded protection for the communist terrorists (CTs) whose aim was to avoid pitched battles in favour of soft targets, the squadrons killed, wounded and captured CTs in a series of operations. They suffered casualties themselves, but both British and Malayan decorations for gallantry were awarded to individual officers and airmen in recognition of their achievements.

Despite this regular commitment to internal security operations with the Army, the squadrons were required to maintain their primary role for the ground defence of the RAF's major bases in Malaya, Hong Kong and Singapore. When the Joint Intelligence Committee reviewed the likely threats to the Far East Air Force in 1954, it was decided that low level air defence would be needed against the possibility of air attack on RAF airfields in Singapore and Malaya. 96 Squadron was formed at Changi in January 1955 and a programme of LAA training was introduced at the depot to convert 92, 95 and 96 Squadrons to the use of 40mm Bofors guns in the LAA role. At the same time, 91, 93 and 94 Squadrons were re-equipped as field squadrons to enhance their ground defence capabilities.

As Malaya and Singapore moved towards independence, the reduction in the RAF's presence in those countries reduced the need for the RAF Regiment (Malaya). Its squadrons were progressively disbanded until the force disappeared with the demise of No.94 Squadron in July 1961.

The redundant officers and airmen of the RAF Regiment (Malaya) were readily absorbed into the Malayan Army and the Royal Malayan Air Force, where many achieved distinguished second careers – due largely to the excellent training and experience which they had gained in serving as part of the RAF Regiment. Although they had done much more than make a continuing contribution to the defeat of the MPLA and the communist insurrection, that part was recognised in the official history of the Emergency by the comment "almost continuously for nearly eleven years…the RAF Regiment (Malaya) had played a valuable role in providing extra troops to assist the Security Forces in the innumerable tasks which arose in combined operations against the terrorists."[33]

World Wide Tasks

For a force whose existence was continually under threat, and which had been reduced to two wing headquarters and ten squadrons world-wide,[34] the RAF Regiment was in great demand at the sharp edge of the Royal Air Force around the world. The UK-based strategic reserve[35] was committed to a series of reinforcement exercises in overseas theatres as well as being deployed to Northern Ireland as and when the IRA threat to RAF stations increased.

Crises seldom arise singly and in 1961 2 Squadron was on standby to reinforce RAF Gatow at the time of the "Checkpoint Charlie" confrontation with the Russians in Berlin when the Iraqi government issued threats against Kuwait and a bomb destroyed an RAF aircraft at Muharraq, in Bahrain. As the only RAF Regiment unit which was available to meet unexpected contingencies at that time, 2 Squadron was deployed to Bahrain instead of Berlin, and when both crises were resolved the squadron returned to the United Kingdom and began its conversion to a fully-parachute trained unit.

In 1963 the armies of the three former British dependencies in East Africa mutinied and 37 Squadron was flown from Aden to secure the airhead in Tanzania from which the Royal Marines mounted the operations which quelled the mutinies. Later in the same year the simmering antagonism between the Greek and Turkish communities erupted into open violence in Nicosia and – when there was a danger that the Turks would gain the upper hand – President Makarios appealed to the British government for military intervention to restore the situation.

The officers and NCOs of 3 Wing were serving Christmas lunch to their airmen at RAF Akrotiri when the order was given to move to Nicosia. Within two hours the entire wing, fully-armed, was on the move, by air and road, to RAF Nicosia. OC 3 Wing established his headquarters in the Ledra Palace Hotel and with orders to separate the warring communities, began intensive patrolling to carry out this difficult task while Cypriots were still exchanging fire with one another – often with scant regard for the Union flags draped over British vehicles which happened to come between them. When the situation had been stabilised, and the Greeks and Turks had been forced into their respective enclaves, Wing Commander Hobden deployed his force along the line which had been marked out – using green chinagraph pencil – on the large-scale town map in the Joint Army/RAF Headquarters on the island. The "Green Line" thus established in 1963 still exists today as the boundary which divides the city of Nicosia between Greek and Turk. The Chief Justice of Cyprus – a Turkish Cypriot – commented subsequently that it was a remarkable achievement, which only the British would have attempted, let alone succeeded in resolving.

3 Wing RAF Regiment (which, had it been a composite Army organisation, would undoubtedly have been named "Hobforce" after its commander) was expanded to include no fewer than five RAF Regiment squadrons[36], two armoured car troops from 14/20 Hussars, a battery of 2nd Royal Horse Artillery and a company of 1st Bn Sherwood Foresters. When the situation stabilised, the force was dispersed and on leaving the Ledra Palace Hotel OC 3 Wing was presented with a bill for C£2,413.175 for accommodation – which he declined to pay on the grounds that, as the President of Cyprus had requested the British intervention, the account should be sent to the presidential palace.[37]

Flying Officer GR Lee and his flight of 34 Squadron had been moved by air from Akrotiri to Nicosia on Christmas Day and he soon found himself and his men carrying out a wide range of duties, ranging from patrolling the streets, dispersing mobs, clearing improvised roadblocks, retrieving hostages taken from one community by the other and recovering civilian dead and wounded from various parts of the city. For this latter task, his vehicles carried the Red Cross as well as the Union flags which they had displayed prominently since their arrival. However, the Red Cross flag meant that the Regiment officers and airmen in the vehicles which flew it had to be unarmed – an order which the gunners were reluctant to obey. However, once Flying Officer Lee had found, and removed, the sub-machine guns hidden in their vehicles by his airmen, the Landrovers started to bring back the bodies of the men, women and children who were the victims of this frenzied inter-communal violence.

From Nicosia 34 Squadron was ordered to move north to Kyrenia where fighting had broken out between Greeks and Turks. When the Regiment column reached the pass where the road wound through the Kyrenia mountains it was brought to a halt by a road

block manned by Turkish irregulars, armed to the teeth and in no
mood to let the British reach Kyrenia and stop the fighting. As
negotiations progressed the Turks were reinforced by larger armed
groups and an impasse was reached. Despite the orders which the
column commander received by radio from higher authority to fight
his way through to Kyrenia, common sense prevailed. The Turkish
commander was told that if the road block was still in place at dawn,
it would be destroyed by the Regiment, supported by the armoured
cars and artillery which were following from Nicosia. This face-saving
solution enabled the Turks to back down during the hours of darkness,
thus avoiding unnecessary bloodshed and political confrontation, and
the column rolled on along an empty road to Kyrenia the next
morning.[38]

When, some weeks later, it was reported that the Greeks were
building improvised tanks by cladding bulldozers with armour plate,
the deployment of a Regiment LAA squadron's 40mm L70 Bofors
guns loaded with armour-piercing ammunition, at strategic points
along the Green Line, had an immediate effect in removing that
particular threat to peace.

One of the valuable lessons which came out of this operation
was that a civilian population which had, as a result of prolonged
anti-British activity, come to regard the Army as a hostile force, more
readily accepted the intervention of RAF ground forces whom they
considered to be neutral and impartial. Accordingly, the RAF
Regiment squadrons in Cyprus had few difficulties in enforcing the
separation of the two communities and were able to establish the
basis of a peace which United Nations forces have since been able to
maintain.

In 1965 political progress in southern Africa was disrupted by
the unilateral declaration of independence (UDI) by the government
of Southern Rhodesia. This was the result of the dissolution of the
federation of that country with Northern Rhodesia and Nyasaland
following the British government's grant of independence to those
two former colonies – but not to Southern Rhodesia, which was ruled
by a white minority government. Northern Rhodesia (renamed
Zambia) feared a military intervention by Southern Rhodesia – which
had the only air force in the three states – and appealed to Britain for
military support. This was another delicate problem for Britain, which

had no wish to become embroiled in a colonial war in Africa, but it was resolved by deploying airfield defence forces (ie the RAF Regiment) to defend the Zambian airport at Lusaka from any attempt at attack by the Rhodesian air force. The first squadron – 51 (which had only been re-formed in late 1964) was en route to Zambia by air within 24 hours of the proclamation of UDI.

The Impact of National Service

In the immediate post-war years British foreign policies were buffeted by a series of unwelcome – and often unforeseen events, most of which had an impact on defence policies. Despite the intended run-down of military bases overseas, the commitments which remained – as well as those which subsequently arose – demanded military forces which were much larger than those which might have been sustained by an all-regular Army and Air Force, for whom conscription – or National Service – was deemed to be the only means of maintaining the required manning levels. (This was not the case for the Royal Navy, which was almost entirely manned to establishment by regular officers and ratings).

Thus between 1946 and 1962 (when the last National Serviceman returned to civilian life) a large training machine had to be provided to produce officers and men who were becoming productive members of the respective Services at about the time they were due for discharge after serving for two years – or less in some periods. It was a costly structure, which required a large number of experienced officers and NCOs to run it, but it did supply the manpower which was needed once the system was operating effectively – which was not until 1948 or 1949.

All basic training for RAF entrants was carried out at Recruit Training Centres, from where those airmen selected for the trade of Gunner (Group V) went on to the Depot at Catterick, where the Training Wing also ran courses for officers and NCOs. At Dumfries a separate training school for airmen was established to deal with the expansion of the Regiment front line after the Korean War. LAA gunnery training for officers, NCOs and airmen took place at Watchet, so in this period the RAF Regiment had three large training schools in being to maintain the professional skills of its wings and squadrons.

Ceremonial

The Band of the RAF Regiment was established in 1942, within the framework of the Royal Air Force's Music Services. This ensured that training and manning were controlled by HQ Music Services under the Organising Director of Music for the RAF and left the Band to work for the RAF Regiment without any of the specialised problems which the Regiment would otherwise have had to manage – without the necessary specialist skills. It was based at the RAF Regiment Depot from 1946 onwards and carried out its duties both as the band of the Corps and a regional band in the North-East of England.

In 1949 the Regiment abandoned the khaki battledress which all ranks had worn as the everyday working dress since 1942 and wore RAF No.2 dress – the blue equivalent of battledress – instead. For training and operations in the field, the early form of khaki combat clothing was used.

On 17th March 1953 Her Majesty The Queen presented her Colour to the RAF Regiment at Buckingham Palace in the presence of the Commandant General and senior RAF officers. The parade warrant officer was, not unexpectedly, Warrant Officer DA Gourd MBE.

As national service provided an adequate flow of Gunners for the RAF Regiment, a Demonstration Flight was formed at the Depot with the aim of assisting in the large training task which was in progress at the time. However, with Flight Lieutenant RC Gahan in charge, and with WO DA Gourd as his warrant officer, the Demonstration Flight soon became a hand-picked and elite unit which continually set new standards in everything it touched. When perfection had been attained in drill, the flight commander and his WO devised a sequence of continuity drill which has developed to the present day and has become a feature of RAF Regiment drill displays.

When the end of national service forced the disbandment of the Royal Air Force's own Ceremonial Drill Unit, the Regiment had little difficulty in manning the new Queen's Colour Squadron (QCS) of the Royal Air Force. Based at RAF Uxbridge, the squadron had responsibility for The Queen's Colour for the Royal Air Force in the United Kingdom as well as being the lead unit for all RAF ceremonial.

It was not long before the QCS established a national reputation, not only for the high standard of its ceremonial parades but also for its unique form of continuity drill – for which it features in the Guinness Book of Records. It was also responsible for the introduction of the stable belt into RAF Regiment – and later RAF – informal dress. When the first RAF Regiment commander of the QCS – Squadron Leader Peter Hutchins[39] – took the QCS to Portugal as part of a tri-Service ceremonial detachment, he was dismayed to see how much smarter the Royal Marines and Brigade of Guards appeared in shirt-sleeve order because of their stable belts. Back in England, preparing for a QCS detachment to the USA in the following summer, he chanced to see a Royal Air Force stable belt in the window of a military outfitters in the Strand. He immediately ordered 150 – and QCS attracted considerable comment from the Americans for their smart appearance in shirt-sleeve order in Madison Square Garden in the heat of a New York summer.

The Queen's Colour Squadron mounts a Royal Guard of Honour for HRH The Duchess of Gloucester.

Meanwhile, the Demonstration Flight at the Depot was renamed the RAF Regiment Colour Guard – and continued to set high standards for drill and ceremonial, albeit on a rather smaller scale and with a lower profile.

Rockapes and the Regiment

The term "rockape" came into use within the RAF in the 1950s as a disparaging term for Regiment officers and airmen – who quickly adapted it as a title of distinction, thus turning the tables on those who had intended to label them with a derogatory nickname. Since then, a wide variety of theories have been advanced as to how and why this term originated, possibly the most bizarre being an attempt to link the RAF Regiment with the Rock of Gibraltar and the Barbary Apes which are maintained there by the British Army. In reality, the truth is simpler than the fiction.

In November 1952, two RAF Regiment officers serving with the APL at Dhala, in the Western Aden Protectorate, decided to amuse themselves by going out to shoot some of the baboons (locally referred to as rock apes) which came down from the mountains in the cool of the evening to forage for food in the plain – and to throw stones at the Levy camp. Each officer took a Service rifle and ammunition from the squadron armoury and set off on foot to look for baboons. Unwisely, they went their separate ways and in the semi-darkness one of the hunters saw a movement on a rocky outcrop some distance away. Taking careful aim, he fired and was delighted to see his target fall – but horrified when he reached the spot to find his colleague lying with a bullet wound in his chest.

Flight Lieutenant Mason was still alive, although the bullet had passed within inches of his heart, and thanks to swift medical attention – including an overnight road journey by a medical team from Aden, and a casevac by air at dawn the following day – he survived to make a good recovery before returning to active duty several months later.[40]

Although the incident itself did not gain much publicity – death or injury to Servicemen in far-flung outposts of the Empire were common enough at that time not to warrant headlines in the British press – a statement made at the subsequent board of inquiry did. Under questioning, the firer of the almost-fatal shot said, in mitigation

of his actions, that his target had "looked just like a rock ape" in the half-light. This remark reverberated throughout the messes on RAF stations wherever members of the Regiment were serving, and it was not long before the term was in general use. But as a burly LAC gunner said to a penguin (the Regiment term for an RAF tradesman) in the NAAFI soon afterwards "you can call me a rockape – but make sure that you smile when you do!"

The 'rockape' mascot of the APL Armoured Car Squadron.

The Achievements of the Immediate Post-War Years

There is no doubt that the National Service intakes served the RAF Regiment well in these troubled days and indeed without them the front-line squadrons would have been unable to carry out their many overseas tasks. However, the other side of the coin was that compulsory service deterred many young men from enlisting as regulars, and with only a small element of long-serving regular junior officers and airmen, and a continuing turnover of the majority of personnel within the timescale of a normal overseas tour, the experience levels of squadrons was usually well below the desired level.

The instability in the Middle East, which lasted throughout this period, made it the most important area for the RAF Regiment until the emergence of the Cold War with the Soviet Bloc concentrated attention on Europe. Wherever RAF airfields and installations were under threat, Regiment squadrons were in demand – to the extent that there were occasions when a single squadron had its flights deployed hundreds, and sometimes thousands, of miles apart.

The challenges of training and leading locally-enlisted forces in the Middle and Far East was a stimulating – and rewarding experience for those RAF Regiment officers and NCOs who were fortunate enough to serve in the RAF Levies Iraq, the Aden Protectorate Levies and the RAF Regiment (Malaya). Sadly, these opportunities ended with the disbandment of two of these forces, and the transfer of the third to Army control – although the retention of some RAF Regiment squadron leader posts in the new battalions of the Aden Protectorate Levies/Federal Regular Army enabled this link to be sustained to the benefit of both parties.[41]

As an example of the wide variety of tasks and postings which faced a Regiment gunner in this period, Corporal Renshaw's service between 1952 and 1957 can be considered as fairly typical. Enlisting on a regular five-year engagement at the age of 18 in 1952, he went to RAF Bridgnorth for recruit training, after which he was posted to RAF Dumfries for his RAF Regiment basic gunner course. At the end of that, he was selected to attend a Junior Gunner Instructors' Course at Catterick as a potential NCO, from where he was posted to 194 Squadron at RAF Ouston. With his flight commander, Pilot Officer Anderson[42], he formed part of the detachment which took part in the Coronation procession in London. Not long afterwards he was posted to 66 Squadron in Aden – in those days a long sea voyage instead of a flight by RAF or chartered transport aircraft. Within weeks he was detached to Kenya to defend forward airstrips used by Harvards of 1340 Flight RAF and the Air Wing of the Kenya Police Reserve. Three months later he was back in Aden, carrying out internal security drills in the Colony and spending time on detachments on the Yemen border at Mukeiras in support of the Aden Protectorate Levies. Tour-expired in 1956, he returned to the UK to become an

NCO instructor at No.5 School of Recruit Training at West Kirby and completed a qualifying course at the Joint School of Chemical Warfare at Winterbourne Gunner before returning to civilian life after what he described as "five happy years".[43]

The Regiment, usually understrength, often under-equipped and almost always over-committed, continued to serve wherever it was needed by the Royal Air Force and to provide the essential elements of defence, security and protection so that the Service's primary role could continue without interference to its operational bases. But times were changing, and the RAF Regiment would have to change with them.

Notes

[1] Air Chief Marshal Sir Edgar Ludlow-Hewitt GCB GBE CMG DSO MC (1886-1973) Inspector-General 1940-45

[2] See Chapter 3 Note 5

[3] AC5(46) 1 Feb 46 (PRO)

[4] See Chapter 2 Note 15

[5] RAF Regiment Association (Birmingham Branch) *Newsletter* No.48 – July 1992

[6] 1 (from 1300), 4 (from 1304), 6 (from 1306) and 16 (from 1316) Wing Headquarters

7   3 (from 2757) and 4 (from 2777) Armoured Car Squadrons, 51 (from 2713), 54 (from 2724), 55 (from 2750), 56 (from 2770), 57 (from 2786), 59 (from 2798), 60 (from 2827), 61 (from 2829), 63 (from 2864), and 64 (from 2897) Rifle Squadrons

8   19 (from 1319) and 20 (from 1320) Wing Headquarters

9   1 (from 2701) and 2 (from 2702) Armoured Car Squadrons, 52 (from 2717), 53 (from 2721), 8 (from 2778), 62 (from 2864), 65 (from 2898) and 66 (from 2899) Squadrons

10 4001 Flight RAF Regiment

11 1307, 1308, 1323, 1324, 1325, 1326, 1327, 1329, 1330 and 1331 Wing Headquarters

12 2706, 2708, 2739, 2743, 2746, 2748, 2759, 2802, 2810, 2837, 2846, 2852, 2854, 2886, 2896, 2941, 2942, 2943, 2944, 2945, 2946, 2958, 2959, 2960, 2961, 2962, 2963, 2964, 2965, 2966, 2967, 2968, 2970, 2971, 2972 and 2981 Squadrons

13 2501, 2502, 2504, 2602, 2603, 2604 (later renumbered 2600), 2605, 2608, 2609, 2611, 2612 and 2616 Squadrons

14 Lee – *Wings in the Sun*, p20

15 Ib p21

16 Mr AM Ferrey – letter 11 January 1996

17 Mr RF Wilcock – letter 14 November 1995

18 19 Wing HQ with 2 Armoured Car and 52 & 62 Rifle Squadrons to Amman; 20 Wing HQ with 58 & 66 Rifle Squadrons to Egypt and Aden. 1 Armoured Car Squadron was disbanded, as were 53 & 65 Rifle Squadrons

19 Mr RS Brett – letter 23 November 1995

20 Report on the Evacuation of the RAF from Palestine by Air Vice-Marshal WL Dawson CB CBE DSO, later Air Chief Marshal Sir Walter Dawson KCB CBE DSO (1902-94)

21 Group Captain MF Hobden OBE – letter 20 May 1996

22 2, 5 & 8 Wing Headquarters

23 26, 27, 28, 34 & 37 Squadrons

24 Mr DR Walker – letter 4 October 1995

25 Lee – op cit p104

26 27, 34 & 37 Squadrons

27 Lee – op cit p59

28 I am grateful to Squadron Leader EJ Gee, who served in the RAF Levies (Iraq) and was sometime Whipper-in to the Royal Exodus Hunt, for this information

29 See "So-called 'Non-Operational' Gallantry Awards" – an article by Sqn Ldr

NG Tucker in the Journal of the Orders & Medals Research Society, Vol 35 No 2 (Summer 1996)

[30] AIR8/1884 (PRO)

[31] Lee – *Flight from the Middle East* p144

[32] I am indebted to Air Commodore GES Bumstead for his very detailed record of the events which occurred while he was commanding 2 Wing of the APL in 1956/58

[33] HMSO – *The Malayan Emergency 1948-60* p145

[34] 3 & 33 Wing HQs; 1, 2, 15, 16, 26, 27, 34, 37, 48 & 63 Squadrons

[35] HQ 33 Wing with 15, 16 and 48 Squadrons

[36] 26, 28 & 34 Squadrons, reinforced by 27 and 16 Squadrons from the UK

[37] Group Captain MF Hobden OBE – letter 20 May 1996

[38] Lee – *From Wales to West Sussex* pp51/52

[39] Later Group Captain P Hutchins OBE, Commandant RAF Regiment Depot 1972-1974

[40] AIR24/2241 (PRO)

[41] De Butts – *Now the Dust Has Settled* p149

[42] Later Air Commodore DD Anderson MBE (Director RAF Regiment 1983-87)

[43] Mr T Renshaw – letter 6 May 1995

10

The Uncertain Future

Qui desiderat pacem, praeparet bellum. (Let him who desires peace, prepare for war).

Vegetius, 4th Century AD.

This makes it even more clear than ever that the overriding consideration must be to prevent war rather than prepare for it.
Statement on British Defence Policy, 1957

The Beginnings of the Cold War

As the political differences between East and West grew in the post-war years, tension between the two blocs widened until it became obvious that there was an increasing risk of war between the USSR and its allies on the one hand and the USA and the countries of western Europe on the other. This situation was exacerbated by the Russian blockade of the American, British and French zones in Berlin, and later by the invasion of South Korea by the North Korean army. The formation of the North Atlantic Treaty Organisation (NATO) provided the framework for a reappraisal of British defence policy which would operate within the framework of a multi-national alliance in peace time.

As early as March 1945 the War Office had written to the Air Ministry[1] to make it clear that the defence of airfields, whether in the United Kingdom or abroad, was a matter in which the Army reserved its right to influence post-war policy. So effective was the War Office in managing this that in 1950 the Chiefs of Staff had "agreed that the Army should be responsible for the LAA defence of airfields and ancillary units at home and overseas, with the exception that the RAF should provide this defence at certain overseas stations outside an Army LAA defence layout."[2] It is difficult to comprehend why, within five years of the ending of a war in which the Army had rarely been able to provide adequate forces for the defence of RAF airfields and installations, the Air Ministry should have accepted, without question, the proposal to reinstate a failed policy.

However, in the following year the War Office admitted that the regular Army could not provide LAA defence for airfields in Germany and the Middle East and suggested that the RAF should provide its own LAA defence there in peace-time.[3] Nevertheless, the Army insisted on retaining responsibility for these tasks in war – ie by deploying Territorial Army LAA batteries to RAF stations at home and overseas after mobilisation. The Air Staff recalled having heard these proposals some twelve years earlier and the Chief of Air Staff (CAS) was deeply concerned at the prospect of a re-run of the events of 1940.

CAS returned to the Chiefs of Staff Committee with a forcefully-worded paper[4] pointing out that the risk of low-level attack was greatest in the opening phases of a war – before reserve Army units could be mobilised and deployed – and that among the many advantages of the RAF providing its own LAA defences was that of economy, in that RAF Regiment units represented a lesser cost to the Defence vote than those provided by the Army. His most telling point, however, was that the Polish Air Force had been destroyed on the ground in 1939 by the failure of the Polish Army to provide adequate defence for its airfields. As a result the Polish ground forces had to fight without air support – and were, inevitably, defeated. In fact, a more pertinent British example would have been the campaign in Malaya and the East Indies in 1941-42, but Supreme Headquarters Allied Powers Europe (SHAPE) was already using the Polish debacle as its justification for airfield defence measures within NATO and the Air Ministry saw merit in linking its own arguments to the NATO case.

The Air Staff made it clear that the RAF was not prepared to run the risk of a Polish situation arising in a British context in a future war and CAS was adamant that, in the absence of dedicated regular Army units assigned to airfield defence tasks in peace, it would be essential for the RAF to provide the defences which it required from its own resources. He stressed that to ignore the Soviet threat would be to risk losing both air superiority for the RAF and air support for the Army at a very early stage in a future war.

Apart from maintaining a heightened state of alert on its bases in Germany, the Regiment squadrons were not directly involved in the Berlin airlift of 1948/49. It was a massive air transport operation from the American, British and French zones of occupation into their respective sectors of Berlin – which were separated by the Russian occupation zone, in which Berlin was situated. The one exception among the Regiment squadrons was Squadron Leader Alex Gordon's 3 Armoured Car Squadron, which was based at Fassberg but had a flight detachment at RAF Gatow, in the British sector of Berlin, where the station boundary bordered on the Russian zone of occupation. Pilot Officer Fisher took his flight – by air – to Gatow to relieve the squadron personnel who had been trapped in Berlin by the blockade, and to defend the airfield with three very tired and elderly Humber armoured cars. It was a cat-and-mouse game of constant patrolling and close encounters with the tanks of a Russian armoured division. Given the disparity of armament and numbers between the flight of British armoured cars and the regiments of Russian battle tanks, diplomacy played a major part in resolving the confrontations which arose from time to time.[5]

In 1949 four field squadrons – 59, 61, 55 and 64 – had been converted to the LAA role to provide LAA defence at RAF Celle and RAF Gutersloh in Germany, and were renumbered 17, 18, 19 and 20 respectively. However, following the reappraisal of the policy for the defence of RAF stations, and the introduction of NATO criteria for the defence of NATO airfields, a further 28 RAF Regiment squadrons were formed, equipped, trained and deployed between June 1951 and December 1952.[6] Although national service provided the necessary manpower without much difficulty, it was an extremely large training task to complete within the allotted timescale. Even more difficult was the requirement to recruit and train the officers and NCOs who were to lead this greatly enlarged force.

At the end of that period, the total strength of the RAF Regiment was 720 officers and 7,196 airmen. In addition, the Regiment's order of battle included two wings (eight squadrons) of the RAF Levies (Iraq), three wings (ten squadrons) of the Aden Protectorate Levies and one wing (five squadrons) of the RAF Regiment (Malaya), representing a further 4,000 locally-enlisted officers and men, with a sprinkling of RAF Regiment officers and NCOs.

In 1953 the Chiefs of Staff had accepted the need for a suitable armoured vehicle to equip RAF Regiment squadrons in order to enhance their ground defence capabilities. The only vehicle available for this role at that time was the Land Rover but – unfortunately – replacing its aluminium bodywork with steel armour plate proved too much for its mobility and the project was abandoned.[7]

In the same year the Air Council agreed to provide a better anti-aircraft gun for the Regiment's LAA squadrons and it was decided to follow the Army's example and introduce the 40mm Bofors L70 gun – with an associated fire control radar named Yellow Fever – as the replacement for the outdated L60 Bofors equipment. Financial stringency prevented a complete re-equipment but plans were made to purchase 230 L70 guns, with a proportion of the fire control radars, to replace 50 per cent of the Regiment's existing LAA guns.[8] The new LAA gun eventually entered RAF Regiment service in 1957.

The British nomenclature for anti-aircraft defence weapons and units had undergone a series of changes since 1939 – and was to continue to change as new concepts were introduced. "Anti-aircraft" (AA) was used by the RAF to describe automatic weapons up to 20mm calibre (usually designed for aircraft use) employed in the ground-to-air role. The introduction of larger calibre weapons, categorised as anti-aircraft artillery, led to the designation "Light Anti-Aircraft" (LAA) for units using such equipment. By the 1960s this had progressed through "Light Air Defence" (LAD) – as used by the Army – to the agreed joint-service term "Low Level Air Defence" (LLAD). Standardisation with NATO terminology in the 1970s replaced this with "Short Range Air Defence" (SHORAD) as the description used for 30mm to 40mm guns and for missile systems such as Rapier. However, the long-established American terminology "anti-aircraft artillery", abbreviated to "triple-A", remained in colloquial use – particularly by aircrew.

1954 was to be the high water mark of the post-war RAF Regiment; from then onwards a series of political decisions and economic pressures, operating either together or separately, progressively reduced British influence – and deployments – overseas and led to reductions in the RAF front-line at home. For one reason or another, Regiment wings and squadrons were to be disbanded to

match the perceptions of changing or disappearing threats and
consequent reductions in the Defence budget. All too often it appeared
that the levels of presumed military threats to national security were
adjusted to accord with the resources which the government of the
day was prepared to allocate to the Defence Vote.

Reappraisals of Defence Policy

Among the many problems which faced British governments
in this unsettled period were those of reconciling vestigial imperial
responsibilities, and the desire to be seen as a great power, with the
economic realities of trying to balance the national budget which
had to sustain an impressive international posture with declining
resources. The unsuccessful attempt to restore British influence in
the Middle East by military intervention in the Suez Canal zone in
1956 was instrumental in eroding British political and economic
credibility on a world-wide basis. It therefore became essential to
formulate a policy which would reduce expenditure on defence while
creating the impression of greater military strength in the international
arena. The 1957 Defence review sought to provide the solution to
the intractable problem of spending less but getting more in return.

NATO's original aim in 1949 had been to respond to any Soviet
aggression by a conventional response appropriate to the size of the
incident. Although the invasion of South Korea was far beyond
NATO's geographical area of interest, the United States and its allies
had observed similar precepts in matching North Korean (and later
Chinese) force levels, even though these had strained the West's
military resources. The plea by General MacArthur for the release of
nuclear weapons to defeat the North Korean and Chinese armies had
been rejected on political grounds by President Truman. However,
by the mid-1950s it had become increasingly attractive to NATO's
military planners to suppose that the threat of massive retaliation,
involving the large-scale use of nuclear weapons, was the only realistic
means of deterring further Soviet expansion.

Apart from anything else, NATO governments saw an
immediate advantage in opting for the tripwire nuclear deterrent,
which promised to be cheaper than maintaining conventional forces
large enough to match the Russians man for man and tank for tank.
Not only was this appealing to a British government facing an

economic crisis, but it also assuaged that body of opinion which believed that international disarmament was the proper course to pursue – and that this might be the first step. There were certainly others who objected to the new policy as they were convinced that unilateral nuclear disarmament by Great Britain was a real option for peace and should be embarked upon to set an example which other nations would have no choice but to follow. These were, of course, the thoughts which had led to the League of Nations in the 1920s – and world war in the 1930s. What was conveniently overlooked in this debate was that there would always be a need for conventional forces to deal with the many subsidiary threats which would face the United Kingdom in the years ahead.

In 1956 the RAF was already studying the implications of a new defence policy which included the possibility of economies resulting from the disbandment of the RAF Regiment because there was no longer any need for LAA defence. Indeed, the members of the Air Council believed that the Army would have no requirement for LAA defence either, but accepted that in this, at least, the Army was not as forward thinking as the RAF. In the interim, the Air Ministry was prepared to offer the new L70 Bofors guns which were on order for the RAF Regiment to the Army.[9]

The Sandys' Axe

The 1957 British Defence White Paper used three premises to introduce dramatic changes in defence policy: it predicated the phasing out of manned aircraft and the introduction of missile systems, and stated that any future war in Europe would involve the use of weapons of mass destruction from the very outset. Conventional military forces, which no longer had a predominant place in the British defence structure in this concept of global war, were to be reduced, if not eliminated, to make way for the new technology.

As far as the RAF Regiment was concerned, its role in Europe disappeared overnight and all nine wing headquarters and 24 squadrons in RAF Germany were disbanded by the end of 1957. A further two wing headquarters and four squadrons were summarily removed from the order of battle in the Middle East, leaving a rump of only four wing headquarters and 12 squadrons[10] in the United Kingdom and overseas.

The AOC-in-C 2TAF was Air Marshal the Earl of Bandon whose war experience made him sceptical of the prediction that low-level air attack on RAF airfields and radar systems was a thing of the past. He made a forceful case for the retention of LAA defences on his airfields in Germany in a letter to CAS[11] but the best offer he received in return was that the guns of the disbanded Regiment squadrons might be left in situ to be manned in an emergency by station personnel. If nothing else, this reinforced the case for politicians, civil servants and serving officers alike to be reminded of Douglas Evill's 1937 dictum on the futility of not preparing for war in times of peace.

Defence policies are, by their very nature, driven by politicians responsible to the electorate – but ministers are constrained by the advice of the Foreign Office and the resources of the Treasury. Given the national tendency to under-estimate an enemy's capabilities and intentions, it is hardly surprising that most wars have begun badly for the British. Even worse, however, is the national flair for forgetting the salutary lessons which were learned in defeat once these are overtaken by the euphoria of victory. Nevertheless, the allocation of limited resources posed the Air Staff with difficult choices which forced valuable RAF assets to be sacrificed in order to balance budgets. The question was, would the RAF Regiment have to be discarded as well?

Of the options which the Chiefs of Staff had already considered, the retention of RAF Regiment LAA squadrons had been rejected as too costly for the needs of the RAF. The second option – to pass the task to the Army – had been promptly turned down by the General Staff as being an unacceptable additional commitment in view of the reductions which the Army had suffered. The first option – to dispense with the low level air defence of RAF airfields and installations was therefore glossed over by the reassuring statement that "there is no global war requirement for LAA guns either now or in the future. In limited war, there may be such a requirement in the Middle East only."[12]

However, as the author of the official study into RAF policies of that period noted "the thinking behind the intention to disband the RAF Regiment is an example of an over-rigorous application of the logic of deterrence and a failure to appreciate the value of the

Regiment if the RAF was to play its part in peacetime policy and internal security operations overseas, especially as the Army, which might otherwise have assumed the RAF Regiment's duties, was to be much reduced in strength."[13]

In fact, the RAF Regiment managed to survive this particular crisis, albeit at the cost of large-scale redundancies among its most experienced officers and NCOs. The training task was drastically reduced at the Depot and the LAA Gunnery School at Watchet was closed. The very limited requirement for the LAA training of Regiment officers and NCOs was to be transferred to the Royal School of Artillery at Larkhill.

The other major casualty of this sweeping review was the Royal Auxiliary Air Force which was "stood down" – a euphemism for disbandment. The twelve field squadrons of the Royal Auxiliary Air Force Regiment disappeared, leaving the RAF Regiment with no formed reserve units.

Events in the Real World

The international situation was such that defence policies had to operate at two or more levels: beneath the confrontation between the superpowers which occupied much of diplomatic and military time there were the recurring threats of insurgency, terrorism and minor wars in those areas where the RAF was based, or to which it was deployed in furtherance of HMG's foreign policies. It was therefore inevitable that the defence structures decided upon in Whitehall were not always the most appropriate ones to deal with the actions taken by the Queen's enemies who were intent on pursuing their own agendas, both in the United Kingdom and elsewhere.

Before long the call for RAF Regiment squadrons was heard again: the resurgence of IRA activity in Northern Ireland created threats to the RAF presence in the Province and 15 and 63 Squadrons, followed by 48 and 194 Squadrons, were deployed to RAF Aldergrove and RAF Ballykelly for security and defence duties. The internal security situation in Cyprus then demanded Regiment reinforcements and 63 and 194 Squadrons were redeployed to Cyprus while 16 Squadron was sent to Northern Ireland to fill the gap caused by another unforeseen contingency.

It was now clear that most of the very much smaller RAF

Regiment front line would have to be based in the UK, and deployed overseas to meet emergencies as they arose, rather than by stationing squadrons in overseas theatres. 33 Wing HQ was subsequently based at RAF Felixstowe, with the Strategic Reserve squadrons, to meet these commitments. The Northern Ireland task continued to be met by squadron roulements but in 1959 48 Squadron had to be flown from the UK to the RAF staging post at Gan in the Maldives to deal with an internal security situation until an RAF Regiment presence could be re-established in the Far East.

In order to maximise the effectiveness of the resources of the rifle squadrons, these units were given new scales of MT, radio equipment and light machine guns. Thus instead of relying on 15-cwt and 3-ton trucks for transport, the rifle flights were equipped with Landrovers and radios down to section level, enabling them to operate more flexibly and deploy more rapidly with greater mobility. This reorganisation was marked by reviving the title "Field" for the new squadrons, to distinguish them from their former "Rifle" organisation. In fact, the use of "Field" to describe what was still a "Rifle" structure was a misapplication of the term first used during the war. Field squadrons were the original multi-role units, with an armoured car flight as well as a heavy weapons flight – which sometimes included artillery. It was not until Regiment squadrons were re-equipped with CVR(T) in the 1980s that the description "Field" could properly be used again but they were named "Light Armoured" squadrons instead. Today's "Field" squadrons – with three rifle flights and a medium mortar flight – are more correctly "Rifle" squadrons in the traditional Regiment pattern.

1 and 2 Squadrons were again in the Middle East: 1, which had been among the squadrons disbanded in Germany, was revived by transferring its number to 62 Squadron at RAF El Adem. In 1959 the squadron received its Standard from Air Marshal Sir Hugh Constantine who, as a junior officer, had served in 1 Armoured Car Company before the war. 2 Squadron had been redeployed from Cyprus to Malta in the same year and received its Standard from Air Chief Marshal Sir Hubert Patch at RAF Luqa. These were the first two Standards to be awarded to RAF Regiment squadrons in recognition of 25 years distinguished service – although in both these cases most of that service was as armoured car companies, which

had not been part of the RAF Regiment.

The loss of the RAF Regiment (Malaya) squadrons left no alternative to the long-deferred deployment of RAF Regiment squadrons to the Far East. 1, 15 and 63 Field Squadrons were deployed to FEAF and stationed at Butterworth, Changi and Tengah respectively – in time to take over the Gan roulement from the UK-based 48 Squadron.

On 1st November 1960 The Queen's Colour Squadron of the Royal Air Force had been formed at RAF Uxbridge as an RAF unit with responsibility for RAF ceremonial duties. Manned by Regiment officers and airmen, it was controlled by P1 (Ceremonial) in the Air Ministry, and not by the RAF Regiment staff, although it was to have a war role as an RAF Regiment field squadron, despite its lack of training and equipment for that task.

Airfield Crash/Rescue Fire Services

The RAF Fire Service had developed from a pre-war part-time activity to a post-war professional organisation, but it lacked the dedicated officers and controlling authority which could manage the resources of manpower and equipment efficiently and effectively. Following a review of the situation in 1959 it was decided to make the RAF Regiment responsible for the RAF Fire Services, with the civilian component forming a separate corporate service (the Air Force

Aircraft crash/ rescue firefighting training at the RAF Regiment Depot, Catterick.

Department Fire Service) with its own officers and its training establishment at RAF Manston. The RAF Fire Training School was moved from Sutton-on-Hull to the Regiment Depot at Catterick and all Service firemen were absorbed into the Regiment trade group and wore the RAF Regiment shoulder title. By 1961 the RAF Regiment, with only 37 per cent of its strength of 5,563 airmen dedicated to its primary combat role, was largely an airfield crash/rescue firefighting organisation – with a limited capability for ground and low level air defence tasks superimposed on it.

Nevertheless, RAF Regiment staff officers and station fire officers were instrumental in raising standards throughout the RAF's Fire Service and training, discipline, motivation and morale all improved. NCOs and airmen responded to the knowledge that – at last – they had officers who were directly responsible for their efficiency and who took an interest in their welfare. As in any military organisation, leadership was the most important factor – and the RAF Regiment provided it for the RAF Fire Service.

Nuclear, Biological and Chemical Defence
Passive defence – the aim of which is to mitigate the effects of enemy weapons – became one of the RAF Regiment's responsibilities in the early days of its existence when it was given the task of training all RAF personnel in protection against chemical attack. This included measures for decontaminating aircraft and equipment so that operations could be continued in spite of the hazards produced by chemical warfare agents. The subsequent addition of biological agents, followed by the effects of radioactive fallout from nuclear weapons, produced a composite package of defensive measures known as NBC – for which the Regiment retained responsibility for training all RAF and WRAF personnel. The Joint School of Chemical Warfare became the Defence NBC Centre and was staffed by both Army and RAF Regiment officer and NCO instructors.

When the teams were assembled for the various British series of A-bomb tests ("Antler" and "Buffalo") in Australia and for the subsequent H-bomb test ("Grapple") at Christmas Island in the 1950s, RAF Regiment specialists were included with particular responsibility for radioactive monitoring and decontamination. Thus the first Service personnel to enter the target areas on the ground after the atomic

Harrier operating in the field in an NBC environment.

Tornado aircraft turn-round by ground crew under NBC conditions.

explosions in Australia were Regiment officers and NCOs.

One of the by-products of the introduction of nuclear weapons into service was the formation of a nuclear accident response organisation which could deal with any spill of radioactive material from damaged nuclear weapons. As the Regiment had conclusively proved its expertise in this field during the weapons testing programme, Regiment officers and NCOs formed part of the Special Safety Organisation teams which were instituted to guard against such incidents. Even though none occurred, the requisite premium was duly paid for the insurance policy.

The Campaign for Nuclear Disarmament

The genuine feelings of many individuals who were concerned about the dangers of nuclear war were, unsurprisingly, cultivated by certain groups and secretly funded by others as a means of exerting pressure on the British government to remove what was, in fact, the greatest factor in preserving peace – the nuclear deterrent which stabilised the East-West balance and restrained the Russians from any precipitate action which could have led to war. Mass demonstrations were orchestrated with the aim of attracting wider support and these had obviously to be handled both sympathetically and firmly when they threatened security on RAF airfields.

The task of mobilising and controlling the necessary Service manpower to deal with such attempts to invade RAF property was given to the Commandant General of the RAF Regiment who, with the Provost Marshal of the RAF, organised – when necessary – a mixed force of RAF Regiment squadrons and RAF Police flights under the title of "The Commandant General's Task Force". Discipline, good humour and leadership combined to make the ad hoc force successful in dealing with a large number of demonstrations, which were not always uniformly peaceful on the part of the demonstrators.

More New Tasks for the Regiment

The attempt to maintain a post-war parachute squadron, which had collapsed in 1949, was revived on a firmer basis in 1962 when the Regiment was authorised to have a parachute capability and 2 Squadron was selected for that role. Selection was carried out by the

Army's "P" Company, which was not necessarily the most appropriate system for the RAF Regiment's purpose. "P" Company was designed to eliminate as many candidates as possible from the large number of Army volunteers for the Airborne Forces. On the other hand, the Regiment requirement was to bring as many volunteers as possible – from a much smaller pool of eligible personnel – to the necessary standard for service in a parachute-trained squadron. The muddled thinking which confused this issue resulted in keeping 2 Squadron under-manned, and therefore with a reduced operational capability, until – eventually – a more appropriate system of selection and training under RAF control was instituted.

In the Middle East, and later the Far East, theatre parachute teams were established for emergency operations and these were almost entirely manned by RAF Regiment officers and airmen. This was invaluable in extending the parachuting ethos more widely throughout the Regiment and in creating a pool of experienced parachutists who were available for this role in the UK and overseas.

Another innovation was the establishment of RAF Regiment NCOs and airmen on the strength of squadrons of the short-range transport force. These gunners played a valuable role in carrying out many routine tasks in the helicopter and light transport squadrons as well as providing their own ground defence expertise when the aircraft were deployed in the field. Later, when side-mounted machine guns were carried by helicopters, these were often manned by the Regiment gunners in the squadrons. Similar RAF Regiment detachments were established on Harrier squadrons and the gunners soon became as adept as those in other flying squadrons at refuelling and rearming their aircraft as well as providing the close defence of the sites when deployed in the field.

Although the strengthening of links with flying squadrons was both welcome and important for the Regiment, there were disadvantages in that there was no Regiment officer in charge and training standards were prone to be the first casualty of misemployment on a variety of non-professional tasks. These were not new problems – they had first arisen in the western desert in 1942, and had reappeared on numerous occasions thereafter when the usefulness and versatility of the Regiment gunner proved irresistible to officers of other branches.

Twenty Years On

The twentieth anniversary of the RAF Regiment's formation was marked by a Royal Visit by HRH The Duchess of Gloucester to the Depot on 18th May 1962. The 21st anniversary in the following year was marked by a series of formal and informal occasions at home and overseas, culminating in a parade, at which CAS[14] took the salute, and a subsequent service at the RAF Church of St Clement Danes. With a force level of only two wing headquarters and ten squadrons – rather less than the equivalent of a weak Army brigade containing both infantry and air defence artillery – it was a very appropriate time to pray for better things in the future.

Confrontation in the Far East

The formation of the Federation of Malaysia in 1962 encouraged the Republic of Indonesia to adopt an aggressive attitude towards the newly independent states with the aim of expanding its territory – particularly at the expense of Eastern Malaysia, which shared a common land frontier with Indonesian Borneo. An urgent reappraisal of requirements for the defence of Malaysia against Indonesian "confrontation" resulted in the conversion of 1 and 63 Squadrons to the LAA role and their reinforcement by 26 LAA Squadron from Cyprus. 15 Squadron, which remained a field squadron, had already been involved in the operations which quelled an attempted coup d'etat in the neighbouring state of Brunei.

1, 26 and 63 LAA Squadrons were deployed at Far East Air Force's major airfields on Singapore Island and near Penang where RAF fighter and bomber squadrons, reinforced from the UK, were at readiness to counter any hostile moves by the Indonesian Air Force. Such was the concentration of aircraft on these airfields that the existing 12 gun defence at each was insufficient to protect all the aircraft dispersals and other vulnerable points. Reinforcements were therefore necessary from outside the theatre and two Royal Artillery Light Air Defence batteries arrived from Germany to join the defences of Changi and Tengah, on Singapore Island, while a Royal Australian Artillery LAA battery was deployed with 1 Squadron at Butterworth, opposite Penang.

The joint LAA defences at each station were fully integrated under the local RAF Regiment commander and all guns were ready for action from September 1964 to August 1966 – a period of almost two years when the gun detachments, and their observation posts, some of which were sited on offshore islands, – lived in the field with their equipments and were at readiness from dawn to dusk for seven days a week. There is little doubt that the deterrent presented by a powerful multi-role Air Force operating from such secure bases was instrumental in discouraging the Indonesians from any serious military adventure against Western Malaysia.

The situation was rather different in Eastern Malaysia, where the border with Indonesia ran through a thousand miles of jungle from Tawau in the north to Kuching in the south. There were no LAA squadrons available to defend the RAF's airheads at Labuan, Kuching and Tawau and – once again – improvisation was the only solution. Surplus 20mm Oerlikon guns were acquired from the Royal Navy's stocks in the Singapore Naval Base and RAF Regiment NCOs were trained in their use. They completed their crash training courses by carrying out live firing practices at sea from RAF marine craft. The instructors and the guns were then airlifted to Borneo where station personnel were trained to use them in an emergency. Such were the anti-aircraft defences deployed on the vital Borneo airfields against an attack by the Indonesian Air Force.

In the depths of the Borneo jungle the British, Malaysian and Gurkha battalions played a cat-and-mouse game with their Indonesian opponents. Air support for the Army was essential and the RAF helicopter force was continually engaged in operations from remote forward sites. 15 Field Squadron, based at Seletar on Singapore Island, maintained a constant presence on jungle airstrips, such as Sepulot, along the Indonesian border and their 3" mortars were often employed in defensive fire tasks against Indonesian infiltrators.

The effectiveness of the field squadron's role was described in a letter from one of the helicopter squadron commanders to the officer commanding 15 Squadron: "I would like you to know how much the efforts of your men are appreciated by the helicopter detachments on forward LZs. Apart from their primary tasks of manning the helicopter machine guns and defending the forward sites from ground attack, they have assisted with the day-to-day administration to such an extent that the helicopter crews have been able to devote all their time to achieving maximum aircraft serviceability."

But there was a price to pay: the permanent employment of four Regiment squadrons in the Far East put an immense strain on the remaining squadrons in the UK and Middle East which were almost continually deployed on a series of emergency deployments. Unaccompanied detachments were the norm – even in the Far East the Regiment gunners saw little of their families who were living there – and the stress of only four-month breaks in the UK between unaccompanied 12-month tours overseas discouraged an increasing number of NCOs and airmen from re-engaging when their service expired.

This loss of experience and manpower was not easy to replace at a time when recruiting for the all-regular Services was generally poor. Manning levels had declined to less than 240 officers and 2,000 gunners and it was becoming increasingly difficult to meet the growing demands for Regiment forces. How different it all might have been had the RAF Regiment (Malaya) survived to undertake the LAA defence of the airfields in Malaya and Singapore as well as being able to provide well-trained and experienced squadrons for jungle operations in Borneo.

Events in the Middle East

The growth of terrorism in Aden added to the general insecurity of the sprawling airfield at Khormaksar and RAF Regiment squadrons returned – on consecutive detachments – to provide security for the RAF installations there. 37, 48 and 2 Squadrons all carried out these tasks in turn from the UK and in order to spread the load, 27 and 34 Squadrons met the Aden task from Cyprus as well.

As if that was not enough to deal with, the unilateral declaration of independence (UDI) by Southern Rhodesia resulted in the unplanned deployment of the newly-raised 51 Squadron to Zambia, where it had to be relieved by 16 Squadron and then by 2 Squadron.

Meanwhile, at Khormaksar the threat had intensified to such an extent that 81mm mortars were being used by terrorists to attack the airfield from the town of Sheikh Othman. In order to co-ordinate the station defences it was decided to appoint a Regiment wing commander to fill the post of Senior Ground Defence Staff Officer at HQ Middle East Command and to act as officer commanding the Security Wing at RAF Khormaksar as well. It is not clear why one officer should have been appointed to two such disparate tasks simultaneously when an RAF Regiment wing headquarters would have been the most suitable organisation for the task, but Wing Commander Mark Hobden was posted to Aden to do both jobs by himself.

The new OC Security Wing organised protection for aircraft against mortar bombs by obtaining thousands of 40 gallon oil drums from the BP refinery at Little Aden, filling them with water from fire tenders and constructing protective walls around the aircraft dispersals. Having taken care of the passive defence requirement, he then organised rapid reaction teams from the resident RAF Regiment squadron and arranged for one such team to be airborne in a Wessex helicopter at all times – by day and by night. With the aircraft protected against stand-off attack and the adoption of an aggressive defence posture, Khormaksar was no longer a soft target for the terrorists.

As the overall situation deteriorated, the Aden government became concerned about their currency reserves – some £16 million – which were deposited in the vaults of the Chartered Bank in Crater. British control over the old town of Crater was spasmodic and it was decided to mount the currency recovery operation in case access to the town finally became impossible. At dead of night, a convoy of RAF Regiment land rovers and trailers, with Currency Board officials and a strong escort of Regiment officers and airmen, drove into Crater and loaded some ten tons of currency into the vehicles. The column returned to Khormaksar where the money was put on board a waiting Britannia aircraft and, with a Regiment escort, flown to the UK. £250,000 of the total was retained at Khormaksar – and kept in a large box under OC Security Wing's desk as a footstool – and an emergency reserve of cash for pay parades.

As the date for the British withdrawal approached, the helicopter squadron commander and the Regiment security commander arranged for two large marine buoys to be delivered to the Wessex squadron dispersal at Khormaksar. Teams of RAF Regiment gunners – with chains, shovels and cement – were lifted by helicopters to the peak of Jebel Shamsan (the feature overlooking Aden) where they dug bases to receive the buoys. Painted with large red, white and blue roundels, the buoys were lowered into place by the helicopters and firmly secured by chains which were set in concrete by the gunners.

As far as is known, these symbols of the RAF's farewell to Aden remain there to this day.[15]

Silver Jubilee

In 1967 the RAF Regiment front line consisted of two wing headquarters, six field and five LAA squadrons variously based in the United Kingdom, Cyprus, Aden and Singapore.

The commemoration of twenty-five years of service was marked by a service of thanksgiving at St Clement Danes in February and the presentation of a new Colour by HM The Queen at a parade at the Depot in June. These were encouraging signs for a Corps whose existence had been constantly under threat since its formation in 1942.

However, there were reminders – for those who needed reminding – of Douhet's doctrine that the simplest way to defeat an air force is to destroy it on the ground. The Arab-Israeli war of 1967 – the "six-day war" – saw 416 Arab aircraft destroyed in the first 48 hours: 23 in the air and 393 on the ground.[16] After that, victory came much more easily to the Israeli army.

In Vietnam, the USAF's air bases suffered aircraft losses out of all proportion to the size of the attacking forces and the simple weapons which they used against the world's most sophisticated air force. Between 1964 and 1973 the USAF incurred losses of almost 100 aircraft destroyed, and more than 1,000 damaged, by ground attacks on their ten major airfields in Vietnam and Thailand.[17]

Although the USAF demonstrated ingenuity and resourcefulness in their air base defence programmes, they were severely handicapped by the US Army's refusal to allow USAF forces to operate outside the airfield perimeters. At the same time, the US Army was reluctant to commit troops to the security of air bases, at the expense of their ground operations, so the USAF airfields remained vulnerable to ground attacks throughout the whole period of the war.

One result of this was that the USAF turned to the RAF Regiment for advice on ground defence planning (as the USAAF had done in Burma in 1943). It so happened that the Air Standardisation Co-ordinating Committee of Working Party 84 – which was responsible for developing NBC Defence procedures among the air forces of the UK, USA, Canada and Australia – was visiting the USA in 1965 and the RAF component of WP 84 consisted mainly of RAF Regiment officers. The RAF head of the working party was Group Captain DA Pocock, the Deputy Director of the Regiment, and he was invited by the air attache at the British Embassy to meet the Chief of USAF Security Police in Washington DC before returning to the UK. The topic was not NBC protection – but active air base defence and as a result of that discussion the ground was laid for the RAF Regiment/USAF Security Police Exchange Programme which continues to the present day.[18]

Thirty years later the American view of the exchange programme was expressed by Lt Col John M Reis, the Chief of Plans and Programmes in the Department of the Chief of Security Police in the Headquarters of the United States Air Force in Washington DC. He wrote "the RAF exchange officer program has provided excellent support to the USAF Security Police for three decades. The positions have been located at the Air Staff, Security Police Academy and for short periods at HQ Tactical Air Command and the 82nd Combat Security Police Wing. The contributions made to the security police mission over the years have been significant. The contributions range from the Regiment's unique perspective on organization to the integral part the HQ USAF exchange officer played in the joint USAF SP/RAF Regiment guard force formed to protect Ground Launched Cruise Missile (GLCM) assets in the UK.[19] The close interaction and familiarity that grew from this large scale integration paid practical dividends when our two nations deployed air base defenders side by side in operation Desert Shield/Desert Storm.

"The early exchange officers arrived in the Vietnam era and provided the RAF perspective on organizing air base defense forces in a more concise manner. Officers at the Air Staff level reviewed after action reports coming from Vietnam and provided expertise in the pursuit of solutions to Air Force Base Defense needs. The Safe-Side program was developed to better protect resources and was designed around combat security police squadrons that deployed in mass to defend forward air bases. The RAF Regiment background of the exchange officers at the Air Staff (Policy) and 82nd Wing (Tactical) level provided uniquely qualified insight during the building process of this program. Upon termination of the Safe-Side program the exchange officers helped in the transition to the follow-on program known as Security Police Elements for Contingencies (SPEC).

"In the late 1970s and early 1980s the focus of the exchange officers was vectored to the issues of nuclear, biological and chemical (NBC) defense and short range air defence (SHORAD). Again, the unique perspective of the RAF Regiment helped the USAF Security Police to introduce fresh ideas and solutions. Today's exchange officers are actively engaged in the training and policy arenas of the Security Police's air base defense mission. They take part in programs to improve the shooting skills of Air Force security men and women and participate in the training of new personnel at our Security Police Academy. They have been involved with management of the Air Force corrections program, the military working dog (MWD) program and as controllers in Joint Chiefs of Staff exercises. They have served at locations throughout the United States, including the Pentagon Washington DC, Fort Campbell Kentucky, Lackland AFB Texas, Langley AFB Virginia and Kirtland AFB New Mexico. RAF Regiment exchange officers are fully functional air force staff officers and they have performed duties up to division chief level. The United States Air Force looks forward to many more productive years from the RAF Regiment Exchange Officer program."[20]

The Regiment possesses a visible reminder of this close association with the USAF in the Kuhn Sword which, since 1970, has always been worn by the officer carrying The Queen's Colour for the RAF Regiment. Presented by Lt Col Byron D Kuhn USAF, one of the first exchange officers to serve with the Regiment, it forms an integral part of the Colour ensemble and is used on all ceremonial occasions when the Colour is paraded or displayed.

The example set by the USAF in Vietnam was recognised by the Royal Australian Air Force when they began to commit their aircraft to Vietnam. The RAAF ensured that they went with their own formed and trained ground defence units to protect their aircraft and installations on the ground. These were the signs of a changing climate in defence thinking which indicated a reawakening of the awareness of the vulnerability of increasingly expensive – and therefore fewer – aircraft to ground attack in a variety of forms by a determined and enterprising enemy.

Full Circle

The dramatic change in defence policy in 1957 should have resulted in – among other things – the disbandment of the RAF Regiment. That it did not was in part due to the Regiment's inherent flexibility in responding to change, and in part to the realisation by others in the RAF that the flying Service needed its own ground combat force to provide defence and security in a wide range of scenarios, for which the Army simply did not have the resources to detach from its primary role for the support of another Service.

Although the Regiment was much reduced in size post-1957, its tasking increased and it was only possible to meet the requirement by exploiting the loyalty and commitment of the Regiment gunners – many of whom spent long periods on unaccompanied overseas tours, under less than adequate living conditions and in unpleasant surroundings, with only brief spells in the UK before being sent back overseas again. Man-management and leadership were critical factors in this equation and ultimately the success of these contingency operations was due to the sterling qualities of the squadron officers and NCOs. Nowhere did the Regiment fail the Royal Air Force in those trying days.

Notes

[1]   AIR2/5732 – 8 Mar 45 (PRO)

[2]   COS (50) 24 – 3 Jan 50 (PRO)

[3]   79/HD/2260(MO5) – 11 Jan 51 (PRO)

[4]   AIR6/102 – 12 Nov 51 (PRO)

[5]   Mr RW Fisher – letters 1 & 30 May 1996

[6]   22, 23, 24, 25, 26, 27, 28, 29, 30, 31, 32, 33, 34, 35, 36, 37, 48, 75, 80, 85, 89, 100, 104, 168, 194, 199, 289, and 533 Squadrons. Most, but not all, were LAA units.

[7]   COS(53)597 (PRO)

[8]   SC(53)35 (PRO)

[9]   SC(56)15 (PRO)

[10] 3, 5, 8 & 33 Wing HQs; 2, 15, 16, 26, 27, 28, 34, 37, 48, 62, 63 & 194 Squadrons

[11] AIR8/2475 (PRO)

[12] COS(57)94 (PRO)

[13] James – *Defence Policy and the RAF 1956-63* p60 n1

[14] Air Chief Marshal Sir Charles Elworthy GCB CBE DSO MVO DFC AFC MA

[15] Group Captain MF Hobden OBE – letter, 20 May 1996

[16] Churchill – *The Six Day War* p86

[17] Vick – *Snakes in the Eagle's Nest* p94

[18] AVM DA Pocock – letter 15 Apr 1996

[19] RAF Greenham Common & RAF Molesworth

[20] Lt Col John M Reis USAF – letter 3 Sep 1996

11

Change and Upheaval

The withdrawal from most of our non-NATO commitments will enable us to reduce the task and size of the RAF Regiment. We are therefore examining the structure of the Regiment to determine how its remaining tasks may be met.

Statement on British Defence Policy, 1974

Non-NATO Commitments

The gradual run-down of RAF commitments overseas encouraged the belief that the Regiment's tasking would be correspondingly reduced; optimism has all too often been the overriding feature of a British Defence Policy which seeks to justify reductions in capability by claims that the smaller, leaner forces which remain will be capable of carrying out all sorts of demanding (but unspecified) tasks in the nation's defence.[1]

As has inevitably happened, withdrawals from one area were all too often followed by contingencies in another and the term "overstretch" was coined to describe official recognition of the widening gap between manpower resources and military commitments. For the Regiment squadrons, this resulted in the continuation of the series of unaccompanied detachments, with shorter and shorter periods in the UK between longer and longer spells overseas: something which had been a feature of their lives for many years.

In the Middle East the withdrawal from Aden (where a Regiment officer was the last member of the RAF to leave) was immediately followed by the rotation of squadrons through Muharraq, in Bahrein, from where detachments were maintained at Sharjah, Salalah and Masirah. When the requirement for Regiment units in Bahrein lapsed, the need for airfield defence became more urgent at Salalah where the effects of a rebellion against the Sultan of Oman impinged on the RAF detachment there. The threat to Salalah increased as the rebels grew in strength and were able to deploy longer-range weapons against the airfield. A series of "hedgehogs" – defended localities sited up to four miles beyond the airfield perimeter – were constructed and the attached Regiment squadron carried the battle from these to the enemy by using 81mm mortars and .50" machine guns against the enemy targets which were detected at night, and in conditions of poor visibility, with the aid of ZB 298 ground radar equipment.

The defence of Salalah was co-ordinated by a Fire Support Co-ordination Centre (FSCC) from which the RAF Regiment squadron commander controlled all ground defence units: the Royal Artillery Locating Troop, the 5.5" medium battery of the Royal Jordanian Artillery and the 25 pounder guns of the Sultan's artillery – as well as the Regiment squadron's assorted weapons – to maximum effect.

A 'hedgehog' at Salalah.

The Regiment squadrons carried out their tasks with distinction and one of the results of this was a request by the Sultan's Armed Forces

for Regiment officers to be loaned for duty as infantry company commanders. Three such posts were approved in 1972 and the success of the incumbents was such that a further request – this time for senior NCOs – was made for more Regiment personnel to serve with SAF. The RAF – and the RAF Regiment – withdrew from Salalah in 1975 but Regiment officers and NCOs remained to serve with the Sultan's forces until 1978. The relationship thus established has been maintained by the Royal Air Force of Oman's continuing policy of sending some of its officers to the RAF Regiment Depot for further training on a regular basis.

1 and 26 Squadrons were withdrawn from the Far East in 1967 and returned to the UK to a temporary home at RAF Bicester. 15 and 63 Squadrons remained in Singapore until 1971 when they, too, returned to the United Kingdom.

Instability in Hong Kong threatened both the RAF station at Kai Tak and the signals unit situated on the peak of Tai Mo Shan, from which radar cover extended into China, and the Regiment presence which had been maintained there by detachments from the Far East squadrons was continued by rotating flights from the UK squadrons for this task.

In the Caribbean, a minor insurrection in Anguilla led to another rotational task for the UK-based squadrons which had to maintain detachments at Coolidge airfield in Antigua for over two years. At one stage, 26 LAA Squadron had its flights operating in the field role in Antigua, Bahrein and Salalah simultaneously – quite a challenge to the effective implementation of command and control, even for a Regiment squadron leader.

In the Mediterranean, the breakdown of negotiations between the British and Maltese governments produced yet another crisis requiring RAF Regiment participation. This time a a Royal Marine Commando, embarked in an LPH, sailed into the Grand Harbour at Valetta while HQ 5 Wing and 15 Squadron secured the airfield at RAF Luqa until an Anglo-Maltese treaty was eventually signed. Within another two years 15 and 26 Squadrons were back in the Mediterranean – this time to Cyprus, where they were flown to reinforce the British Sovereign Base Area at Akrotiri and the signals unit at Troodos – following the Turkish invasion of the island in 1974. Together with the two Cyprus-based squadrons (27 and 34) of 3 Wing, the augmented Regiment force protected RAF installations and evacuated British civilians from threatened areas in a divided island.

Tigercat

Short Brothers had developed a guided missile system – Seacat – for the defence of RN ships against low-level attack. It sold well to other navies and Shorts saw an opportunity to market a land-based system before British Aerospace had developed their ET 316/Rapier SAM system to the stage where it could be brought into British Army and RAF Regiment service. After intense political lobbying, it was agreed that the Regiment should have one squadron equipped with three Tigercat launchers as a sales platform for British industry. 48 Squadron was selected for this role in 1968 and apart from the fact that this gave the Regiment a (very) limited airportable low-level air defence capability, it produced logistic and training headaches as the result of the "one-off" status of 48 Squadron within the RAF.

The squadron's sales task was reflected in the large number of overseas missions which were directed towards the Depot – where 48 Squadron was based – by the Defence Sales staff. Among the successes were sales to Argentina – which later enabled the Regiment to recover a Tigercat fire unit for its Museum from those left by the Argentine Air Force in the Falklands – but it was an unwelcome addition to the Regiment's many other roles as it effectively kept 48 Squadron out of roulement tasking and so added to the workload of the remaining squadrons.

All this changed in 1972 when British Honduras (later to acquire independence as Belize) was threatened by Guatemala, which considered it had a justifiable claim to Honduras if and when the British departed. 48 Squadron was rapidly deployed to the airhead in British Honduras – and immediately became the centre of a political storm when the Organisation of American States accused Britain of moving "missiles" (then a very emotive term, after the Cuban missile crisis) into Central America. Tigercat was subsequently replaced by a more conventional L70 Bofors gun defence – with all the airlift problems which this involved – for several years.

In 1977 the threat to Belize increased and 48 Squadron's Tigercats were once more deployed to the airfield there – this time to

**RAF Regiment
40/70 LAA gun
detachment at
Belize airport.**

**Tigercat
launcher
deployed in
Belize.**

reinforce the Bofors guns which had provided the defence there since Tigercat had been withdrawn five years earlier. When Rapier became operational in the RAF Regiment in 1978, a flight of four Rapier systems took over the low level air defence of Belize airport. The last 40mm Bofors L70 squadron – 66 – was disbanded at Catterick in 1978 and the Regiment's three Tigercat systems were given to Zambia, which was still nervous of Rhodesia's intentions, as a goodwill gesture by the British prime minister. After enduring ten years of being the only Tigercat unit in British service – with all the operational and logistic problems which this generated – 48 Squadron was rewarded by being re-equipped with Rapier.

John Bull's Other Island

The resurgence of the terrorist campaign by the IRA and its various factions, and the subsequent actions by Loyalist paramilitaries, drew an increasing number of Army units into internal security duties in Ulster. The three RAF stations in the Province – Aldergrove, Ballykelly and Bishop's Court – were all candidates for Regiment support from 1969 onwards and again this task fell to the UK-based squadrons on a rotational basis. A last-minute requirement to replace a Royal Marine Commando in the Northern Ireland roulement resulted in 33 Wing being deployed to Omagh, Enniskillen, Dungannon and Armagh with 16, 37 and 48 Squadrons, and 4th (Sphinx) Battery Royal Artillery, under command. Collocated with 17/21 Lancers at Omagh, HQ 33 Wing became responsible for a large area adjoining the border with the Irish Republic.

In addition to the roulement tasks at the three RAF stations, Regiment squadrons (2 and 15) reinforced the Army in Belfast at critical periods. In 1973 the British Army of the Rhine was tasked to provide a battalion-strength unit from Germany for duty in Londonderry and the choice fell on 22 Light Air Defence Regiment Royal Artillery – which had, ten years earlier, provided the Light Air Defence reinforcement batteries for the RAF Regiment LAA squadrons in Singapore. In order to bring 22 LAD Regiment up to the required strength, 26 LAA Squadron stationed at RAF Gutersloh was attached to the Army for this task. When the squadron commander broke the news to his officers and men that they were to be detached to Londonderry for four months, there was a stunned silence, broken only by a question "where is the airfield in Londonderry, sir?" Squadron Leader Alan Collinge's quick response "on the streets" had a salutary effect on his audience.

On the day that the squadron assumed responsibility for its tactical area, bombs were carefully planted in various locations along sub-unit boundaries. A bomb exploded without warning in a city store and while picking through the debris caused by the first bomb, a second bomb detonated, hurling Flight Lieutenant France and Flight Sergeant Abbott into the street. Although bleeding from their wounds and with their flak jackets in shreds, they survived – to be hospitalised and withdrawn from duty. Despite a number of other incidents, 26 Squadron completed its tour without incurring any fatalities.

Although the threat of further injuries was ever-present throughout the arduous and demanding aspects of the remainder of the squadron's tour of duty, SAC Gallacher remembers his time in Londonderry with 26 Squadron as one of the most challenging and rewarding experiences of his service in the Regiment.[2]

As this pattern continued – without interruption, despite the lip-service paid to the importance of the NATO task – it was not unusual for Regiment personnel to complete eight or more detachments of three to four months in Northern Ireland while serving a theoretical home tour on a UK-based squadron. This made the earlier cycle of a series of twelve-month unaccompanied tours – with short but generally uninterrupted breaks at home stations – seem almost more attractive to the gunners serving on squadrons.

Until 1988 the RAF Regiment maintained a continuous presence by rotating UK-based squadrons to defend RAF installations in Northern Ireland. This pattern ceased when 3 Squadron, which had been disbanded in 1957, was re-formed and based at RAF Aldergrove where the security of the airfield was a major commitment.

As RAF assets in Northern Ireland were concentrated at RAF Aldergrove – which is adjacent to Belfast's civil airport – the Regiment's TAOR (tactical area of responsibility) there expanded. Helicopters were increasingly used to deploy patrols and establish vehicle check points and this energetic pattern of counter-terrorist action enabled the Regiment squadron to foil an ingenious attempt to use remotely-fired mortars to attack the airport.

One of the prime tasks for the resident Regiment squadron was to control vehicle movement to and from Aldergrove and this resulted in the establishment of a pattern of road blocks and vehicle check points. One of these – Checkpoint Delta – developed into one of the busiest – and most effective – security features in the Province and most of the gunners who served in Northern Ireland remember the many hours spent on duty there, in all weathers, with mixed feelings.

At particular times of heightened tension, the resident Regiment squadron was reinforced by detachments from other UK-based squadrons and this sequence of deployments resulted in some gunners spending more time in Northern Ireland than elsewhere in the United Kingdom during what was theoretically a home tour at their parent station. The vulnerability of Regiment personnel in Ulster to attacks on their vehicles had been reduced in 1977 by the provision of long wheelbase Landrovers fitted with macrolon plastic armour – a distinct improvement on the level of protection previously afforded by canvas and aluminium!

Despite the pious sentiments contained in the 1974 Defence Review, the fundamental problem of "overstretch" was never addressed at unit level and Regiment officers and airmen in the UK-based squadrons were still spending up to nine months out of twelve away from their parent stations. The Germany-based squadrons (all assigned to NATO) were temporarily spared this degree of separation – but their time would come!

A New Look at the Cold War

Although the RAF Regiment remained committed to maintaining a presence in Central America (Belize), the Middle East (Salalah) and the Far East (Hong Kong) as well as in Northern Ireland, these tasks were viewed as transitory – and therefore irrelevant to the long-term future of the Regiment. Meanwhile, the Defence Planning Staffs once more focussed their attention on the case for reinstating conventional defence in Europe to replace the nuclear strategy which – because of the massive overkill capabilities on both sides – was becoming to look less and less credible as a means of dealing with the smaller-scale situations which seemed more likely to arise between NATO and the Warsaw Pact countries. The Supreme Allied Commander Europe (SACEUR) formally approved this change to a policy of "flexible response" and with it the Regiment's return to the 2nd Tactical Air Force in Germany became inevitable.

The introduction of Harrier, with its V/STOL capability and the consequent development of close air support from field locations in the Army's area of operations, made it obvious that such deployments would depend on effective local defence for the Harriers. 51 Squadron was redeployed to the Harrier main base at RAF Wittering, where it was joined by 15 Squadron and HQ 5 Wing to form a field wing with the primary task of operating with Harrier squadrons.

At the same time, 1 and 26 Squadrons were deployed to Laarbruch and Gutersloh respectively to provide LAA gun defences there, while 16 and 37 Squadrons remained in the United Kingdom but were earmarked for similar tasks at Bruggen and Wildenrath in an emergency.

The joint-Service Rapier Pilot Battery was formed by 9th (Plassey) Light Air Defence Battery Royal Artillery and 63 Light Anti-Aircraft Squadron RAF Regiment in 1973 and in 1974 63 Squadron became the first operational Rapier unit in the British forces. Joint-service development programmes for new small-arms and improved combat clothing also involved Regiment staffs, working with the Army and Royal Marines, and Regiment units participated in the trials and evaluation processes.

Reduction and Reorganisation

The size and shape of the Regiment front-line set out in the Defence White Paper in 1974 slashed the 1972 forecast of six Rapier and eight Field squadrons to five Rapier and five Field squadrons. This further reduced the manpower available for non-NATO tasks, even after taking into account the lower manning levels which resulted from the transition from 40mm gun squadrons to Rapier. The importance given to the NATO tasking was reflected in the redeployment to Germany of HQ 33 Wing when it moved from Catterick to Wildenrath to co-ordinate the field squadron contribution to the Harrier Force. In addition, HQ 4 Wing was re-formed at Bruggen to exercise control of the four Rapier squadrons which were to be deployed at Bruggen, Wildenrath, Laarbruch and Gutersloh.

Outside the NATO area, the Regiment tasks in the Middle and Far East eventually ended in 1975 and 1976 respectively. However, the Belize commitment was to continue, with Rapier defence provided on a roulement basis from the Rapier squadrons in the UK and RAF Germany, instead of Tigercat and 40mm Bofors guns, until 1990. The last L70 Bofors guns in any British regular unit – those of 66 Squadron – were trooped off parade at Catterick in 1978 when the squadron disbanded and the guns – which, with their L60 predecessors, had served the Regiment so well – became museum pieces.

The Security Branch

As the Regiment had now been reduced in size beyond the forecast in the 1974 White Paper, further studies were initiated into a more economical structure for what was left of the Corps. The Regiment and the RAF Police had always worked together well in emergency situations but there were fundamental differences in their training, organisation and roles. RAF policemen were trained to operate independently in their primary roles of law enforcement and crime prevention, and the policeman's ultimate sanction was that of arrest. RAF Regiment gunners, on the other hand, were trained to operate in teams, to use a wide range of weapons in their primary role of defending RAF installations – and their ultimate sanction was the application of lethal force. A number of studies had been carried out in the post-war years to find ways of rationalising the tasks of the Regiment and the Police, but all had concluded that there was insufficient common ground between the two bodies to justify any integration of one with another.

Despite these earlier investigations into the agencies responsible for quite different roles, it was decided that a single Security Branch, combining both RAF Regiment and the Provost Branch under a single two-star Director-General of Security, should be formed in 1976. It was confidently expected that this would be the most cost-effective answer to whatever problems might have otherwise arisen by allowing two small branches to continue their independent existence.

While it was unlikely that anyone in the Ministry of Defence believed that NCOs and airmen of the Regiment and Police trades would be interchangeable, it was hoped that there would be opportunities for the cross-posting of officers above the rank of wing commander – and Regiment group captains and above were ordered to remove their shoulder titles to avoid indicating any branch allegiances. Unpopular though that might have been for the officers concerned, it was deeply resented by the gunners who saw this as a blow to the Regiment in which they were proud to serve – and so it was. Fortunately, the effect on morale caused by this trifling with trifles was sufficient to make the MOD restore the Regiment badge to all Regiment officers.[3]

A new Trade Group 8 was created to contain the separate trades of gunner, firemen and policeman – which were not interchangeable – and the firemen ceased to wear the Regiment shoulder badge which they had worn since 1959.

The Queen's Silver Jubilee – and other Ceremonial

The Queen's Colour Squadron, with the Queen's Colour for the RAF, formed part of the tri-Service guard mounted at Buckingham Palace in June 1977 when Her Majesty drove to St Paul's Cathedral for the anniversary service. In July of the same year The Queen presented her new Colour to the RAF at a commemorative parade held at RAF Finningley.

1 and 2 Squadrons had received their Standards largely on the basis of their service as armoured car companies, but in 1975 15 Squadron – which had not been formed until after World War II – received its Standard. Others soon followed and – by the judicious transfer of squadron numbers when disbandments were forced upon the Regiment – squadrons were able to build up the required twenty-five years of service which is the minimum qualification for the award of a squadron Standard.

The Queen's Colour Squadron represented the Royal Air Force in numerous ceremonial events – the furthest afield being the laying-up of the Queen's Colour – which had been replaced by the one presented by The Queen at Finningley in July 1977 – in Wellington Cathedral (in New Zealand) in the October of the same year, in the presence of MRAF Sir Charles Elworthy. QCS took part in the RAF's 60th anniversary celebrations in 1978 and in that year the squadron participated – as usual – in the Festival of Remembrance in the Albert Hall on Remembrance Sunday. On this occasion the difference was that the Squadron wore the uniforms, and carried the No.4 rifles of the 1950s, as a tribute to the originators of the Regiment's ceremonial drill displays – the Demonstration Flight of the RAF Regiment Depot. The Demonstration Flight warrant officer then had been Warrant Officer "Danny" Gourd – and now, as Flight Lieutenant D A Gourd MBE, he was to command the Queen's Colour Squadron at the Festival of Remembrance twenty-five years later.

Airfield Crash/Rescue Fire Services – and Diversions

The Director of the RAF Regiment was also Director of RAF Fire Services and between 1974 and 1978 a new generation of airfield fire vehicles were introduced in order to improve the safety standards at RAF airfields. The new range of vehicles – and the fluorosynthetic and fluoroprotein foam agents which they carried – was designed to deal with the increasing hazards resulting from larger and heavier aircraft which carried more fuel and more passengers and crew.

However, such esoteric attitudes were relegated to second place following the national strike by local authority firemen throughout the United Kingdom in November 1977. RAF Regiment fire officers

**Airfield Crash/
Rescue Fire
vehicle.**

and NCOs embarked on a rapid training programme for almost half the 20,000 personnel, from all three Services, who were tasked to fill the gap. A number of the venerable "Green Goddess" fire vehicles from the Home Office reserve stocks were trundled out to replace the modern local authority fire vehicles and for nine weeks this scratch force provided the fire cover for the nation and answered almost 40,000 emergency calls.

Broadening the Field of Experience

The Regiment had experienced loan service by sending officers to the Army to spend tours of duty with the APL and by attaching both officers and NCOs to the Sultan of Oman's Armed Forces. The approval for an officer exchange scheme between the Regiment and the USAF Security Police for airfield defence planning and training was implemented by having one officer from each air force in a staff appointment and a second in a training post.

Nearer home, an NCO exchange post was established with the Royal Marines, with the Regiment NCO at the Commando Training Centre at Lympstone and the Royal Marine NCO at the Regiment Depot. Another Regiment sergeant joined the instructional staff of the School of Infantry at Warminster, and three officers and four warrant officers were members of the Rapier training wing at the Royal School of Artillery at Larkhill.

In a less obvious way, the Regiment's links with another part of the Army were maintained by providing volunteers to serve with the Special Air Service.

The Rapier Force

Although anti-aircraft guns continued to be developed after the war, they became heavier and more labour-intensive as they progressed to greater rates of fire, with more effective ammunition although with the greater accuracy provided by radar fire control systems. Nevertheless, it became clear that the speed and manoeuvrability of new types of aircraft would inevitably make gun defences less cost-effective, and studies began in the 1950s to develop a low-level missile system to replace the LAA gun.

The British Aircraft Corporation, later to become British Aerospace (BAe), began work on a project code-named PT428, but the Ministry withdrew funding for this in 1962. Funding recommenced in 1963 on the same system – now called ET 316 – which would be optically controlled and used in conjunction with an all-weather American LLAD system ("Mauler") which would be purchased for British use. By 1965 it was clear that the American system would not meet its design criteria and ET 316 was hastily reprogrammed as an all-weather system and the first ET 316 Blindfire firing took place in 1967.

The system was named "Rapier" while No.21 Joint Services Trials Unit (JSTU), manned by Royal Artillery and RAF Regiment officers and men, was carrying out trials at Woomera in 1968. Development work continued with No.23 JSTU and in cold weather trials in Canada. The first Rapier unit in British service – 63 Squadron RAF Regiment – was deployed to RAF Germany in 1974 and achieved operational NATO status shortly thereafter. By 1976, five Regiment squadrons and nine Royal Artillery batteries had been equipped with optical Rapier; the first Blindfire Rapier unit came into service in 1978 – this time it was 27 Squadron RAF Regiment which led the way.

All Rapier equipments were now at Field Standard "A" level but by the 1980s the policy of improving in-service equipment had raised the level to Field Standard "B1" for both Army and RAF Regiment Rapiers. However, by 1987 the differing requirements of the two Services led to the Army having its Rapier fire units rebuilt to Field Standard "B2" while the RAF opted for a mid-life improvement programme to raise the level to Field Standard "B1M" for its Rapier force – by now six squadrons following 48 Squadron's re-roling from Tigercat to Rapier – deployed at Leuchars and Lossiemouth in Scotland and at Bruggen, Wildenrath, Laarbruch and Gutersloh in Germany.

SACEUR's criteria for the level of air base defence within NATO included SHORAD and any nation which failed to meet the full range of criteria was liable to lose its share of NATO funding, as well as earning ignominy for its failure to support the alliance. USAF air bases in Germany could rely on the US Army to provide their SHORAD , but this was not the case in the UK. After some agonising, a remarkable compromise was achieved: the USAF bought Rapier equipment, and the RAF Regiment manned, it to defend three USAF bases in England. HQ 6 Wing, with 19, 20 and 66 Squadrons, became under the operational control of the USAF in the UK for this purpose.

Lightening the Load

As a result of the decision to reduce the Regiment front-line to only ten squadrons, the demands made on this small force were such that it could not meet the war roles laid down for it. In Germany, the ground threat to airfields – and to Harrier squadrons deployed off-base – from Soviet special forces trained specifically to neutralise NATO airfields and aircraft was such that another squadron had to be provided to fill the obvious gap in the RAF's defences. 58 Field Squadron, which had been disbanded in Aden in 1957, was accordingly re-formed as a Rapier squadron in 1974 and added to the order of battle. However, a study of the more sophisticated ground threat revealed that the soft-skinned Land Rovers and the sections

Spartan CVR(T).

travelling in them outside the airfield perimeter would be extremely vulnerable to ambush by small groups of special forces. Furthermore, the field squadron's main support weapon – the 81mm mortar – an indirect fire weapon with a slow reaction against unregistered targets – was unlikely to be effective against the expected threat.

The solution was to re-equip the field squadrons with light armoured vehicles of the Combat Vehicle Reconnaissance (Tracked) range manufactured by Alvis. This gave the squadrons excellent mobility across any terrain, protection against enemy fire and the capability to engage targets directly with 76mm turret-mounted guns and 7.62mm cupola-mounted machine guns in armoured vehicles. The range of CVR(T) equipment for each squadron included armoured vehicles (Scorpions) with turret-mounted 76mm guns capable of firing a wide variety of ammunition, armoured personnel carriers (Spartans) for the rifle sections, an armoured command post (Sultan) for squadron HQ and an armoured recovery vehicle (Samson). This enabled a single squadron to dominate the large area of ground from which stand-off weapons could be fired against airfields and aircraft as well as providing the rapid concentration of firepower and manpower to deal with enemy incursions onto the airfield itself. The armoured car – this time with tracks – had returned into RAF service after a gap of more than thirty years and gave the Regiment back the capabilities of the wartime field squadrons.

The training task for the conversion of the field squadrons to the light armoured role was a formidable one but with the ready co-operation of the Royal Armoured Corps Centre at Bovington and the RAC training regiment at Catterick garrison, the Regiment squadrons began to re-equip in 1981 and the conversion was completed by 1983. Two light armoured squadrons were deployed in Germany and Cyprus, but the strategic reserve wing remained based in the UK.

Unfortunately, it was to prove increasingly difficult to maintain the necessary levels of CVR(T) skills when the light armoured squadrons were continually committed to contingency tasks in the infantry role. These constant interruptions to the very demanding training cycle of maintaining, operating and tactically employing armoured vehicles inevitably degraded operational capability in the war role in favour of internal security tasks of the type on which the Regiment squadrons had routinely been employed since 1946.

The Royal Auxiliary Air Force Regiment

As is the nature of things, much time and effort is expended in military circles – as in many other fields of human endeavour – on such innovative tasks as re-inventing the wheel, and similar pioneering activities.[4] Thus by 1979 it became time for the Royal Auxiliary Air Force Regiment to be resuscitated in order to provide ground defence units to defend RAF bases in the United Kingdom against the same threats which faced RAF bases in Germany. In the next three years a total of six field squadrons were raised on RAF stations as far apart as Lossiemouth and St Mawgan and, unlike the regular squadrons, both men and women were recruited as gunners.

The traditional four-figure numbers were used for the new series of RAuxAF Regiment field squadrons, which were organised as four Landrover-borne rifle flights. They were provided with additional automatic weapons to compensate for the absence of mortars and anti-armour weapons, which it was considered would unnecessarily complicate the training task.

In 1985 a seventh auxiliary squadron was raised at RAF Waddington to man the radar-controlled 35mm Oerlikon anti-aircraft guns which had been captured from the Fuerza Aerea Argentina in the Falklands campaign. In 1989 a second air defence squadron was formed at the same station with the aim of introducing Rapier to the RAuxAF Regiment on a cadre basis.

In order to foster a competitive spirit which would develop esprit-de-corps and raise both individual and collective skills, an inter-squadron competition was established for all auxiliary squadrons and conducted under the direction of regular officer and NCO judges.

Operation Corporate

The British reaction to the Argentinian seizure of the Falkland Islands in 1982 was to mount an improvised recovery operation under circumstances in which success would have been considered improbable – if not impossible – by any respectable military staff college.

One of the first steps was to establish a staging post at Wideawake airfield on Ascension Island and in order to provide the necessary level of defence there against the possibility of an attack by Argentine special forces, HQ 33 Wing was deployed, with a field flight under command, for this task.

63 Squadron, equipped with Blindfire Rapier, was at seven days readiness at RAF Gutersloh; it was given forty-eight hours notice to embark on the Queen Elizabeth II which sailed for the Falklands on 5th May with an Army brigade on board. What air defences there were on the QE II – .5" machine guns and Blowpipe missiles – were manned by the Regiment whose existence was otherwise largely ignored by the embarked Army contingent.

Meanwhile, the first RAF Regiment gunners to reach the Falklands were those in 18 Squadron, whose Chinook helicopters landed there on 6th May. These gunners were to be the first Regiment personnel to see action in the Falklands when they manned the side-mounted machine guns of the Chinooks on operational flights. There were, of course, other Regiment gunners with 1 (Harrier) Squadron, as well as those embarked on the merchant ships – principally the North Sea ferries – which carried troops to the war zone. As the vessels approached the Falklands the threat of air attack increased and the gunners participated in manning their GPMGs in the anti-aircraft role when the occasion demanded.

Operation Corporate – 63 Squadron landing by Mexefloat at San Carlos.

When 63 Squadron came ashore at San Carlos, there were obvious difficulties in locating, and unloading, their Rapier equipment and vehicles from the Atlantic Causeway while the squadron personnel, who had transhipped from the QE II in South Georgia to the Canberra and the Norland, did not land as a formed unit. These were not unlike the problems which Regiment LAA flights and squadrons had encountered in Operations Torch and Husky almost forty years earlier. It took over 12 hours to land 59 Land Rovers and 57 trailers – including the

Rapier equipment – by Mexefloats from the Atlantic Causeway and it was another 24 hours before the last of the squadron personnel was ashore from the passenger vessels. The squadron commander had received no briefing on his tasks, no preliminary reconnaissance of fire unit sites had been possible and the logistic and administrative support left something to be desired – there were, for example, only twenty-four sets of Arctic clothing for the whole squadron.

The Falklands Air Defence cell on shore was manned by the Army and although an additional Regiment squadron leader was utilised as the RAF representative there, he was not included in the subsequent move of the cell from San Carlos to Port Stanley. Despite these – largely avoidable – difficulties, the usual Regiment energy and initiative were successfully employed to gather the Rapiers and their supporting equipment on shore and to deploy them operationally in the shortest possible space of time.

63 Squadron replaced the Rapier defence of the San Carlos airhead, which had until then been carried out by T Light Air Defence Battery of the Royal Artillery. The battery then moved forward to

Rapier deployed in the Falklands.

provide air defence for the brigade area in the advance to Port Stanley. What was noticeable was the difference in tactical doctrine – and therefore in operational procedures – between the SHORAD provided by the Army and the RAF Regiment. The Army requirement is for SHORAD well forward in an hostile air environment in which their priority is to protect the ground forces from air attack; any presence of friendly aircraft is a secondary consideration.

Conversely, the RAF Regiment task is to provide SHORAD in an environment in which friendly aircraft are constantly operating (eg airfields and airheads) and where aircraft procedures and weapon control are essential for safety. Thus the Army Rapier deployment at the airhead had made no provision for safe lanes and appropriate operating procedures for friendly aircraft and 63 Squadron had to introduce the conventional procedures for the defence of an airhead.

It was indeed fortunate that the war ended at this stage as the style of the Regiment's commitment was reminiscent of 1940-43 and a serious war, against a determined enemy, might have produced unpleasant results for the Royal Air Force. The deployment of RAF Regiment airmen, scattered as individuals through flying squadrons without any officers to provide specialist advice, let alone command and control, effectively reduced the ground defence representation to the level provided by the ACH/GD/Ground Gunners in 1940-41.

In World War II the Regiment had managed to be among the first – if not the first – British troops to enter a variety of interesting places and this tradition was continued in the Falklands when a Spanish-speaking Regiment officer – Flight Lieutenant G H Bransby – who had been deployed to assist in the interrogation of prisoners of war, was among the very early arrivals in Port Stanley. He was an even earlier arrival at Government House – then the residence of the Argentine army commander – and one of the results of that is the handsome bronze statuette of General San Martino which now resides in the Depot officers' mess.

However, the Regiment participation in Operation Corporate provided salutary reminders of some earlier operations which had not been entirely satisfactory. The deployment of a single squadron, without an adequate Regiment command structure for example, was reminiscent of the North African landings in 1942. This inevitably resulted in weaknesses which could – and should – have been avoided in a classic joint-service operation. In a brigade environment, a minor unit (a company or squadron commanded by a major) has no independent standing unless it is part of a major unit (ie a lieutenant-colonel's command) or attached to the brigade HQ (eg a Signals or Engineer squadron). Thus an RAF Regiment squadron, commanded by a squadron leader and without a higher-ranking formation to command it, was largely ignored by the Army – and, to a certain extent, even by the small RAF command element which was fully occupied with the task of aircraft operations.

The deployment of a wing HQ, with only one flight from a squadron under command, to Ascension Island was a tasking more appropriate to a Regiment squadron, with one or more of its flights. This could have enabled the Regiment wing HQ to be deployed to the Falklands, where it would have transformed the situation – not least for the Rapier squadron which had an integrated joint-service task there. These lessons were obviously taken to heart before the next major joint-service operation arose in the Gulf in 1990.

Once the campaign was over, it became clear that short range air defence would have to be a continuing feature of the defence of the airfield at Port Stanley and of the much larger airfield which was subsequently constructed at Mount Pleasant. Thus began yet another roulement for the Regiment – this time for the Rapier force which had to maintain a flight of four Rapier fire units in the Falklands, as well as in Belize, from the Regiment squadrons in the UK and RAF Germany.

Terrorism in Germany

As a part of widening the IRA's campaign of death and destruction beyond the boundaries of Northern Ireland – and undoubtedly because of the need to find softer targets than those in Ulster – a terrorist campaign was mounted against British Service personnel and their bases in Europe. Inevitably, innocent civilians were to be killed and injured as well in these indiscriminate actions. In May 1988 two groups of off-duty RAF Regiment personnel were attacked in Holland, by a car bomb in one instance and by fire from automatic weapons in the other. In one attack, two airmen from 1 Squadron were killed, and another injured, when their car was blown up.[5] In the other, two airmen from 16 Squadron and one from HQ 4

Wing were shot, one fatally.[6] None of the victims were, of course, either armed or in uniform.

Steady Progress

In this period the Regiment had survived against the odds and had, in fact, been able to demonstrate its value to the RAF as a whole in a variety of roles which had not been considered when successive policy statements on defence were being prepared and published. The importance of air base defence had been recognised by the introduction of the Rapier missile system to replace the LAA gun and by the re-equipment of the field squadrons with light armoured vehicles to enhance the ground defence of vulnerable airfields.

The mass of overseas roulement commitments had gradually been slimmed down, and the establishment of a squadron in Northern Ireland had stabilised that task, although short-term reinforcements were required at critical times in the Province. However, the continuation of the LLAD task in Belize, and the emergence of another in the Falklands, placed a heavy burden on the Rapier squadrons.

Internal organisation had been improved by a clearer distinction between gunners and firemen – a move welcomed by both groups – although the training and supervision of RAF airfield crash/rescue crews remained a Regiment responsibility, with policy matters in the hands of the Director RAF Regiment as Director RAF Fire Services.

The existence of the Security Branch did little other than to buttress the continuation of the two-star Commandant-General/ Director-General of Security (a General Duties branch post) against the threat of disestablishment. This was to come, eventually, when the realities of the situation became too obvious to ignore any longer and the Regiment and the Provost branch subsequently returned to their separate existences, each under its own professional one-star head.

The 1974 defence review had envisaged the RAF Regiment as one of the sacrificial lambs which would be placed on the altar of economy. What had not been thought through was the continuing ground and air threat to the RAF's bases and installations, and how this was to be countered – apart from hoping that it would simply go away. Events inevitably proved that an air force's assets were too attractive to an enemy – particularly those who understood Douhet's arguments – and that if not defended on the ground they would be lost before they could be used in the air.

All in all, the RAF Regiment could begin to look forward to the 1990s with rather more confidence than it had faced the 1960s and 1970s.

Notes

[1] "Hope springs eternal in the human breast" Alexander Pope 1711

[2] Mr R Gallacher – letter 4 November 1995

[3] "Men are led by baubles". Napoleon Bonaparte (on instituting the Legion d'honneur in 1802)

[4] "The thing which has been, it is that which shall be; and that which is done is that which shall be done: and there is no new thing under the sun." Ecclesiastes ch.1 v.9

[5] SAC JD Baxter (killed) SAC JM Reid (killed) SAC AB Kelly (injured)

[6] SAC IL Shinner (killed) SAC IW Lewis (seriously injured) SAC Garth (wounded)

12

A Return to Stability

The RAF Regiment will continue to provide ground-based air defence protection for RAF main operating bases.
Statement on British Defence Policy, 1992

E vents in eastern Europe in general, and in the USSR in particular, transformed the international scene by ending the cold war. In the euphoric situation which followed, the British government lost no time in reducing its armed forces – summer had come, and chimneys which were no longer needed could be pulled down. Unfortunately, the international stability which had been one of the results of great-power confrontation was soon to be replaced by outbreaks of instability in areas outside Europe.

"Options for Change", as the unilateral restructuring of the British Services was termed, cut more deeply in some areas than others but the main result was the loss of large numbers of skilled and experienced personnel. There was an understandable decline in the morale of those who remained in uniform, wondering what they were being retained to do and how long it would be before they would be declared redundant.

Whatever doubts may have lingered about the cost-effectiveness of retaining the RAF Regiment in an RAF which was under continual financial pressure were soon dispersed by the Iraqi invasion of Kuwait in August 1990 and the consequent threat to the stability of the Middle East. With the prospect of having to deploy combat aircraft to forward bases in another country, SHORAD and the ground defence of RAF assets became the first priority, with NBC defence and ground defence training for all deployed RAF personnel following close behind.

Operation Granby resulted in the deployment of RAF aircraft and equipment to Cyprus, Bahrain and Saudi Arabia. RAF Regiment officers and NCOs were distributed throughout the force, carrying out a range of duties which included NBC monitoring, ground defence advisers and other specialised tasks. The mobile field laboratory responsible for identifying any biological or chemical agents used by the Iraqis deployed a number of field teams, each of which was commanded by a Regiment NCO, while the helicopter squadrons took their own Regiment personnel with them into the desert.

The RAF Regiment units in the theatre were deployed at Akrotiri, Muhurraq, Dharan, Riyad and Tabuk as part of the Allied operation Desert Shield and included four wing headquarters[1], three Rapier squadrons[2], four light armoured squadrons[3], and one field squadron[4]. All in all, RAF Regiment personnel made up 19% of the total RAF force deployed to the Gulf.

The Iraqi air force made no attacks on targets in Kuwait, Bahrain or Saudi Arabia – to the great disappointment of the Rapier squadrons. While the other light armoured squadrons were utilised for airfield defence tasks, 1 Squadron deployed in support of the RAF helicopter squadrons operating with 1st (UK) Armoured Division. Once operation Desert Storm began, and the ground forces advanced, it was not long before 1 Squadron was once more back in Iraq, where it had been formed some 70 years earlier! With the abrupt ending of the campaign, the Regiment squadrons were withdrawn from the Gulf and returned to their parent stations in the UK and Germany.

Nevertheless, the RAF Regiment was able to notch up another "first into..." to add to the list of places which Regiment units – or

Operation Desert Storm – 1 Squadron returns to Iraq.

individuals – had entered ahead of the main bodies of British forces. Flight Lieutenant Bell and Sergeant Baldwin had been tasked with locating chemical weapons left behind by the retreating Iraqi forces. Moving independently of other British forces, they were halted at a US Army checkpoint outside Kuwait City and told that only Arab coalition forces were allowed beyond this point and that they should rejoin the British Army, twenty miles down the road. Bell replied "we're not British Army – we're RAF Regiment" – and the American officer in charge waved them through the checkpoint. They were thus the first western allied military personnel to enter Kuwait City and reached the airport just before the first RAF Hercules landed there.[5]

Fifty Years Old

The 1st of February 1992 marked the 50th anniversary of the formation of the RAF Regiment and the year saw a series of commemorative events which began with a Service of Thanksgiving in the RAF Church of St Clement Danes in London.

General Sir Peter de la Billiere, who had commanded the British forces in the Gulf, named a British Rail Class 91 locomotive "The RAF Regiment" at a ceremony held at King's Cross station.

A major ceremony of Beating Retreat by the Regiment, with the massed bands of the RAF, was held on Horse Guards Parade in June. It was supported by a static demonstration of RAF Regiment equipment and personnel, demonstrating the differences between 1942 and 1992. The Regiment was well represented at both the Royal Tournament in July and the Edinburgh Tattoo in August – where the RAuxAF Regiment were on parade as well.

The major event of the anniversary year, however, was the visit by Her Majesty The Queen to the RAF Regiment Depot at Catterick in October. At an impressive ceremonial parade, held in the west hangar because of the unpredictability of the weather, The Queen presented her new Colour to the Regiment. After visiting the Sergeants' Mess, and lunching in the Officers' Mess, Her Majesty attended a very successful regimental muster of serving and retired personnel and their families during which she spoke to many of those present.

The old Colour, which was presented to the Regiment by the

Queen at Catterick in 1967, was subsequently laid up in the RAF Regiment Memorial Chapel in the Catterick Village parish church of St Anne. It remains there, despite the subsequent move of the Depot to Honington, and with the Memorial Chapel is a reminder of the RAF Regiment presence in North Yorkshire from 1946 to 1994.

Her Majesty The Queen with the senior officers of the Regiment in the Richmond Room of the Officers' Mess at the RAF Regiment Depot, Catterick, 1992.

Looking Ahead

Fittingly, the Regiment's golden jubilee coincided with the first positive statement about the Regiment in a Defence white paper. This recognised the contribution made by the Regiment to the security of the RAF's operations in peace and war and indicated an awareness of the importance of the ground and short range air defence role in the future.

Although the light armoured vehicles in squadrons were to be phased out as squadrons reverted to the field role, the Rapier force was to be re-equipped with Field Standard C fire units, at an estimated cost of £1.9 billion – a clear statement of the value of the Regiment to the Air Force whose much smaller front line represented increasingly valuable aircraft assets which had to be properly defended on the ground in order to ensure that they would be available to fight in the air.

In the wider context of "surviving to operate" the importance of every man and woman in the RAF being able to carry out his or her duties in war accentuated the importance of personal protection measures in an NBC environment and the need for every combatant in uniform to be able to use personal weapons effectively in the defence of RAF installations. Churchill's demand for "every airfield to be a stronghold of fighting air-groundmen" is readily accepted in the modern Air Force and the planning, organisation and implementation of these measures has become a vital role for officers and NCOs of the Regiment.

The professional skills of the Regiment are thus even more closely than ever interwoven into the fabric of the RAF. By ensuring that operational capability can be maintained in the face of enemy attack as well as by providing the highly specialised ground defence and SHORAD squadrons to defend vital resources, the Regiment provides the remainder of the RAF with the assurance of being able to operate from secure bases in war.

Considerable as the achievements of the Regiment have been, the future depends on the motivation and ability of all serving officers and airmen. Unless each and every one strives to reach higher goals, takes a personal pride in the attainments of individuals and squadrons and develops an esprit-de-corps second to none, the possibility of failure will always be present. Those who fought in the adverse conditions which faced the Regiment in operational theatres between 1942 and 1946 set the example for those who live in easier, and more comfortable, times. Difficult days will return, as surely as winter succeeds summer, and the lessons learned at such cost in the past should be studied in peace – and heeded in war.

Notes

[1]   3, 4, 6 & 33 Wings

[2]   20, 26 & 66 Squadrons

[3]   1, 34, 51 & 58 Squadrons

[4]   2 Squadron (at RAF Akrotiri to replace 34 Squadron)

[5]   Allen – *Thunder & Lightning* p125

13

Past, Present and Future

*The man is the first weapon of combat: let us then study the soldier
in battle, for it is he who brings reality to it.*

Ardant du Picq

Field Marshal Slim once said of the infantry that there were no
bad battalions in the British Army – but there were some
battalions which had bad officers. This was one of those cryptic
statements which attracted attention by having sufficient truth in it
to cause the subject of military leadership to be taken seriously. In
reality, the problem goes much deeper than simply posting the right
officers to the right units: it is dependent on the selection, motivation
and training of the soldier and his junior NCOs as well as on the
qualities of man-management and leadership exercised by senior
NCOs and officers.

It was possibly because the foundling RAF Regiment was so
short of material and equipment that those in command realised that
its only real assets were in its manpower. As a result, training and
leadership – at all levels – gained an importance in the Corps which
has never been lost. This was accentuated by the function of size –
the squadron is a unit which is too small for anyone to escape notice
but large enough for esprit-de-corps to develop and flourish.

This is not to suggest that every RAF Regiment squadron has
been without fault; some were very good indeed, most were good
but there have undoubtedly been some which were less good than
they could – or should – have been. Throughout the Regiment's history
it has been the skill and determination of the well-led gunner – alone,
in a small fire team or together with his comrades in his flight or
squadron – which has enabled the Regiment to carry out whatever
task it has been set. It is undeniably the quality, skill and courage of

the well-trained and well-led junior ranks which have stood the
Regiment in such good stead in the past – and hopefully will do so in
the future. As Wellington said, pointing to a British private soldier in
Paris before Waterloo "it all depends on that article whether we do
the business or not."[1]

The Armoured Car Companies

The post-World War I economic situation made service in the
armed forces an attractive option to unemployment, but the small
size of the RAF, in particular, enabled recruiting to be carried out on
an extremely selective basis. The results were obvious in the high
standards which prevailed in the RAF between the wars. The
armoured car companies were manned occasionally by volunteers
but more usually by drafting airmen of various ground trades to Iraq
and Transjordan for three-year tours as "armoured car crewmen".
With only a brief familiarisation course before sailing from the UK,
most adapted easily to the unfamiliar role and the achievements of
the armoured car companies in the Middle East in 1940-43 bear
witness to the professional ability of those who served in them. Due
partly to the separate identity of the armoured car companies
throughout the war, and the mass exodus from the Service in 1945-
46, very few of those who had served in 1 and 2 Armoured Car
Companies chose to transfer to the RAF Regiment into which the
companies were incorporated in 1946. Those who did, and those
who remained in the RAF in other branches and trades, added to the
experience levels which were needed in the immediate post-war years.

Ground Gunners

The need for AA defence of airfields became increasingly
obvious in the run-up to the outbreak of war and Ground Gunner
became a sub-trade within the all-embracing one of Aircrafthand
General Duties (ACH/GD). The organisation of AA defences relied
heavily on the Ground Gunners themselves and although they were
formed into defence squadrons, with their own officers, in 1941,
there was still ample scope for initiative by individual airmen who
had to improvise in order to carry out their multifarious tasks.

The Ground Gunners were, of course, the foundation on which
the RAF Regiment was built when the RAF's 150 defence squadrons

became the first RAF Regiment squadrons in February 1942. Interestingly enough, the introduction of Regiment airmen into the establishment of support helicopter (SH) and Harrier (V/STOL) squadrons is a reversion to the early system of allocating ground gunners to stations and flying wings where they were employed under non-Regiment officers. As in 1940/41, the adaptability and skill levels of the modern gunners has enabled them to carry out a variety of essential roles as members of flying units.

The Modern RAF Regiment

Success in war depends on a combination of leadership, training and equipment. Napoleon would have added "luck", but that is not a factor on which one can rely in preparing for war; all the more important, therefore, to ensure that the factors under one's control are polished to the highest possible standards.

The lessons are clear: officers and airmen must be carefully selected on entry, given sound basic training and placed in units where experienced NCOs and officers are thoroughly professional in their duties. Individual, continuation, specialist and collective training in the multifarious roles of the modern Regiment is essential if smaller numbers are to be able to make a greater contribution to the Royal Air Force's role of exercising air power wherever this is required. At the end of the day, the best weaponry and most sophisticated equipment are only as good as the men who use them: this is well understood in the General Duties branch – and it is equally applicable to the RAF Regiment.

Competition is an obvious stimulus to achievement – after all, there is no more competitive arena than combat – and there are a number of structured Regiment competitions in existence to encourage this.

The Lloyds Cup

Shortly after the RAF Regiment was formed in 1942, its first Commandant – Major-General Claude Liardet, himself a member of Lloyds – persuaded the Committee of the Corporation of Lloyd's of London to present a trophy for skill-at-arms competition by RAF Regiment squadrons. It was originally awarded on the basis of range results achieved by every officer and airmen on the strength of each squadron. More recently the competition has been refined and it is now fired by selected teams from regular squadrons, thus encouraging the best shots in each unit to take part in other small-arms competitions. The competition for the Lloyds Cup, which is the premier Regiment trophy, has resulted in a high proportion of the competitors at the RAF meeting at Bisley being drawn from RAF Regiment squadrons.

The Vaux Trophy

Major Hugh Vaux, a member of the prominent brewing family in the North East of England, was second-in-command of 1st Bn Durham Light Infantry on Cos in 1943. He assumed command of the British forces on the island when his commanding officer was wounded, and was captured – with most of the garrison, including the RAF Regiment element – when the Germans overran the island. After the war he transferred to the RAF Regiment and was commanding 2 Wing of the RAF Levies Iraq when he was appointed to take command of the Force and promoted to the rank of group captain. He was returning from a visit to Amman when his aircraft crashed in a dust storm when attempting to land at Habbaniya and both he and the pilot were killed. The trophy was presented to the Regiment, in his memory, by the directors of his family firm in 1970. It is awarded to the most improved student on the Junior Regiment Officers' Training Courses held at the Depot.

The Higginson Trophy

Squadron Leader J S Higginson led 2777 Armoured Car Squadron into Brussels on 5th September 1944 and ended the war with them in Germany in 1945. On demobilisation he returned to his family business in Northern Ireland and when the RAuxAF Regiment came into being in 1947 he raised – and commanded – 2502 (Ulster) Squadron, which was one of the few RAuxAF Regiment units to be fully manned for most of its existence. It was rumoured that one of the requirements for employment in the Higginson family firm was enlistment in 2502 Squadron! Squadron Leader Higginson presented his trophy for competition among the regular units of the Regiment to mark both his war-time squadron service and to emphasise the links between the regular and auxiliary units of the Regiment. In recognition of his outstanding contribution as an Auxiliary officer, he was granted the honorary rank of wing commander when the RAuxAF Regiment squadrons were disbanded in 1957.

The Barnard Trophy

Group Captain Arthur Barnard's brilliant career was cut short by terminal illness, which he endured with great courage, setting an outstanding example to all who knew him. As Deputy Director of the Regiment he had been a key figure in bringing Rapier into RAF Regiment service and after his death his widow, Mrs Dorothy Barnard, presented a trophy bearing his name for competition among the Rapier squadrons.

The Strickland Trophy

Air Commodore Roy Strickland, Director of the RAF Regiment from 1981 to 1983, had been involved in planning the revival of the RAuxAF Regiment and much of the success of the auxiliary squadrons in the 1980s was due to his continued interest in the project. Conscious of the need for a challenging competition which would raise training standards and develop team spirit, he presented a trophy for annual competition among the squadrons of the RAuxAF Regiment.

Royal Auxiliary Air Force Regiment personnel training for the Strickland Trophy competition.

The RAF Regiment Prize Essay

Group Captain Kingsley Oliver, as a winner of the Bertrand Stewart (Army) and Trench Gascoigne (RUSI) essay competitions during his service, endowed the prize for an annual essay competition in order to encourage individual thought and the free expression of ideas within the Regiment. He suggested that entry should be restricted to junior officers and that the essays should be directed at topics which were likely to be of relevance to the future development of the RAF Regiment.

The Kapuscinski Sword

Flying Officer Stephen Philip Andrew Kapuscinski was a student on the Junior Regiment Officers' Course at the Depot when he was tragically killed in a road traffic accident in September 1984. His family presented a sword, as the prize for the best student on subsequent Junior Officers' Courses, in his memory.

The Roberts Trophy

Group Captain David Roberts MBE MM had a distinguished career in the RAF Regiment from its inception in 1942. In fact, as a young PAC Operator, he was awarded the Military Medal for gallantry during the Battle of Britain when he brought down an enemy bomber at RAF Kenley. As a trainer of officers and airmen (and flight cadets at the RAF College Cranwell), and as a commander in junior and senior ranks, he well understood the importance of good leadership at all levels and he emphasised this by presenting a trophy in 1991 for annual award to the junior Regiment officer who had best demonstrated his qualities of leadership under demanding conditions anywhere in the world.

Skill at Arms Competitions

The Royal Air Force Skill at Arms Match (RAFSAM) is an annual event at Bisley. RAF Regiment competitors have to qualify at the Corps Concentration, which is shot concurrently with the Lloyds Cup each year. The winner is awarded the title Champion Shot of the RAF Regiment and the twenty-two highest-scoring competitors go forward to compete in the RAFSAM, which takes the form of ten days of intense competition firing the Service Rifle (SR) and the

Service Pistol (SP) on the Bisley ranges. The final of the SR competition is a match for the best thirty competitors and the ultimate winner is awarded the Queen's Medal for the Champion Shots of the Air Forces. Of the twenty-seven post-war Queen's Medallists, four have been from the RAF Regiment.

The National Rifle Association (NRA) matches are then held between foreign competitors and the best shots from the British Services; RAF Regiment personnel have achieved considerable success in these NRA matches. The military competition includes team matches, the most prestigious of which is the Methuen Cup. This is a Corps level competition which attracts some thirty teams from all three Services; it has yet to be won by the Regiment. The final day of Bisley is used for RAF and British matches – and RAF Regiment shots have won places in both the RAF and the British teams in recent years.

The Cambrian Patrol

This is the British Army's most important test of military skills at patrol level. It is an annual event which takes place in the Brecon Beacons area of Wales in October/November – when the weather can be relied upon to add to the competitors' problems – and is open to teams from regular and reserve units of the Army, Royal Marines and RAF Regiment. Selected foreign teams are invited to participate as well.

The competition is a particularly arduous 48 hour event which takes place over some fifty miles of very challenging terrain. The exercise is designed to test both individuals and teams in a variety of modern military skills. These include: reconnaissance and fighting patrols, leadership, weapon handling and marksmanship, map reading and navigation, first aid and relations with the media. Each team has to submit a detailed report at the end of the competition and individuals are subjected to testing debriefing sessions. Gold, silver and bronze medals are awarded sparingly, but both RAF Regiment and RAuxAF Regiment teams have achieved consistently good results over the years, winning a number of medals to mark their success.

USAF Security Police Competitions

The RAF Regiment/USAF Security Police exchange

programme resulted in an annual small arms competition between teams from the two forces and this led to the RAF Regiment being invited to participate in the Rodeo and Peace Keeper Challenge competitions held in the USA each year.

The Rodeo Competition, held annually at McCord Air Force Base (AFB) in Washington State, includes a competition to test ground defence security teams in all aspects of air base defence such as rifle and pistol shooting, physical fitness and tactics. Up to forty teams from the major USAF commands and NATO countries participate in this competition – in which the RAF Regiment has achieved excellent results, including first place.

The Peace Keeper Challenge (PKC) competition is considered to be the "Olympics of Air Base Defence" and takes place at Kirtland AFB in New Mexico each year. Up to twenty participating teams come from the air forces of the USA, Australia, Canada and the United Kingdom and are first tested in physical fitness and marksmanship with rifles, pistols, machine guns and grenade launchers. Subsequent tactical exercises, in a variety of settings, complete the competition. An indication of the intensity of the contest is that although individual members of RAF Regiment teams have won gold medals, the highest team placing achieved – so far – by the RAF Regiment is 5th.

The Proof of the Pudding

Despite its small size, the Regiment embraces a wide range of skills which ensures that its personnel are adaptable and versatile. The Queen's Colour Squadron of the Royal Air Force (63 Squadron RAF Regiment) sets the benchmark for RAF ceremonial and – because its officers, NCOs and aircraftmen return to other units after a tour of duty with QCS – raises the standard of ceremonial within the Regiment as a whole.

2 Squadron has maintained its parachute role for over thirty years and in that time has leavened other units with a steady flow of experienced parachutists while continuing to demonstrate the value of an airborne capability within the Regiment. As a recognised airborne unit, it participates regularly in joint-service exercises in the UK and abroad.

Selected RAF Regiment officers and NCOs fill exchange and instructional posts in the British Army and in foreign forces as well

RAF Regiment team in the USAF 'Peacekeeper' competition.

2 Squadron parachute training.

as participating in United Nations monitoring operations in countries such as Iraq & Kuwait, Cambodia, and parts of the former Yugoslavia. In addition to the long-running USAF exchange programme, Regiment officers are serving on the instructional staff of the Royal Military Academy Sandhurst, in junior officer posts in British Army units and in a German SHORAD regiment, on loan service in Oman and with military training teams in overseas and Commonwealth countries. The Joint Arms Implementation Group, recently commanded by a Regiment group captain, continues to have RAF Regiment representation in it.

Senior NCOs are serving in exchange posts in the Royal Marines and the Parachute Regiment. Even within the Royal Air Force itself, a number of Regiment personnel are employed in non-Regiment posts because of their particular skills and the contribution which these enable them to make to the wider RAF mission.

Extra-regimental posts such as these are not easily come by and the fact that RAF Regiment personnel are sought after by others is an indication of their professional competence and the skills which they have to offer in a broad spectrum of challenging tasks. Equally important is the fact that on returning to the Regiment, they bring with them wider experience, better understanding of others and enhanced professional skills.

Notes

[1]   *Creevey Papers* p127

14

Epilogue

For our future security we must look forward from the past and its lessons, not back to the past.

MRAF Lord Tedder

This history is concerned with the first 50 years of the existence of the Royal Air Force Regiment. It has been necessary to survey the development of the Royal Air Force from its inception almost twenty-five years before that in order to understand the reasons for the creation of a ground fighting element within the structure of a Service whose raison d'etre is the exercise of air power.

Although this work has been published on the 55th anniversary of the Regiment's formation, it is silent on the events of the last five years. The reason for that is quite simple - contemporary events, momentous though they may be to those living through them, cannot be seen in an historical perspective until sufficient time has elapsed to enable them to be set against events which preceded them. There is also the matter of the source material which is available to the researcher; that which is in the public domain - principally in the Public Record Office, other accessible archives and published documents - can be used freely but classified government material is not normally released until the perceived need for security has disappeared. For those reasons, no classified source material has been reproduced in this book - and while this might make the contents less exciting, it avoids problems of departmental security.

As Lord Tedder has said, progress is based on learning from the past when laying plans for the future. Despite its unpropitious beginnings, the Regiment has, in its comparatively short life, carried out an amazing variety of tasks and earned for itself a reputation for reliability and professional competence. The past therefore provides a wide range of experience - often gained at some cost - on which to build for the future.

The first point to establish is what the Regiment is not. It is not a static "guard force" to obviate the need for all combatant personnel to carry out routine guard duties to protect their installations - and the lives of their comrades - against intruders and terrorists. Nor is the Regiment concerned with security and control of entry, which are among the tasks of the RAF Police. The Regiment is not a "private army" of soldiers wearing air force blue, nor is it a part-time and partly-trained security force carrying out only limited military tasks within airfield perimeters.

The RAF Regiment is a highly-trained and thoroughly professional military force which provides mobile ground combat and air defence units which are capable of being deployed wherever the RAF operates. Its personnel are also responsible for advising commanders and staff officers on defence matters and for training all members of the RAF to withstand hostile action while under attack. It is this close relationship within the framework of the Royal Air Force which gives the Regiment its credibility and ensures that its personnel and their roles are readily accepted by all ranks in the Service.

The Regiment is unique within the British Services in that - despite its small size - it has the capability for parachute assault, for mobile infantry tasks, for air defence missile operations and for ceremonial to the demanding standards of public duties in London and elsewhere. It includes some of the roles of the Parachute Regiment, the Royal Artillery, the infantry and the Guards - with personnel who are interchangeable within those varying roles. Its total manpower is less than that of an Army brigade but it is much more cost-effective than comparable Army units as Regiment units are supported by the RAF's administrative system and do not require separate - and expensive - support services.

The additional role of Regiment officers and NCOs extends throughout the Royal Air Force in training all RAF personnel in the active and NBC defence skills which are necessary to carry out their primary tasks in peace and war. The integration of the Regiment within the Air Force is not only the most economical solution to these problems but it also ensures that these resources remain under RAF command and control and can be utilised to meet the RAF's requirements, whenever and wherever they arise.

In essence, therefore, the lessons of the past sixty and more years are that the RAF requirement for air base defence - including the management of all its resources for maximum effectiveness when under attack - can only be properly achieved by its own in-house organisation. Reliance upon the Army has proved to be impractical and inefficient for both Services. This is understandable when the Army's primary task is to fight, and win, the land battle - for which a favourable air situation is essential. The absence of an adequate base defence capability for the RAF would leave the Army with two equally unpalatable choices - to detach much-needed forces from the land battle to defend air bases, or to fight without air support - and accept the inevitable defeat which would follow. Learning from the past, and looking to the future, the conclusion must be that the RAF Regiment is one of the best allies which the Army can have.

The other lesson worth remembering is that the RAF Regiment should never become larger than is absolutely essential for the fulfilment of its commitments to air operations. It must aim at meeting its many and varied tasks by a combination of flexibility, superior training and equipment - and sheer professional ability - and not by substituting quantity for quality.

When the parade and flypast arranged to mark the 75th Anniversary of the Royal Air Force in 1993 were cancelled due to appallingly bad weather, a disgruntled member of the public was heard to ask where the RAF's expensive all-weather fighters were that day. His neighbour promptly responded "the only all-weather fighters in the RAF are in the RAF Regiment."

Perhaps the last words on this subject should be those written by Douglas Evill in 1937: no works or equipment not provided in peace, and no measures of defence and protection not practised in advance, will be found of any effect in the opening stages of an emergency when the need for them will be at its height.

Per Ardua

"Down with work: the curse of the drinking classes!"
Oscar Wilde

From *RAF Types* by Chris Wren (1946).

With acknowledgements to Aeroplane Monthly and the RAF Club.

Light Armour

Operation Desert Storm – 1 Squadron in Iraq.   *© Crown copyright.*

Scorpion CVR(T) on a training exercise in Yorkshire.   *© Crown copyright.*

40/70 gun detachment at RAF Akrotiri, Cyprus, 1970.
From an original painting by Penelope Douglas GAvA. (Reproduced by kind permission of the artist)

50th Anniversary Celebrations on Horse Guards Parade

The March On.   *© Crown copyright.*

On Parade in 1942 uniform.   *© Crown copyright.*

The Queen's Colour Squadron on Horse Guards Parade.   *© Crown copyright.*

Naming a British Rail locomotive *The RAF Regiment* at King's Cross Station.
© Crown copyright.

50th Anniversary Review at the RAF Regiment Depot, Catterick, 1992

Her Majesty The Queen escorted by the Commandant-General, Air Vice-Marshal David Hawkins.   *© Crown copyright.*

Squadron Standards on Parade.   *© Crown copyright.*

Presentation of the third Queen's Colour for the RAF Regiment. *© Crown copyright.*

The post-Parade muster: Her Majesty The Queen escorted by Air Vice-Marshal Donald Pocock. *© Crown copyright.*

Rapier Field Standard C – missile launch.
© British Aerospace.

RAF Regiment Squadrons 1942-1946

Notes:

(1)   In April 1941, 150 RAF defence squadrons were formed but not numbered.

(2)   On 19th December 1941 these squadrons were numbered 701 to 850 inclusive.

(3)   On 1st February 1942 these squadrons were re-numbered 2701 to 2850 inclusive.

(4)   * Indicates squadrons with continuous existence from 1st February 1942 to December 1946.

Squadron

Number	Remarks
2701*	London 1941 – Depot 1943 – Catterick, February 1944 – LAA 2 TAF, April 1944 – N.W. Europe, August 1944 – Merged with No.1 Armoured Car Company, 31st October 1946. Renumbered 1 Squadron, February 1947.
2702*	Harrow 1941 – Yatesbury April 1943 – LAA May 1943 – Disbanded February 1945 – Reformed on merger with No. 2 Armoured Car Company, 31st October 1946. Renumbered 2 Squadron, February 1947.
2703	Worcester 1941 – Depot 1942 – Catterick 1943 – LAA 2 TAF, April 1944 – NW Europe, D + 8 – Disbanded Flensburg, November 1945.
2704	Llanbedr 1941 – Depot 1942 – Tangmere 1944 – LAA May 1943 – Disbanded Folkingham, October 1945.
2705	Fairwood Common 1941 – Depot 1942 – North Coates 1943 – LAA May 1943 – Disbanded, July 1944.

2706   Andreas 1941 – Depot 1942 – Hemswell 1943 – LAA May
            1943 – ACSEA August 1944 – Akyab – Hong Kong –
            Disbanded, May 1946.

2707   Ballykelly 1941 – LAA May 1943 – Hawkinge, West Malling
            1944 – Disbanded, October 1945.

2708   Northolt 1941 – Oakington 1943 – LAA May 1943 – ACSEA
            October 1944 – Meiktila – Hong Kong – Disbanded, May
            1946.

2709   Henlow 1941 – Biggin Hill 1942 – LAA May 1943 –
            Tangmere 1944 – Disbanded Folkingham, October 1945.

2710   Valley 1941 – West Malling 1942 – Field March 1943 – Rifle
            July 1944 – NW Europe May 1945 – Disbanded Schleswig,
            May 1946.

2711   Crosby 1941 – Croydon 1942 – Pevensey 1943 – LAA July
            1943 – Disbanded, June 1944.

2712   Ballyherbert 1941 – Mildenhall 1942 – LAA May 1943 –
            Disbanded, July 1944.

2713*   HQ Fighter Command 1941 – Field October 1943 – 2 TAF
            April 1944 – Rifle July 1944 – NW Europe August 1944 –
            Bonn, Hesselburg 1945 – Luneburg 1946 – Renumbered 51
            Rifle Squadron 1947

2714   Wormwell 1941 – Skuabrae 1942 – LAA May 1943 –
            Disbanded, July 1944.

2715   Dishforth 1941 – Depot 1942 – Manston 1943 – LAA May
            1943 – 2 TAF April 1944 – Rifle December 1944 – LAA
            January 1945 – NW Europe February 1945 – Gilze Rijen –
            Disbanded, December 1945.

2716   Finningley 1941 – Depot 1942 – LAA May 1943 – Disbanded,
            July 1944.

2717*   Hemswell 1941 – Tangmere 1943 – Field March 1943 – 2
            TAF April 1944 – Rifle July 1944 – NW Europe August 1944
            – BAFO to MEAF October 1945. Renumbered 52 Rifle
            Squadron 1947

2718	Leeming 1941 – Hornchurch 1942 – LAA May 1943 – Disbanded, June 1945.
2719	Lindholme 1941 – Coltishall 1942 – Wittering 1943 – 2 TAF April 1944 – Rifle July 1944 – NW Europe November 1944 – Disbanded Detmold, April 1946.
2720	Linton-on-Ouse 1941 – LAA June 1943 – Disbanded, September 1945.
2721*	Mildenhall 1941 – Kenley 1942 – Field October 1942 Middle East – Italy – Palestine – Rifle January 1946. Renumbered 53 Squadron, June 1947
2722	Newton 1941 – Hendon 1942 – LAA May 1943 – Rifle October 1944 – Disbanded, April 1945.
2723	Oakington 1941 – Tangmere 1942 – LAA May 1943 – Disbanded, September 1945.
2724*	Scampton 1941 – Depot 1942 – Feltwell 1943 – Field March 1943 – Rifle September 1944 – NW Europe November 1944 – Gilze Rijen – Fassberg – Gatow. Renumbered 54 Squadron August 1947.
2725	Stradishall 1941 – LAA July 1943 – Disbanded, April 1945.
2726	Swinderby 1941 – Depot 1942 – Field March 1943 – 2 TAF April 1944 – Rifle August 1944 – NW Europe August 1944 – Disbanded Lubeck, December 1946.
2727	Syerston 1941 – Henlow 1943 – LAA July 1943 – Disbanded, February 1946
2728	Waterbeach 1941 – LAA October 1942 – Disbanded, June 1944
2729	Waddington 1941 – Depot 1942 – Field March 1943 – Rifle July 1944 – NW Europe August 1944 – Disbanded, Gatow March 1946.
2730	Wyton 1941 – LAA October 1942 – Disbanded, June 1944.
2731	Abingdon 1941 – LAA May 1943 – Rifle October 1944 – NW Europe February 1945 – Disbanded Hamburg, August 1946.

2732   Bassingbourne 1941 – LAA July 1943 – Disbanded Llanbedr,
            April 1945.

2733   Benson 1941 – Manston 1943 – LAA May 1943 – Disbanded,
            April 1945.

2734   Bicester 1941 – LAA May 1943 – 2 TAF April 1944 – NW
            Europe D + 11 – Volkel, Fassberg – Disbanded Lubeck,
            November 1945.

2735   Bramcote 1941 – Martlesham 1942 – LAA May 1943 –
            Disbanded, April 1945.

2736   Cottesmore 1941 – Feltwell 1943 – LAA May 1943 – 2 TAF
            April 1944 – NW Europe D + 11 – Wunstorf 1945 –
            Disbanded, November 1945.

2737   Harwell 1941 – LAA July 1943 – Disbanded, December 1945.

2738   Upper Heyford 1941 – St. Eval 1942 – LAA May 1943 –
            Rifle October 1944 – NW Europe, January 1945 – Disbanded,
            Bonn July 1946.

2739   Upwood 1941 – Depot 1942 – Field March 1943 – 2 TAF
            April 1944 – ACSEA August 1944 – Rifle March 1946 –
            Disbanded, April 1946.

2740   Moreton-in-Marsh 1941 – LAA May 1943 – Rifle October
            1944 – NW Europe, February 1945 – Disbanded Gatow,
            September 1946.

2741   Pershore 1941 – Northolt 1942 – LAA May 1943 – Rifle
            October 1944 – NW Europe, January 1945 – Disbanded,
            August 1946.

2742   Wellesbourne Mountford 1941 – Depot 1942 – Field March
            1943 – 2 TAF April 1944 – Armoured Car August 1944 –
            NW Europe, November 1944 – Palestine October 1945 –
            Disbanded, August 1946.

2743   Topcliffe 1941 – LAA May 1943 – ACSEA October 1944 –
            Argatala 1945 – Disbanded 1946.

2744   Dyce 1941 – Depot 1942 – Field October 1942 – Middle
            East – Italy – Austria – Disbanded, June 1946.

2745	Leuchars 1941 – Skuabrae 1942 – LAA July 1943 – Disbanded, October 1943.
2746	Lossiemouth 1941 – LAA May 1943 – ACSEA October 1944 – Disbanded, April 1945.
2747	Kinloss 1941 – LAA May 1943 – Disbanded, October 1945.
2748	Wick 1941 – Tangmere 1942 – Sumburgh 1943 – LAA May 1943 – Absorbs 2778 Squadron – September 1944 – ACSEA October 1944 – Malaya 1945 – Disbanded, April 1946.
2749	Grantham 1941 – Wick 1942 – Scampton 1943 – LAA May 1943 – 2 TAF August 1944 – Rifle – NW Europe April 1945 – Rifle September 1944 – Disbanded Wahn, September 1946.
2750*	Carew Cheriton 1941 – Duxford 1942 – Wittering 1943 – LAA June 1943 – 2 TAF April 1944 – Rifle September 1944 – NW Europe December 1944 – Bonn, Osnabruck 1945 – Wahn 1946. Renumbered 55 August 1947.
2751	Sullom Voe 1941 – Detling 1942 – LAA May 1943 – Disbanded, July 1944.
2752	Stranraer 1941 – LAA July 1943 – Disbanded, April 1945.
2753	Turnhouse 1941 – Depot 1942 – LAA May 1943 – Disbanded, November 1945
2754	Limavady 1941 – LAA May 1943 – Disbanded, July 1944.
2755	Lough Erne 1941 – West Raynham 1943 – LAA May 1943 Disbanded, July 1944
2756	Eglington 1941 – LAA May 1943 – Disbanded, July 1944
2757*	Nutts Corner 1941 – Depot 1942 – Field March 1943 – 2 TAF April 1944 Armoured Car July 1944 – NW Europe August 1944 – Wunstorf 1945 – Gutersloh 1946 – Celle 1947. Renumbered 3 Squadron August 1947
2758	Aberporth 1941 – Depot 1942 – LAA May 1943 – Disbanded, August 1945.
2759	Andover 1941 – Field March 1943 2 TAF April 1944 – ACSEA August 1944 – Malaya 1945 – Disbanded, April 1946.

2760   Bodorgan 1941 – Sumburgh 1942 – LAA June 1943 – 2 TAF
            August 1944 – Rifle December 1944 – LAA January 1945 –
            NW Europe February 1945 – Hamburg 1945 – Disbanded,
            December 1946.

2761   Bottisham 1941 – LAA June 1943 – Disbanded, April 1945.

2762   Cardiff 1941 – Depot 1942 – LAA May 1943 – Disbanded,
            July 1945.

2763   Doncaster 1941 – LAA May 1943 – Disbanded, April 1944.

2764   Perton 1941 – Field October 1942 – Disbanded, June 1943.

2765   Gatwick 1941 – LAA May 1943 – Rifle October 1944 – NW
            Europe February 1945 – Disbanded, August 1946.

2766   Kidsdale 1941 – LAA May 1943 – Disbanded, October 1945.

2767   Manorbier 1941 – Depot 1942 LAA May 1943 – Disbanded,
            October 1945

2768   Odiham 1941 – Depot 1942 LAA May 1943 Rifle December
            1944 LAA January 1945 – NW Europe February 1945 –
            Disbanded, Volkel October 1945

2769   Old Sarum 1941 – LAA June 1943 – Disbanded, October
            1945.

2770   Sawbridgeworth 1941 – Depot 1942 LAA May 1943 – 2 TAF
            April 1944 Rifle September 1944 – NW Europe October 1944
            – Krefeld 1945 – Gutersloh 1946. Renumbered 56 Squadron
            August 1947

2771   Cleave 1941 – Depot 1942 – Field April 1942 – Middle East
            – Italy – Aegean – Greece – Austria – Palestine – Rifle March
            1946 – Disbanded, April 1946.

2772   Towyn 1941 – Depot 1942 – LAA May 1943 – Disbanded,
            April 1945.

2773   York 1941 – Depot 1942 – LAA May 1943 – 2 TAF April
            1944 NS Europe August 1944 – Disbanded, December 1945.

2774   Longkesh 1941 – LAA October 1942 – Disbanded, April
            1945.

2775   Newtonards 1941 – LAA October 1942 – Disbanded, October
            1943.

2776   Helensburgh 1941 – LAA May 1943 – Rifle October 1944 –
            Disbanded, February 1945.

2777*   Evanton 1941 – Field March 1943 – 2 TAF April 1944 –
            Armoured Car July 1944 – NW Europe August 1944 – Gilze
            Rijen – Ahlhorn 1945 – Celle 1946. Renumbered 4 Squadron
            August 1947

2778   Jurby 1941 – Manston 1942 – LAA May 1943 – Absorbed
            by 2748 Squadron September 1944.

2779   Netheravon 1941 – North Weald 1942 – LAA July 1943 –
            Disbanded, April 1945.

2780   Penrhos 1941 – Depot 1942 – LAA May 1943 – Disbanded,
            April 1945.

2781   Peterborough 1941 – Field March 1943 – 2 TAF April 1944
            – Armoured Car July 1944 NW Europe August 1944 –
            Schleswig, Kiel, Sylt 1945 – Disbanded Lubeck, July 1946.

2782   Manby 1941 – LAA May 1943 – Disbanded, July 1945.

2783   Upavon 1941 – LAA July 1943 – Disbanded, April 1945.

2784   West Freugh 1941 – LAA May 1943 – Rifle October 1944 –
            Disbanded, February 1945.

2785   Chivenor 1941 – LAA May 1943 – Disbanded, July 1944.

2786*   Boscombe Down 1941 – Netheravon 1943 – LAA May 1943
            – Rifle October 1944 – NW Europe April 1945 – Uetersen
            1946 – Renumbered 57 Squadron August 1947

2787   Swanage 1941 – LAA July 1943 – Disbanded, April 1945.

2788*   South Cerney 1941 – Depot 1942 – Field March 1942 –
            Middle East – Italy – Greece – Palestine – Rifle January 1946.
            Renumbered 58 Squadron June 1947.

2789   Montrose 1941 – LAA May 1943 – Disbanded, October 1944.

2790   Worcester 1941 – LAA May 1943 – Disbanded, October 1944.

2791	Cranfield 1941 – LAA May 1943 – 2 TAF August 1944 – Rifle December 1944 – LAA January 1945 – NW Europe February 1945 – Celle – UK – Disbanded Folkingham, December 1945.
2792	Kidlington 1941 – Depot 1942 – LAA May 1943 – Disbanded, October 1945.
2793	Grantham 1941 – Depot 1942 – LAA May 1943 – Disbanded, December 1945.
2794	Watchfield 1941 – LAA May 1943 – 2 TAF April 1944 – NW Europe D + 10 – Disbanded Flensburg, December 1945.
2795	Bovington 1941 – Depot 1942 – LAA May 1943 – Disbanded, October 1945.
2796	Ronaldsway 1941 – Eastchurch 1943 – LAA May 1943 – Disbanded, October 1945.
2797	North Luffenham 1941 – LAA May 1943 – Disbanded, April 1945.
2798*	Church Lawford 1941 – Depot 1942 – Field March 1943 – 2 TAF April 1944 – Rifle July 1944 – NW Europe July 1944 – Husum – Kiel – Sylt 1945 – Flensburg 1946 – Wahn 1947. Renumbered 59 Squadron August 1947
2799	Grangemouth 1941 – Depot 1942 – LAA May 1943 – Disbanded, October 1945.
2800	Pembrey 1941 – Colerne 1942 – LAA May 1943 – 2 TAF April 1944 – NW Europe August 1944 – Disbanded Dedelsdorf, December 1945.
2801	Stornoway 1941 – Northolt 1942 – LAA July 1943 – Disbanded, April 1945.
2802	Cardington 1941 – Depot 1942 – LAA May 1943 – ACSEA October 1944 – Malaya 1945 – Disbanded, February 1946.
2803	Sealand 1941 – Peterhead 1942 – LAA May 1943 – Disbanded, October 1945.
2804	Cosford 1941 – Halton 1942 – Field March 1943 – 2 TAF

April 1944 – Armoured Car July 1944 – NW Europe September 1944 – Disbanded Gatow, June 1946.

2805   Hawkinge 1941 – LAA May 1943 – Rifle October 1944 – NW Europe January 1945 – Disbanded Schleswig, June 1946.

2806   Cranwell 1941 – Field March 1943 – 2 TAF April 1944 – Armoured Car July 1944 – NW Europe July 1944 – Disbanded Lubeck, April 1946.

2807   Yatesbury 1941 – LAA May 1943 – Rifle October 1944 – NW Europe February 1945 – Disbanded Wahn, April 1946.

2808   Polebrook 1941 – LAA May 1943 – Disbanded, October 1944.

2809   Snaith 1941 – Wittering 1942 – Field October 1942 – LAA May 1943 – 2 TAF April 1944 – NS Europe D + 1 – Disbanded Schleswig, November 1945.

2810   Pocklington 1941 – LAA May 1943 – ACSEA October 1944 – Parachute – Malaya 1945 – Disbanded Changi, April 1947.

2811   Molesworth 1941 – LAA May 1943 – 2 TAF April 1944 – Rifle September 1944 – NW Europe November 1944 – Disbanded Ghent, March 1946.

2812   Holme 1941 – Coltishall 1942 – LAA May 1943 – 2 TAF August 1944 – Rifle December 1944 – LAA January 1945 – NW Europe February 1945 – Disbanded Epinoy, November 1945.

2813   Thurleigh 1941 – Middle Wallop 1942 – LAA May 1943 – Disbanded, July 1945.

2814   Stapleford 1941 – LAA May 1943 – 2 TAF April 1944 – Rifle September 1944 – NW Europe May 1945 – Disbanded Hildesheim, July 1946.

2815   Atcham 1941 – Kenley 1942 – Field October 1942 – LAA May 1943 – Disbanded, October 1944.

2816   Tempsford 1941 – Field April 1942 – 2 TAF April 1944 – Rifle July 1944 – NW Europe August 1944 – Disbanded Celle, June 1946.

2817   Bottesford 1941 – LAA May 1943 – 2 TAF April 1944 – NW
            Europe D + 2 – Brussels 1944 – Disbanded Uetersen,
            December 1945.

2818   Theale 1941 – Depot 1942 – LAA May 1943 – Rifle October
            1944 – Disbanded, April 1945.

2819   Chelveston 1941 – LAA May 1943 – 2 TAF April 1944 –
            NW Europe D + 1 – Eindhoven 1944 – Luneburg – Lubeck
            1945 – Disbanded Travemunde, December 1945.

2820   Millom 1941 – Kenley 1942 – LAA May 1943 – Disbanded,
            April 1943.

2821   Perth 1941 – Thorney Island 1942 – LAA May 1943 – Rifle
            May 1945 – Disbanded, October 1945.

2822   Colerne 1941 – Carlisle 1942 – Field March 1943 – Rifle
            January 1945 – NW Europe May 1945 – Disbanded Gutersloh,
            April 1946.

2823   Derby 1941 – LAA May 1943 – 2 TAF April 1944 – Rifle
            December 1944 – LAA January 1945 – NW Europe February
            1945 – Hamburg – Disbanded Stade, May 1946.

2824   Fairoaks 1941 – Biggin Hill 1942 – LAA May 1943 – Rifle
            December 1944 – LAA January 1945 – NW Europe February
            1945 – Disbanded Gilze Rijen, December 1945.

2825   Booker 1941 – Duxford 1942 – Field May 1942 – Middle
            East – Italy – Aegean – Austria – Rifle March 1946 –
            Disbanded, April 1946.

2826   Cambridge 1941 – Hawkinge 1942 – LAA May 1943 – 2
            TAF April 1944 – Rifle December 1944 – LAA January 1945
            – NW Europe February 1945 – Disbanded Flensburg,
            December 1945.

2827*   Castle Bromwich 1941 – Wittering 1942 – LAA May 1943 –
            2 TAF April 1944 – Rifle July 1944 – NW Europe July 1944
            – Volkel 1945 – Hamburg 1946 – Luneburg 1946. Renumbered
            60 Squadron August 1947.

2828   Honeybourne 1941 – LAA May 1943 – Disbanded, August
            1945.

2829*   Chipping Warden 1941 – Depot 1942 – Field March 1943 –
            2 TAF April 1944 – Rifle September 1944 – NW Europe
            November 1944 – Celle 1945 – Lubeck 1946 – Buckeburg
            1947 – Renumbered 61 Squadron August 1947

2830   Clyffe Pypard 1941 – Southend 1942 – LAA July 1943 –
            Disbanded, December 1945.

2831   Inverness 1941 – LAA May 1943 – 2 TAF August 1944 –
            NW Europe September 1944 – Rifle September 1944 –
            Disbanded Detmold, March 1946.

2832   Honiley 1941 – LAA May 1943 – Disbanded, April 1945.

2833   Hadley 1941 – Driffield 1943 – LAA May 1943 – Disbanded,
            July 1944.

2834   Wigtown 1941 – Wittering 1943 – LAA May 1943 – 2TAF
            April 1944 – NW Europe D + 1 – Volkel 1944 – Fassberg
            1945 – Disbanded Flensburg, November 1945.

2835   Woodvale 1941 – LAA May 1943 – Disbanded, April 1945.

2836   St. Angelo 1941 – West Raynham 1943 – LAA May 1943 –
            Disbanded, July 1944.

2837   Thruxton 1941 – LAA May 1943 – ACSEA August 1944 –
            Cox's Bazaar 1945 – Disbanded, March 1946.

2838   Dalcross 1941 – Leighton Buzzard 1942 – LAA May 1943 –
            2 TAF August 1944 – Rifle December 1944 – LAA January
            1945 – NW Europe February 1945 – Melsbroek – Disbanded
            Gutersloh, December 1945.

2839   Marston Moor 1941 – LAA May 1943 – Disbanded, August
            1945.

2840   Ossington 1941 – Depot 1942 – LAA May 1943 – Disbanded,
            August 1945.

2841   Benbecula 1941 – Leighton Buzzard 1942 – LAA June 1943
            – Disbanded, February 1945.

2842   Tiree 1941 – Binbrook 1943 – LAA May 1943 – Disbanded,
            July 1944.

2843   Thame 1941 – Field March 1943 – 2 TAF April 1944 – Rifle
          September 1944 – NW Europe November 1944 – Gilze Rijen
          – Celle 1945 – Disbanded Ahlhorn, August 1946.

2844   Barrow 1941 – Depot 1942 – Field October 1942 – LAA
          May 1943 – Rifle October 1944 – NW Europe 1945.
          Disbanded Luneburg, March 1946.

2845   Drem 1941 – Depot 1943 LAA May 1943 – 2 TAF April
          1944 – NW Europe September 1944 – Rifle December 1944
          – Disbanded Delmenhorst, December 1945.

2846   Leuchars 1941 – LAA May 1943 – ACSEA October 1944 –
          LAA February 1945 – Malaya – Disbanded, March 1946.

2847   Llandow 1941 – LAA May 1943 – Trondheim May 1945
          Disbanded, December 1945.

2848   Angle 1941 – LAA December 1943 – 2 TAF February 1944
          – Rifle September 1944 – NW Europe November 1944 –
          Disbanded Fassberg, July 1946.

2849   Wing 1941 – Debden 1942 – LAA July 1943 – Disbanded,
          June 1944.

2850   Weston-on-the Green 1941 – St. Athan 1942 – LAA October
          1942 – Disbanded, April 1945.

2851   Formed Ludham May 1942 – Disbanded, November 1943.

2852   Formed Greencastle May 1942 – ACSEA 1944 – Malaya 1945
          – Disbanded, March 1946.

2853   Formed Lough Erne May 1942 – Disbanded, April 1943 –
          Reformed Rifle 1944 – NW Europe April 1945 – Bad
          Godesburg – Disbanded, December 1945.

2854   Formed Carew Cheriton May 1942 – LAA May 1943 –
          ACSEA August 1944 – Akyab – Malaya 1945 – Disbanded,
          April 1946.

2855   Formed May 1942 – Sicily – Italy – Disbanded, January 1944.

2856   Formed May 1942 – Sicily – Italy – UK July 1944 – Rifle
          October 1944 – NW Europe January 1945 – Copenhagen –
          Disbanded Rendsburg, March 1946.

2857	Formed May 1942 – Sicily – Italy – UK July 1944 – Disbanded, November 1944.
2858	Formed Dyce May 1942 – Sicily – Italy – Rifle September 1944 – NW Europe May 1945 – Disbanded Celle, April 1946.
2859	Formed May 1942 – Sicily – Italy – Rifle October 1944 – Disbanded, April 1945.
2860	Formed May 1942 – LAA May 1943 – Italy – UK May 1944 – Disbanded, June 1944.
2861	Formed May 1942 – LAA May 1943 – Tunisia – Disbanded, November 1944.
2862	Formed May 1942 – LAA June 1943 – Malta – Sicily – Italy – UK July 1944 – Rifle October – NW Europe January 1945 – Jever – Disbanded Delmenhorst, March 1946.
2863	Formed May 1942 – LAA June 1943 – Italy – Rifle September 1944 – NW Europe November 1944 – Disbanded Wahn, December 1945.
2864	Formed May 1942 – LAA June 1943 – Sicily – Italy – Palestine – Rifle September 1944 – Renumbered 62 Squadron June 1947.
2865	Formed May 1942 – LAA June 1943 – Italy – Rifle October 1944 – NW Europe January 1945 – Gatow 1946 – Fassberg 1947. Renumbered 63 Squadron August 1947.
2866	Formed May 1942 – LAA June 1943 – Corsica – Rifle September 1944 – Austria 1945 – Disbanded, April 1946.
2867	Formed May 1942 – LAA June 1943 – Italy – Aegean – Disbanded, November 1944.
2868	Formed Stradishall May 1942 – LAA June 1943 – Sicily – Italy – UK June 1944 – Rifle October 1944 – NW Europe April 1945 – Copenhagen – Disbanded Uetersen, March 1946.
2869	Formed May 1942 – LAA June 1943 – Sardinia – UK May 1944 – Disbanded, June 1944.
2870	Formed Sealand May 1942 – LAA June 1943 – Tunisia – Disbanded, January 1944.

2871   Formed Exeter May 1943 – LAA in 2 TAF April 1944 – NW
            Europe September 1944 – Rifle September 1944 – Disbanded,
            December 1945.

2872   Formed Hawkinge May 1943 – LAA in 2 TAF April 1944 –
            NW Europe August 1944 – Disbanded Dedelsdorf, December
            1945.

2873   Formed Depot May 1943 – LAA in 2 TAF April 1944 – NW
            Europe August 1944 – Disbanded Dedelsdorf, December
            1945.

2874   Formed Tangmere May 1943 – LAA in 2 TAF April 1944 –
            NW Europe August 1944 – Disbanded Dedelsdorf, December
            1945.

2875   Formed Lympe July 1943 – LAA in 2 TAF April 1944 – NW
            Europe D + 12 Fassberg, Flensburg, Sylt 1945 – Disbanded
            UK, December 1945.

2876   Formed Tangmere July 1943 – LAA in 2 TAF April 1944 –
            NW Europe D + 2 – Eindhoven 1944 – Uetersen 1945 –
            Disbanded Sylt, June 1946.

2877   Formed Detling July 1943 – Disbanded, October 1946.

2878   Formed Upavon June 1943 – 2 TAF April 1944 – Rifle
            September 1944 – NW Europe May 1945 – Disbanded
            Delmenhorst, September 1946.

2879   Formed Castle Camps June 1943 – 2 TAF April 1944 – Rifle
            October 1944 – NW Europe November 1944 – Gilze Rijen –
            Dortmund 1945 – Disbanded May 1946.

2880   Formed Kingscliffe June 1943 – 2 TAF April 1944 – NW
            Europe August 1944 – Disbanded Wunstorf June 1946.

2881   Formed Snailwell June 1943 – 2 TAF April 1944 – NW Europe
            August 1944 – Disbanded Travemunde, November 1945.

2882   Formed Northolt June 1943 – Disbanded, April 1945.

2883   Formed Redhill June 1943 – Rifle October 1944 – NW Europe
            April 1945 – Disbanded Wahn, December 1945.

2884   Formed Thruxton May 1942 – Disbanded, November 1943.

2885   Formed Northolt May 1942 – Disbanded, October 1943.

2886   Formed Debden May 1942 – ACSEA October 1944 –
            Disbanded, October 1945.

2887   Formed Castle Camps May 1942 – Disbanded, November
            1943.

2888   Formed Christchurch May 1942 – Disbanded, October 1943.

2889   Formed Fairlop October 1942 – Disbanded, May 1945.

2890   Formed Waddington October 1942 – Disbanded April 1945.

2891   Formed Atcham October 1942 – Disbanded April 1945.

2892   Formed Squires Gate October 1942 – Disbanded, April 1945.

2893   Formed Valley October 1942 – Disbanded, October 1944.

2894   Formed Tangmere October 1942 – Disbanded, April 1945.

2895   Formed Hawkinge October 1942 – Disbanded, October 1944.

2896   Formed Warmwell October 1942 – ACSEA October 1944 –
            Secunderabad – Singapore 1945 – Disbanded, June 1946.

2897   Formed Ford October 1942 – 2 TAF April 1944 – Rifle July
            1944 – NW Europe August 1944 – Detmold 1945 – Bad-
            Eilsen 1946 – Lubeck 1947. Renumbered 64 Squadron August
            1947

2898   Formed Manston October 1942 – Field November 1943 –
            Rifle March 1946 – Absorbed 2908 Squadron 1947.
            Renumbered 65 Squadron June 1947.

2899   Formed North Luffenham June 1943 – Disbanded October
            1943 – Reformed by absorbing 2924 Squadron January 1947.
            Renumbered 66 Squadron June 1947.

2900   Formed Middle East May 1943 – LAA December 1943 –
            Disbanded, November 1944.

2901   Formed Middle East May 1943 – Field November 1943 –
            Disbanded February 1944.

2902	Formed Middle East May 1943 – Field November 1943 – Greece – Palestine – Rifle January 1946 – Disbanded, April 1946.
2903	Formed Middle East May 1943 – Field November 1943 – Disbanded, February 1944.
2904	Formed Middle East May 1943 – Sicily – Italy – Disbanded, February 1944.
2905	Formed Middle East May 1943 – Italy September 1943 – UK May 1944 – Disbanded, June 1944.
2906	Formed Middle East May 1943 – Sicily – Italy – Disbanded, February 1944.
2907	Formed Middle East May 1943 – LAA November 1943 – Aegean – Disbanded, November 1944.
2908	Formed Middle East May 1943 – Field November 1943 – Greece 1944 – Palestine 1945 – Rifle March 1946 – Absorbed by 2898 Squadron January 1947.
2909	Formed Middle East May 1943 – LAA August 1943 – Cos October 1943.
2910	Formed Middle East May 1943 – LAA November 1943 – Disbanded, June 1944.
2911	Formed Middle East May 1943 – Field November 1943 – Disbanded, June 1944.
2912	Formed Middle East May 1943 – LAA November 1943 – Disbanded, June 1944.
2913	Formed Middle East May 1943 – LAA December 1943 – Disbanded November 1944.
2914	Formed Middle East May 1943 – Field November 1943 – LAA January 1944 – Aegean – Greece – Austria 1945 – Disbanded March 1946.
2915	Formed Middle East May 1943 – LAA December 1943 – Disbanded, June 1944.

2916	Formed Middle East May 1943 – LAA November 1943 – Disbanded, November 1944.
2917	Formed Middle East May 1943 – LAA November 1943 – Disbanded, June 1944.
2918	Formed Middle East May 1943 – LAA November 1943 – Disbanded, June 1944.
2919	Formed Middle East May 1943 – Field November 1943 – Disbanded, March 1944.
2920	Formed Middle East March 1943 – Hadera – Disbanded June 1944.
2921	Formed Middle East May 1943 – Hadera – Disbanded June 1944.
2922	Formed Middle East May 1943 – LAA November 1943 – Disbanded, June 1944.
2923	Formed Middle East May 1943 – LAA December 1943 – Greece 1944 – Palestine 1945 – Rifle 1945 – Disbanded, April 1946.
2924	Formed Middle East June 1943 – Field November 1943 – Aegean – Greece – Palestine – Rifle January 1946 – Absorbed by 2899 Squadron January 1947.
2925	Formed Middle East June 1943 – Sicily – Italy – Disbanded, February 1944.
2926	Formed Middle East June 1943 – LAA November 1943 – Greece – Austria – Disbanded, March 1946.
2927	Formed Middle East June 1943 – LAA November 1943 – Disbanded, June 1944.
2928	Formed Middled East June 1943 – Disbanded, March 1944.
2929	Formed Middle East June 1943 – LAA November 1943 – Disbanded, January 1944.
2930	Formed Middle East as "A" Squadron RAF Regiment, February 1943 – LAA December 1943 – Disbanded, January 1944.

2931	Formed Middle East as "B" Squadron RAF Regiment, February 1943 – LAA November 1943 – Disbanded, June 1944.
2932	Formed Middle East as "C" Squadron RAF Regiment, February 1943 – Adriatic (Vis) 1944 – Austria 1945 – Disbanded, March 1946.
2933	Formed Middle East as "D" Squadron RAF Regiment, February 1943 – LAA November 1943 – Disbanded 1944.
2934	Formed Middle East June 1943 – NWAAF September 1943 – Disbanded, June 1944.
2935	Formed Middle East October 1943 – Disbanded, June 1944.
2936 – 2940	Not Used.
2941	Formed India April 1943 – Imphal-Arakan 1944/1945 – Meiktila – Disbanded, June 1946.
2942	Formed India May 1943 – Imphal-Arakan 1944/1945 – Disbanded, December 1946.
2943	Formed India May 1943 – Burma – Java, 1945 – Disbanded, March 1946.
2944	Formed India June 1943 – Burma – Imphal – Sumatra 1945 – Disbanded, January 1946.
2945	Formed India June 1943 – Burma 1945 – Disbanded, June 1946.
2946	Formed India June 1943 – Cox's Bazaar – Imphal – Burma 1945 – Disbanded January 1946.
2947	Formed Daxsham 1943 – LAA April 1944 – Disbanded, April 1946.
2948	Formed Danby Beacon 1943 – LAA May 1944 – Disbanded April 1946.
2949	Formed Longcross 1943 – LAA April 1944 – Stavanger – Oslo May 1945 – Disbanded December 1945.
2950	Formed Longcross 1943 – LAA December 1944 – Disbanded, April 1945.

2951 Formed Longcross 1943 – LAA December 1944 – Disbanded, April 1945.

2952 Formed North Luffenham 1943 – LAA June 1943 – Disbanded, October 1943.

2953 Formed Wellingore 1943 – LAA June 1943 – Disbanded, October 1943.

2954 Formed Driffield 1943 – LAA June 1943 – Rifle September 1944 – Disbanded, September 1945.

2955 Formed St. Athan 1943 – LAA June 1943 – Disbanded, April 1945.

2956 Formed Waddington 1943 – LAA June 1943 – Disbanded, November 1944.

2957 Formed Locking 1943 – LAA July 1943 – Disbanded, June 1944.

2958 Recce Squadron in SEAC – LAA May 1944 – Chittagong – Burma 1945 – Disbanded, January 1946.

2959 Recce Squadron in SEAC – LAA June 1944 – Cox's Bazaar – Ramree 1945 – Disbanded, January 1945.

2960 Formed Secunderabad as LAA July 1944 – Imphal – Burma 1945 – Disbanded, May 1946.

2961 Formed Secunderabad as LAA July 1944 – Burma 1945 – Sumatra 1945 – Disbanded, January 1946.

2962 Formed Secunderabad as LAA August 1944 – Burma – Cocos Islands – Java 1945 – Rifle March 1946 – Disbanded, August 1946.

2963 Formed Secunderabad as LAA July 1944 – Meiktila, Saigon 1945 – Disbanded, March 1946.

2964 Formed Secunderabad as LAA July 1944 – Field November 1944 – Malaya 1945 – Disbanded, March 1946.

2965 Formed Secunderabad as LAA August 1944 – Burma 1945 – Disbanded, April 1946.

2966	Formed Secunderabad as Field July 1944 – Akyab 1945 – Disbanded, August 1946.
2967	Formed Secunderabad as Field July 1944 – Ramree 1945 – Saigon 1945 – Disbanded, February 1946.
2968	Formed Secunderabad as Field July 1944 – Meiktila – Sumatra 1945 – Disbanded, January 1946.
2969	Formed Acerra as Rifle March 1945 – Disbanded, April 1946.
2970	Formed Secunderabad as Armoured Car February 1945 – Disbanded, March 1946.
2971	Formed Secunderabad as Armoured Car February 1945 – Disbanded March 1946.
2972	Formed Secunderabad as Armoured Car February 1945 – Disbanded, March 1946.
2700	Formed as LAA in UK June 1946. Renumbered 15 Squadron June 1947.

RAF Regiment Squadrons
1947-1992
Active Units (as at 1st February 1992)

Squadron
Number   **Remarks**

2*   No. 2 Armoured Car Company incorporated into the RAF
               Regiment and re-numbered 2702 Squadron 3rd October 1946
               in Palestine. Re-numbered 2 (Armoured Car) Squadron 25th
               February 1947 at Ramleh (Palestine). Amman – Habbaniya
               – Sharjah – Habbaniya – Nicosia – Luqa – Felixstowe –
               Colerne (Parachute role) – Catterick – Hullavington. Op
               Granby 1990.

               Total Service 69 years 10 months 13 days. Continuous
               existence since 7th April 1922.

1*   No. 1 Armoured Car Company incorporated into the RAF
               Regiment and re-numbered 2701 Squadron 3rd October 1946
               at Quastina (Palestine). Re-numbered 1 (Armoured Car)
               Squadron 25th February 1947. Ramleh August 1947.
               Disbanded Ramleh – Re-formed Sundern – Lubeck –
               Luneberg – Wunstorf Disbanded Wunstorf Re-formed – El
               Adem – Butterworth – Bicester – Laarbruch – Op Desert
               Storm 1991.

               Total Service 63 years 9 months 11 days.

63   Re-numbered 63 Squadron from 2865 21st August 1947 at
               Gatow. Fassberg – Upavon – Middleton St.George – Pembrey
               – Ouston – Felixstowe – Malta – Felixstowe – Cyprus –
               Tengah – North Luffenham – Gutersloh. Op Corporate 1982.

               Total Service 48 years 8 months.

15   Re-numbered 15 Squadron from 2700 Squadron 8th June
               1947 at Nethertown. Watchet – Upavon – Pembrey – Thornaby

– Innsworth – Changi – Seletar – Wittering – Leeming. Op Corporate 1982. Op Roust 1983-85.

Total Service 45 years 8 months.

16   Formed Watchet 12th January 1948 – Upavon – Wattisham – Innsworth – Felixstowe – Upwood – Catterick – Wildenrath. Total Service 44 years 19 days.

51*   Re-numbered 51 Squadron from 2713 Squadron at Luneburg 21st August 1947 – Utersen – Fassberg – Celle – Disbanded Celle – Reformed Catterick – Wittering. Op Granby and Op Desert Storm 1990-91.

Total Service 43 years 2 months 18 days.

26   Formed Yatesbury 27th August 1951 – Abu Sueir – Habbaniya – Amman – Tymbou – Nicosia – Changi – Bicester – Gutersloh – Laarbruch. Op Granby and Op Desert Storm 1990-91.

Total Service 40 years 5 months 4 days.

27   Formed Yatesbury 3rd September 1951 – Canal Zone – Nicosia – Akrotiri – Leeming – Akrotiri – North Luffenham – Leuchars.

Total Service 40 years 4 months 30 days.

48   Formed Chivenor 3rd October 1951 – Rudloe Manor – Op Musketeer – Felixstowe – Upwood – Catterick.

Total Service 40 years 3 months 28 days.

34   Formed Yatesbury 19th November 1951 – El Hamra – Kasfareet – Abu Sueir – Nicosia – Akrotiri – Khormaksar – Mehrabad – Cyprus. Op Granby 1990.

Total Service 40 years 2 months 11 days.

37   Formed Yatesbury December 1951 – Abu Sueir – Nicosia – Akrotiri – Upwood – Khormaksar – Catterick – Bruggen.

Total Service 40 years 1 month 14 days.

58*	Re-numbered 58 Squadron (Rifle) from 2788 Squadron 8th June 1947 at Wali Road (Palestine) – Aden – Disbanded Khormaksar – Re-formed North Luffenham Laarbruch – Catterick – Op Desert Storm 1991.
	Total Service 33 years 3 months 30 days.
66	Re-numbered 66 Squadron from 2899 Squadron 8th June 1947 at Lydda – El Hamra – Aden 1948 – Disbanded Aden Re-formed North Luffenham – Bruggen – Catterick – Disbanded Catterick – Re-formed West Raynham Op Granby and Op Desert Storm 1990-91.
	Total Service 25 years 7 months 25 days.
19*	Re-numbered 19 Squadron 1st May 1949 from 55 Squadron at Gutersloh – Disbanded Laarbruch – Re-formed Brize Norton.
	Total Service 23 years 6 months.
20*	Re-numbered 20 Squadron 1st May 1949 from 64 Squadron at Gutersloh – Disbanded – Reformed Operation Granby 1991
	Total Service 22 years 6 months 28 days.
3*	Re-numbered 3 Squadron from 2757 Squadron 21st August 1947 at Gutersloh – Disbanded Oldenburg – Re-formed from 168 Squadron Disbanded Oldenburg – Re-formed Hullavington – Aldergrove.
	Total Service 20 years 2 months 5 days.

Inactive Units (as at 1st February 1992)

54*	Re-numbered 54 Squadron 21st August 1947 Disbanded Wildenrath 1st January 1958
	Total service 15 years 11 months
17*	Re-numbered 17 Squadron 1st May 1949, from 59 Squadron at Celle – Disbanded Celle 30th September 1957.
	Total Service 15 years 8 months.

18*   Re-numbered 18 Squadron 1st May 1949, from 61 Squadron at Celle – Disbanded Celle 30th September 1957.

             Total Service 15 years 8 months.

57*   Re-numbered 57 Squadron from 2786 Squadron 21st August 1947 at Blankenese – Disbanded Gutersloh 30th September 1957.

             Total Service 15 years 8 months.

60*   Re-numbered 60 Squadron from 2827 Squadron 21st August 1947 at Hamburg Altona – Disbanded Oldenburg – Re-formed from 199 Squadron Disbanded Oldenburg 30th September 1957.

             Total Service 15 years 8 months.

21   Re-numbered 21 Squadron 1st August 1949 from 52 Squadron. Amman – Aden – Mafraq – Habbaniya – Disbanded Nicosia 15th June 1957.

             Total Service 15 years 4 months 12 days.

56*   Re-numbered 56 Squadron from 2770 Squadron 21st August 1947 at Gutersloh – Disbanded Shallufa 14th January 1956.

             Total Service 13 years 11 months 14 days.

28   Formed Yatesbury 17th September 1951 – Canal Zone – Akrotiri – Nicosia – Disbanded Nicosia 1st January 1964.

             Total Service 12 years 3 months 13 days.

194   Formed Pembrey 1st January 1952 – Akrotiri – Disbanded Akrotiri 16th November 1960.

             Total Service 8 years 10 months 16 days.

24   Formed Yatesbury 30th July 1951 – Disbanded Wildenrath 1st January 1958.

             Total Service 6 years 5 months 1 day.

25   Formed Yatesbury 4th August 1951 – Disbanded Wildenrath 1st January 1958.

             Total Service 6 years 4 months 27 days.

30   Formed Yatesbury 8th October 1951 – Disbanded Laarbruch
                1st January 1958.

                Total Service 6 years 2 months 23 days.

22   Formed Yatesbury 9th July 1951. Disbanded Gutersloh 30th
                September 1957.

                Total Service 6 years 2 months 22 days.

23   Formed Yatesbury 16th July 1951 – Disbanded Gutersloh 30th
                September 1957.

                Total Service 6 years 2 months 15 days.

53*   Re-numbered 53 Squadron from 2721 Squadron 8th June
                1947 at Ein Shemer – Disbanded 5th February 1948.

                Total Service 5 years 11 months 29 days.

31   Formed Yatesbury 15th October 1951 – Disbanded Wunstorf
                30th September 1957.

                Total Service 5 years 11 months 16 days.

32   Formed Yatesbury 29th October 1951 – Disbanded Wunstorf
                30th September 1957.

                Total Service 5 years 11 months 2 days.

33   Formed Yatesbury 5th November 1951 – Disbanded
                Oldenburg 30th September 1957.

                Total Service 5 years 10 months 25 days.

29   Formed Yatesbury 24th September 1951 – Canal Zone –
                Mafraq 1956 – Disbanded Nicosia 15th June 1957.

                Total Service 5 years 8 months 21 days.

75   Formed Hawarden 16th June 1952 – Disbanded Geilenkirchen
                1st January 1958.

                Total Service 5 years 6 months 14 days.

65   Re-numbered 65 Squadron from 2898 Squadron 8th June
                1947 at Ein Shemer – Disbanded 5th February 1948.

                Total Service 5 years 5 months 29 days.

80   Formed Hawarden 7th July 1952 – Disbanded Geilenkirchen
            1st January 1958.

            Total Service 5 years 5 months 24 days.

85   Formed Hawarden 28th July 1952 – Disbanded Bruggen 1st
            January 1958.

            Total Service 5 years 5 months 3 days.

89   Formed Hawarden 28th July 1952 – Disbanded Bruggen 1st
            January 1958.

            Total Service 5 years 5 months 3 days.

100   Formed Hawarden 15th September 1952 – Disbanded Wahn
            31st May 1957.

            Total Service 4 years 8 months 15 days.

104   Formed Hawarden 6th October 1952 – Disbanded Wahn 31st
            May 1957.

            Total Service 4 years 7 months 25 days.

35   Formed Yatesbury 26th November 1951 – Disbanded
            Kasfareet 31st March 1956.

            Total Service 4 years 4 months 4 days.

289   Formed Catterick 1st May 1952 – Disbanded Wattisham 29th
            February 1956.

            Total Service 3 years 10 months.

533   Formed Hereford 1st July 1952 – Disbanded Thornaby 29th
            February 1956.

            Total Service 3 years 8 months.

36   Formed Yatesbury 10th December 1951 – Disbanded Ismailia
            1st May 1955.

            Total Service 3 years 4 months 21 days.

Notes

(1)   Number-plate seniority is determined by the rules governing periods of qualifying service for award of The Standard. Under these rules, precedents for counting time under previous number-plates were authorised provided that the change in number-plate was for administrative reasons and there had been continuity of service by the squadron personnel then concerned.

(2)   An asterisk indicates units directly descended from those squadrons formed on 1st February 1942, when the Royal Air Force Regiment was raised.

(3)   The crediting of service from one number-plate to another prevents the former unit from being re-formed. Consequently, the following post-1947 squadrons are omitted from the seniority list:

No. 4*   Re-numbered from 2777 Squadron 21st August 1947, at Celle and subsequently absorbed into 1 Squadron 15th March 1948.

No.52*   Re-numbered from 2717 Squadron 8th June 1947, at Jerusalem and subsequently re-numbered 21 Squadron 1st August 1949.

No.54*   Re-numbered from 2724 Squadron 21st August 1947 at Celle and subsequently re-numbered 15 Squadron 1st August 1990.

No.55*   Re-numbered from 2750 Squadron 21st August 1947 at Wahn and subsequently re-numbered 19 Squadron 1st January 1958.

No. 59*   Re-numbered from 2798 Squadron 21st August 1947 at Wunstorf and subsequently re-numbered 17 Squadron 1st May 1949.

No. 61*   Re-numbered from 2829 Squadron 21st August 1947 at Lubeck and subsequently re-numbered 18 Squadron 1st May 1949.

No. 62   Re-numbered from 2864 Squadron 8th June 1947 at Wali Road and subsequently re-numbered 1 Squadron 1st June 1958.

No. 64*   Re-numbered from 2897 Squadron 21st August 1947 at
           Bad-Eilsen and subsequently re-numbered 20 Squadron
           1st May 1949.

No.168   Formed Hawarden 27th October 1952 and subsequently
           re-numbered 3 Squadron 1st January 1956.

No.199 Formed Hawarden 17th November 1952 and subsequently
           re-numbered 60 Squadron 1st January 1956.

ANNEX "C"

Squadron Standards and Battle Honours

Squadron Number	Emblazoned	Not Emblazoned
1	Habbaniya Iraq 1941 Egypt & Libya 1941-43 Gulf 1991	Kurdistan 1922-23 Kurdistan 1930-31 Palestine 1936
2	Egypt & Libya 1940-43 Iraq 1941 Syria 1941 El Alamein North Africa 1943	Transjordan 1924 Palestine 1936-39
63	Italy 1943-45 France & Germany 1945 South Atlantic 1982	
51	France & Germany 1944-45	Gulf 1991
26	Nil	Gulf 1991
34	Nil	Gulf 1991
58	Home Defence 1941-42 North Africa 1942-43 Italy 1943-45 Gustav Line May 1944 France 1944 South East Asia 1944-45	Gulf 1991

Squadrons Without Standards

66	Home Defence 1941-42	Gulf 1991
	France & Germany 1944-45	
19	Home Defence 1941-42	
	France & Germany 1944-45	
20	Home Defence 1941-42	
	France & Germany 1944-45	
3	Iraq 1923-25	
	France & Germany 1944-45	

ANNEX "D"

RAF Regiment
Wing Headquarters
1944-1946

Wing
Number

1300   Formed as 1300 (Mobile) Wing 1st April 1944 – NW Europe D + 2 – Disbanded 15th February 1945 – Re-formed as 1300 Wing 1st October 1945 – Altona Hamburg December 1945 – Re-numbered 1 Wing 21st August 1947.

1301   Formed April 1944 – NW Europe D + 9 – Disbanded Eggebek June 1946.

1302   Formed April 1944 – NW Europe D + 2 – Disbanded Lubeck March 1946.

1303   Formed April 1944 – NW Europe D + 9 – Disbanded Sylt April 1946.

1304   Formed as 1304 (Mobile) Wing 1st April 1944 – NW Europe D + 1 – Disbanded 15th April 1945 – Re-formed as 1304 Wing 1st October 1945 – Celle December 1945 – Re-numbered 4 Wing 21st August 1947.

1305   Formed April 1944 – NW Europe D + 1 – Disbanded Eggebek January 1946.

1306   Formed as 1306 (Mobile) Wing 1st April 1944 – NW Europe D + 10 – Disbanded 15th February 1945 – Re-formed as 1306 Wing 1st October 1945 – Gatow September 1946 – Re-numbered 6 Wing 21st August 1947.

1307   Formed April 1944 – NW Europe D + 11 – ACSEA December 1944 – Meiktila – Disbanded Saigon March 1946.

1308   Formed April 1944 – NW Europe D + 11 – India December 1944 – Burma March 1945 – Java October 1945 – Disbanded Batavia April 1946.

1309	Formed April 1944 – NW Europe D + 2 – Disbanded Helmond February 1945.
1310	Formed June 1944 – NW Europe August 1944 – Disbanded 1946.
1311	Formed June 1944 – NW Europe August 1944 – Disbanded Delmenhorst September 1946.
1312	Formed June 1944 – NW Europe August 1945 – Disbanded Grimbergen January 1945.
1313	Formed June 1944 – NW Europe August 1944 – Disbanded Gutersloh September 1946.
1314	Formed June 1944 – NW Europe August 1944 – Disbanded December 1946.
1315	Formed June 1944 – NW Europe August 1944 – Disbanded Wahn April 1946.
1316	Formed as 1316 (Mobile) Wing 1st April 1944 – NW Europe August 1944 – Disbanded 15th February 1945 – Re-formed as 1316 Wing 1st October 1945 – Surdern December 1945 – Re-numbered 16 Wing 21st August 1947.
1317	Formed June 1944 – NW Europe July 1944 – Disbanded Gatow July 1946.
1318	Formed June 1944 – NW Europe D + 2 – Disbanded Oslo July 1945.
1319	Formed Italy 9th March 1944 – Palestine December 1945 – Ramleh June 1946 – Re-numbered 19 Wing 8th June 1947.
1320	Formed Italy 9th March 1944 – Austria May 1945 – Ein Shemer March 1946 – Re-numbered 20 Wing 8th June 1947.
1321	Formed Italy April 1944 – Balkan Air Force – Greece October 1944 – Palestine March 1945 – Disbanded Ramleh December 1946.
1322	Formed Aboukir July 1944 – Disbanded Naples November 1944.

1323   Formed India July 1944 – Burma – Sumatra – Disbanded
            Medan March 1946.

1324   Formed India July 1944 – Burma – Malaya September 1945
            – Disbanded Kallang February 1946.

1325   Formed India October 1945 – Disbanded Secunderabad March
            1946.

1326   Formed Burma October 1944 – Penang September 1945 –
            Disbanded Singapore May 1946.

1327   Formed Burma September 1944 – Rangoon May 1945 –
            Disbanded Kuala Lumpur February 1946.

1328   Formed Italy September 1944 – Balkan Air Force – Disbanded
            Graz April 1946.

1329   Formed UK November 1944 – India January 1945 – Penang
            September 1945 – Disbanded Tengah February 1946.

1330   Formed UK December 1944 – India January 1945 – Burma –
            Disbanded Rangoon March 1946.

1331   Formed India February 1945 – Burma – Hong Kong October
            1945 – Disbanded Kai Tak May 1946.

1332   Formed Bradwell Bay January 1945 – Disbanded Bradwell
            Bay September 1945.

1333   Formed Manston January 1945 – Disbanded Bradwell Bay
            September 1945.

1334   Formed Kenley January 1945 – Disbanded Gatwick September
            1945.

1335   Formed Kenley January 1945 – Disbanded Gatwick September
            1945.

1336   Formed Detling January 1945 – Disbanded Trondheim July
            1945.

1337   Formed Colerne January 1945 – Disbanded Gatwick October
            1945.

1338   Formed Detling January 1945 – Disbanded Llanbedr October
            1945.

ANNEX "E"

RAF Regiment
Wing Headquarters
1947-1992

Active Units (as at 1st February 1992)

**Wing
Number**

3   Formed El Hamra 20th August 1951 – Nicosia December
            1955 – Akrotiri March 1956 – Catterick January 1975 – Op
            Corporate 1982 – Op Granby 1990.

            Total Service 40 years 5 months 11 days.

33   Formed Innsworth 20th October 1952 – Felixstowe January
            1960 – Upwood July 1962 – Catterick April 1964 – Wildenrath
            July 1973 – Laarbruch March 1976 – Gutersloh August 1980
            – Op Granby 1990.

            Total Service 39 years 3 months 11 days.

4   Re-numbered 4 Wing from 1304 Wing at Celle 21st August
            1947 – Luneberg 1949 – Jever 1952 – Laarbruch 1955 –
            Oldenburg 1956 – Absorbed 51 Wing 1st January 1956 –
            Disbanded Oldenburg 30th September 1957 – Re-formed
            Catterick 3rd December 1973 – Bruggen January 1974 –
            Wildenrath June 1978 – Op Corporate 1982 – Op Desert
            Storm 1991.

            Total Service 30 years 1 month 28 days.

6   Re-numbered 6 Wing from 1306 Wing at Gatow 21st August
            1947 – Wahn February 1949 – Celle September 1949 –
            Disbanded Celle 30th September 1957 – Re-formed West
            Raynham 1st July 1983 – Op Desert Storm 1991.

            Total Service 21 years 5 months 14 days.

Inactive Units (as at 1st February 1992)

5
Formed Yatesbury 10th September 1951 – El Hamra November 1951 – Habbaniya November 1954 – Mafraq February 1956 – Nicosia August 1956 – Akrotiri October 1956 – Nicosia July 1958 – Disbanded Nicosia 1st January 1964 – Re-formed Bicester 1st April 1967 – Wittering October 1970 – Hullavington 11th October 1982 – Disbanded 31st July 1990.

Total Service 35 years 7 months 20 days.

20
Re-numbered 20 Wing from 1320 Wing at Ein Shemer 8th June 1947 – Khormaksar May 1948 – Disbanded Khormaksar 30th June 1957.

Total Service 13 years 3 months 21 days.

16
Re-numbered 16 Wing from 1316 Wing at Gutersloh 21st August 1947 – Sundern February 1949 – Gutersloh May 1950 – Laarbruch March 1955 – Disbanded Laarbruch 1st January 1958.

Total Service 13 years 1 month 15 days.

19
Re-numbered 19 Wing from 1319 Wing at Ramleh 8th June 1947 – Amman January 1948 – Disbanded Amman 20th July 1953 – Re-formed at Kabrit 15th September 1953 – Amman May 1955 – Mafraq October 1956 – Habbaniya May 1957 – Disbanded Habbaniya 15th June 1957.

Total Service 13 years 1 month 12 days.

1
Re-numbered 1 Wing from 1300 Wing at Hamburg 21st August 1947 – Fassberg November 1947 – Gutersloh August 1956 – Disbanded Gutersloh 30th September 1957.

Total Service 12 years 10 months 14 days.

2
Formed Upavon 1st January 1948 – Disbanded Upavon 16th March 1951 – Re-formed Yatesbury 9th July 1951 – Uetersen August 1951 – Wildenrath February 1952 – Disbanded Wildenrath 1st January 1958.

Total Service 9 years 8 months 8 days.

8   Formed Yatesbury 12th November 1951 – Elhamra December
             1951 – Kasfareet October 1955 – Abu Sueir December 1955
             – Nicosia April 1956 – Disbanded Nicosia 16th November
             1960.

             Total Service 9 years 4 days.

7   Formed Yatesbury 1st October 1951 – Wunstorf October 1951
             – Disbanded Wunstorf 30th September 1957.

             Total Service 6 years.

25   Formed Hawarden 9th June 1952 – Luneburg July 1952 –
             Geilenkirchen May 1953 – Disbanded Geilenkirchen 1st
             January 1958.

             Total Service 5 years 6 months 21 days.

55   Formed Hawarden 21st July 1952 – Luneburg August 1952 –
             Bruggen July 1953 – Disbanded Bruggen 1st January 1958.

             Total Service 5 years 5 months 10 days.

38   Formed Hawarden 8t September 1952 – Luneburg October
             1952 – Wahn May 1954 – Disbanded Wahn 31st May 1957.

             Total Service 4 years 8 months 22 days.

9   Formed El Hamra 1st September 1951 – Disbanded Shallufa
             September 1953.

             Total Service 1 year 11 months.

21   Formed Pembrey 1st January 1952 – Ouston September 1952
             – Disbanded Ouston 10th October 1953.

             Total Service 1 year 9 months 10 days.

Note: No. 51 Wing is omitted from the seniority list since it was absorbed
by No. 4 Wing on 1st January 1956, and its number cannot, therefore, be re-
used.

ANNEX "F"

Honours and Awards
For Gallantry/Gallant Conduct

Award	Armd Cars (*)	Ground Gunners (*)	RAF Regt (*)	Iraq Levies (*)	Aden Levies (*)	RAF Regt (M) (*)	Firemen (*)	RAF Regt Bnd (*)	RAuxAF Regt
CBE(*)			3						
OBE(*)			6						
MBE(*)			7				3		
MC	10		11		6 Regt 4 APL				
GM		3	2				12		
DSM			1						
MM	3	5	20		1 Regt 3 APL	1 Regt 3 Malay	1		
BEM(*)		3	15				47		
K/QCBC(*)			8		1 Regt		3		
MID(*)	14	22	242		2 Regt	32 Regt 33 Malay	7		
AOC's			10				2		
CBC(*)									

Foreign Awards

USA
Bronze Star	1
Soldiers Medal	2

Belgium
Croix de Guerre	26

France
Croix de Guerre	10

Oman
DSM	1
Commendation Medal	1

Selangor
CGM   2 Malay

Negri Sembilan
DCM   1 Malay

For Meritorious Service

Award	Armd Cars (*)	Ground Gunners (*)	RAF Regt	Iraq Levies (*)	Aden Levies (*)	RAF Regt (M) (*)	Firemen (*)	RAF Regt Bnd (*)	RAuxAF Regt (*)
CB			7		1 Regt				
OBI				1 Levy					
KBE			2						
CBE(*)			10	1 Regt	1 Regt				
OBE(*)		2	21	1 Levy	1 Regt 1 APL	1 Regt			1
MBE(*)	1	2	91	5 Levies	3 Regt 4 APL	3 Regt	8	2	5
BEM(*)			73		2 Regt 1 APL	3 Regt 2 Malay	16		5
RVM			1				2		
QCVS			2						

Foreign Awards

Belgium

Order of Crown	2
Order of Leopold	4

Norway

King Haakon Freedom Cross	1
King Haakon Freedom Medal	18

Oman

DSM	2
Commendation Medal	2

Miscellaneous

Queens Medal for Champion Shots in Air Forces	4

(*) Indicates that lists/figures are not conclusive

ANNEX "G"

Trophies and Competitions
(1942 – 1992)

The Lloyd's Cup
(1942)

1944: No.2824 Squadron

1945: No.2727 Squadron

1946: Not Awarded

1947: No. 64 Squadron

1948: No. 57 Squadron

1949: No. 54 Squadron

1950: No. 15 Squadron

1951: No. 1 Squadron

1952: No. 1 Squadron

1953: No. 57 Squadron

1954: No. 57 Squadron

1955: Not Awarded

1956: No. 100 Squadron

1957: No. 62 Squadron

1958: Not Awarded

1959: No. 16 Squadron

1960: No. 1 Squadron

1961: No. 48 Squadron

1962: No. 16 Squadron

1963: No.48 Squadron

1964: No.16 Squadron

1965: Not Awarded

1966: No.2 Squadron

1967: No.63 Squadron

1968: No.27 Squadron

1969: No.27 Squadron

1970: HQ Sqn 3 Wing

1971: No.1 Squadron

1972: No.26 Squadron

1973: The Queen's Colour Squadron

1974: No. 34 Squadron

1975: The Queen's Colour Squadron

1976: No.51 Squadron

1977: Not Awarded

1978: No.2 Squadron

1979: No.2 Squadron

1980: No.2 Squadron

1981: No.2 Squadron

1982: No.2 Squadron

1983: No.2 Squadron

1984: No.2 Squadron

1985: No.2 Squadron

1986; No.2 Squadron

1987: No.66 Squadron

1988: No.19 Squadron

1989: Not Awarded

1990: No.2 Squadron

1991: Not Awarded (Gulf War)

1992: No.34 Squadron

The Higginson Trophy
(1955)

1956: No. 6 Wing

1959: No. 1 Squadron

1960: No. 16 Squadron

1961: No. 63 Squadron

1962: No. 3 Wing

1972 Station Regiment Squadron (RAF Brize Norton)

1973: Flight Lieutenant J.R. Caley

1974: No. 15 Squadron

1975: No. 16 Squadron

1976: No. 51 Squadron

1977: The Queen's Colour Squadron

1978: No. 1 Squadron

1979: No. 48 Squadron

1980 No. 16 Squadron

1981: No. 27 Squadron

1982: No. 63 Squadron

1983: No. 2 Squadron

1984: No. 1 Squadron

1985: No. 4 Wing

1986: No. 63 Squadron

1987: No. 15 Squadron

1988: No. 3 Squadron

1989: The Queen's Colour Squadron

1990: No. 26 Squadron

1991: No. 1 Squadron

1992: No. 34 Squadron

The Vaux Trophy
(1970)

1971: Pilot Officer RC Moore

1971: Flying Officer JW Gilbert

1972: Pilot Officer JA Ingham

1976: Pilot Officer GJ Evans

1978: Pilot Officer M Brook

1981: Pilot Officer LB Brunt

1982: Pilot Officer MJ Steward

1982: Flying Officer E Adey

1983: Flying Officer P Brightman

1984: Pilot Officer S Tomkins

1984: Pilot Officer P Richardson

1985: Flying Officer A Gilroy

1985: Pilot Officer F Richardson

1986: Pilot Officer JA Jackson

1986: Pilot Officer MJ Payne

1987: Flying Officer CA Wilson

1987: Pilot Officer WJ Rooney

1988: Flying Officer MRL Allen

1988: Pilot Officer AG Williams

1989: Flying Officer AC Wilkinson

1989: Flying Officer JH Gunn

1990: Pilot Officer A Wilson

1990: Pilot Officer MJ Gavars

1991: Flying Officer RA Davies

1991: Pilot Officer AM Hindley

1992: Pilot Officer FD Garwood

The Barnard Trophy
(1976)

1977: No. 27 Squadron

1978: No. 26 Squadron

1979: Not Awarded

1980: No. 27 Squadron

1981: No. 26 Squadron

1982: No. 37 Squadron

1983: No. 26 Squadron

1984: No. 26 Squadron

1985: No. 27 Squadron

1986: No. 27 Squadron

1987: No. 63 Squadron

1988: No. 63 Squadron

1989: Not Awarded

1990: Not Awarded

1991: Not Awarded

1992: Not Awarded

The RAF Regiment Prize Essay
(1978)

1979: Flight Lieutenant A Davie

1980: Flight Lieutenant AH Mann

1981: Flight Lieutenant RG Smith

1982: Not Awarded

1983: Pilot Officer M Pound

1984: Flying Officer GM Jones

1985: Flight Lieutenant DM Beckwith

1986: Flight Lieutenant EJ Adey

1987: Flight Lieutenant EI Rees

1988: Flight Lieutenant KS Balshaw

1989: Flying Officer D Fountain

1990: Flight Lieutenant ES Kendall

1991: Flight Lieutenant MJ Burt

1992: Flight Lieutenant G Jones

The Strickland Trophy
(1984)

1985: No 2625 (County of Cornwall) Squadron

1986: No 2625 (County of Cornwall) Squadron

1987: No 2622 (Highland) Squadron

1988: No 2622 (Highland) Squadron

1989: No 2622 (Highland) Squadron

1990: No 2503 (County of Lincoln) Squadron

1991: No 2623 (East Anglian) Squadron

1992: No 2625 (County of Cornwall) Squadron

The Kapuscinski Sword
(1984)

1984: Pilot Officer RJ Kinnell

1985: Flying Officer G Leonard

1985: Pilot Officer J McEvoy

1986: Flying Officer JA Kirkpatrick

1986: Pilot Officer GP Hellard

1987: Flying Officer MJ Bates

1987: Flying Officer MD Brabon

1988: Flying Officer GP Brown

1988: Flying Officer AJC Glazebrook

1989: Flying Officer CAM Bishop

1989: Pilot Officer WJ Kendall

1990: Pilot Officer JM Banbrook

1990: Flying Officer MP Donoghue

1991: Flying Officer GM Burchill

1991: Flying Officer AD Finch

1992: Flying Officer LB Taylor

The Roberts Trophy
(1991)

1991: Flight Lieutenant PM Stokes

1992: Flight Lieutenant RJ Webster

The Royal Auxiliary Air Force Regiment (1947-1957)

Squadron Number

2501 (County of Gloucester)	Formed as LAA 1st May 1947 – Filton – Disbanded 10th March 1957
2604 (County of Middlesex)	Formed as LAA 1st May 1947 – Stanmore Park – Re-numbered 2600 Squadron 1st June 1949
2605 (County of Warwick)	Formed as LAA 1st May 1947 – Honiley – Disbanded 10th March 1957
2609 (West Riding)	Formed as LAA 1st May 1947 – Yeadon – Disbanded 10th March 1957
2611 (West Lancashire)	Formed as LAA 1st October 1947 – Woodvale – Disbanded 10th March 1957
2502 (Ulster)	Formed as LAA 1st December 1947 – Aldergrove – Disbanded 10th March 1957
2504 (County of Nottingham)	Formed as LAA 1st December 1947 – Hucknall – Disbanded 10th March 1957
2602 (City of Glasgow)	Formed as LAA 1st December 1947 – Bishopbriggs – Disbanded 10th March 1957
2603 (City of Edinburgh)	Formed as LAA 1st December 1947 – Turnhouse – Disbanded 10th March 1957
2608 (North Riding)	Formed as LAA 1st December 1947 – Thornaby – Disbanded 10th March 1957
2612 (City of Aberdeen)	Formed as LAA 1st December 1947 – Dyce – Disbanded 10th March 1957
2616 (South Yorkshire)	Formed as LAA 1st December 1947 – Doncaster – Disbanded 10th March 1957
2600 (City of London)	Formed from 2604 Squadron on 1st June 1949 – Biggin Hill – Disbanded 10th March 1957

APPENDIX "H"

The Royal Auxiliary Air Force Regiment (1979-1992)

Squadron Number

2503 (County of Lincoln)	Formed as Field 1st July 1979 – Scampton
2622 (Highland)	Formed as Field 1st July 1979 – Lossiemouth
2623 (East Anglian)	Formed as Field 1st July 1979 – Honington
2624 (County of Oxford)	Formed as Field 1st November 1982 – Brize Norton
2625 (County of Cornwall)	Formed as Field 1st November 1982 – St. Mawgan
2620 (County of Norfolk)	Formed as Field 1st March 1983 – Marham
2729 (City of Lincoln)	Formed as SHORAD 1st April 1985 – Waddington
2890 (Non Affiliated)	Formed as SHORAD 1st October 1989 – Waddington

Wing Number

1310	Formed 13th June 1989 – Catterick
1339	Formed 1st October 1989 – Waddington

Bibliography

Published Sources

Air Ministry/Central Office of Information – Wings of the Phoenix (HMSO) 1949

Allen, C – Thunder & Lightning (HMSO) 1991

Allen, L – Burma – The Longest War (Dent) 1984

Armitage, Air Chief Marshal Sir Michael – The Royal Air Force (Arms & Armour Press) 1993

Batt, Gp Capt MK – A Short History of the RAF Regiment (RAF Regiment Fund) 1982

Browne, Brigadier JG – The Iraq Levies, 1915-1932 (RUSI) 1932

Boyle, Andrew – Trenchard – Man of Vision (Collins) 1962

Buckley, C – Greece & Crete 1941 (HMSO) 1977

Buckley, C – Five Ventures (HMSO) 1977

Churchill, Winston S – The Second World War, Volumes I to VI (Cassell) 1950

Churchill, Randolph S & Winston S – The Six Day War (Heinemann) 1967

Collier, Basil – The Defence of the United Kingdom 1939-45 (HMSO) 1957

Creevey, Thomas – The Creevey Papers (ed John Gore) (London) 1934

Croker, John Wilson – The Croker Papers 1808-1857 (London) 1884

De Butts, Brigadier FM – Now the Dust has Settled (Tabb House) 1995

de Chair, S – Morning Glory (Merlin) 1988

Douhet, General Giulio – The Command of the Air (Il dominio dell'aria) (1921) (Office of Air Force History, Washington DC) 1983

Elliott, WA – Esprit de Corps: A Scots Guards Officer on Active Service 1943-45 (Michael Russell) 1996

Ellis, Major LF – Victory in the West Vol I (HMSO) 1962

Franks, Norman L – The Battle of the Airfields (Grub Street) 1994

Freeman, Sqn Ldr FA – The Volunteer Reserves of the Royal Air Force (Air Historical Branch) 1996

Gelb, Norman – Desperate Venture – Operation Torch (Hodder & Stoughton) 1992

Glubb Pasha – War in the Desert (Hodder & Stoughton) 1960

Guiver, Peter F – Britain's Modern Royal Air Force (Patrick Stephens) 1994

Harris, Air Vice-Marshal JH – A Brief History of the RAF Regiment 1942-1960 (RAF Regiment Fund) 1960

Her Majesty's Stationery Office – The Malayan Emergency 1948-60 (HMSO) 1970

Hogg, IV – Anti-Aircraft – A History of Air Defence (McDonald & Janes) 1978

Hughes, H Stuart – Consciousness & Society: The Reorientation of European Social Thought 1890-1930 (Harvester Press) 1979

Jackson, General Sir William – The North African Campaign 1940-43 (Batsford) 1975

Jackson, W G F – History of the Second World War – The Mediterranean & Middle East (HMSO) Vol VI Pt II, 1987 & Vol VI Pt III, 1988

James, TCG – Defence Policy and the Royal Air Force 1956-63 (Air Historical Branch) 1987

Kirby, Maj-Gen SW – The War Against Japan (Vols I to V) (HMSO) 1957-69

Lee, Air Chief Marshal Sir David – Wings in the Sun: The RAF in the Mediterranean 1945-1986 (HMSO) 1989

Lee, Air Chief Marshal Sir David – Eastward: The RAF in the Far East 1945-1972 (HMSO) 1984

Lee, Air Chief Marshal Sir David – The Royal Air Force in Germany 1945-78 (HMSO) 1979

Lee, Air Chief Marshal Sir David – Flight From The Middle East (AHB) 1978

Linklater, E – The Campaign in Italy (HMSO) 1977

Lunt, Major-General J – Imperial Sunset (McDonald) 1981

Martin, Lt-Gen HJ & Orpen, Col N – The South African Forces in World War II (Vol VI) – Eagles Victorious (Purnell) 1977

Middlebrook, M – Operation Corporate (Viking) 1985

Molony, CJC – History of the Second World War – The Mediterranean & Middle East (HMSO) Vol V 1973, Vol VI Pt I 1984

North, J – NW Europe 1944-5 (HMSO) 1977

Oliver, Wg Cdr KM – A Short History of the RAF Regiment (RAF Regiment Fund) 1st Ed 1970, 2nd Ed 1971, 3rd Ed 1974

Orpen, Colonel N – The South African Forces in World War II (Vol V) – Victory in Italy (Purnell) 1975

Percival, Lieutenant-General AE – The War in Malaya (Eyre & Spottiswoode) 1949

Peters, R J – Armoured Cars of the RAF (Military Modelling) 1972

Pitt, Barrie – Special Boat Squadron (Century Publishing) 1983

Playfair, I S O – History of the Second World War – The Mediterranean and Middle East (Vol I 1954), (Vol II 1956), (Vol III 1960), (Vol IV 1966) (HMSO)

Playfair, ISO & Molony CJC – History of the Second World War – The Mediterranean & Middle East (Vol IV) (HMSO)

Powell, Dilys – The Villa Ariadne (Efstathiadis) 1973

Price, Alfred – The Hardest Day (Arms & Armour Press) 1988

Probert, Sqn Ldr HA – History of Changi (RAF Changi) 1965

Probert, Air Cdre HA – The Rise and Fall of the German Air Force 1933-45 (Arms & Armour Press) 1983

Probert, Air Cdre HA – The Forgotten Air Force (Brassey's) 1995

Richards, D – The Royal Air Force 1939-45 (Vol 1) The Fight at Odds (HMSO) 1974

Richards, D & Saunders, H – The Royal Air Force 1939-45 (Vol 2) The Fight Avails (HMSO) 1975

Ross, Tony (Ed) – 75 Eventful Years – The Royal Air Force 1918-1993 (Wingham Aviation Books) 1993

Routledge, Brigadier NW – Anti-Aircraft Artillery 1914-55 (History of the Royal Regiment of Artillery) (Brassey's) 1994

Saunders, H – The Royal Air Force 1939-45 (Vol 3) The Fight is Won (HMSO) 1975

Sherbrooke-Walker, Colonel R – Khaki and Blue (St Catherine Press) 1952

Slim, Field Marshal Sir William – Defeat into Victory (Cassell) 1956

Smith, ED – Counter-Insurgency Operations: Malaya & Borneo (Ian Allan Ltd) 1985

Smith, PC & Walker, E – War in the Aegean (William Kimber) 1974

Strawson, Major-General J – The Italian Campaign (Secker & Warburg) 1987

Tedder, MRAF The Lord – Air Power in War (Hodder & Stoughton) 1948

Thompson, Brigadier Julian – Ready for Anything: The Parachute Regiment at War (Weidenfeld & Nicolson) 1982

Trevenen James, AG – The Royal Air Force (Macdonald & Jane's) 1976

Witherow, Air Cdre M S – Flying Soldiers in Blue Khaki (The Army Quarterly) 1988

Wood, SGP – Faithful: The Story of the Durham Light Infantry (Nelson) 1962

Vick, Alan – Snakes in the Eagle's Nest: A History of Ground Attacks on Air Bases (Rand for Project Air Force) 1995

Wigglesworth, Air Marshal Sir Philip – Disarmament Report (1947) published as "The Dissolution of the Luftwaffe" (HMSO) 1995

Unpublished Sources

Bryant, Wg Cdr TH – The RAF Regiment 1942-45 (AHB Narrative) 1947

Eyles, CAG – A Prisoner of War in Arbeit Kommando 107E, 1943-45 (MS) 1995

Godsave, Sqn Ldr GE – Tales of the Tin Trams (MS) 1930 – Ed. Wg Cdr KM Oliver 1969

Hardy, Sqn Ldr WWG – A History of No.2 Squadron RAF Regiment (Pamphlet) 1971

La Forte, Sqn Ldr RW – The First 75 Years: A History of No.1 Squadron RAF Regiment (Pamphlet) 1996

Lee, Sqn Ldr GR – From Wales to West Sussex: An Autobiography (MS) 1995

Ministry of Defence, A Short History of Royal Air Force Catterick (Pamphlet) 1981

Salmon, Col H Morrey – Blue Hats in the Line (MS) 1971

Slee, Wg Cdr MJ & others – 2873 Squadron RAF Regiment (Formed June 43 Disbanded Dec 45) (Pamphlet) 1946

Stewart, DAW – 2875 AA Squadron Went to War, or From Normandy to Norway (Pamphlet) 1981

Tucker, Sqn Ldr NG – In Adversity: Exploits of Gallantry and Awards in the RAF Regiment and its Associated Forces. (MS) 1995

Westrope, EF – Memories of a Ground Gunner: the History of No.2819 Squadron RAF Regiment 1942-46 (MS) 1994

Index

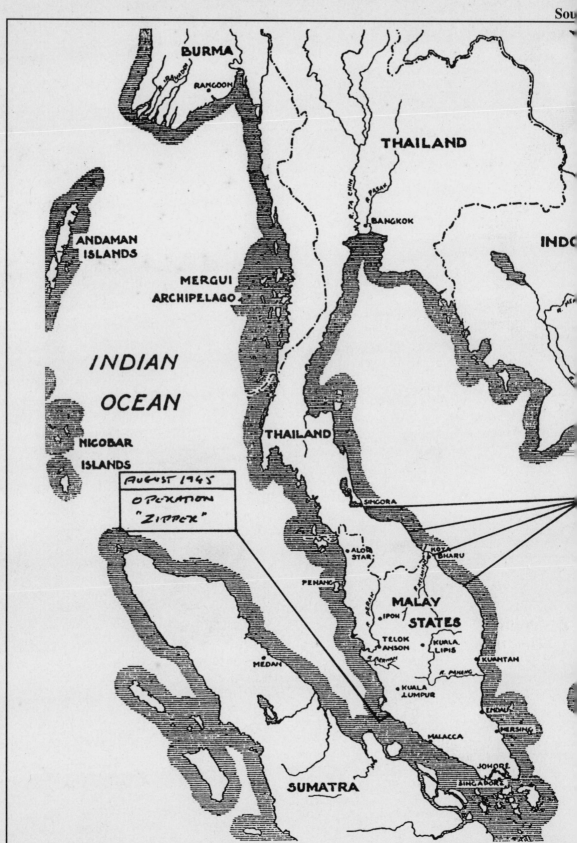